Identity, Ideology, and the Future of Jerusalem

IDENTITY, IDEOLOGY, AND THE FUTURE OF JERUSALEM

DAVID HULME

First published in 2006 by
PALGRAVE MACMILLAN™
175 Fifth Avenue, New York, N.Y. 10010 and
Houndmills, Basingstoke, Hampshire, England RG21 6XS
Companies and representatives throughout the world.

PALGRAVE MACMILLAN is the global academic imprint of the Palgrave Macmillan division of St. Martin's Press, LLC and of Palgrave Macmillan Ltd. Macmillan® is a registered trademark in the United States, United Kingdom and other countries. Palgrave is a registered trademark in the European Union and other countries.

ISBN-13: 978–1–4039–7424–2
ISBN-10: 1–4039–7424–1

Library of Congress Cataloging-in-Publication Data
    Identity, ideology, and the future of Jerusalem / by David Hulme.
        p. cm.
    Includes bibliographical references and index.
    ISBN 1–4039–7424–1
        1. Jerusalem—International status. 2. Nationalism—Palestine.
    3. Group identity—Palestine. 4. Ideology—Political aspects—Palestine.
    5. Statesmen—Palestine—Biography. 6. Jerusalem—Ethnic relations.
    I. Title.

DS109.95.H85 2005
956.94′4205—dc22   2005054530

A catalogue record for this book is available from the British Library.

Design by Newgen Imaging Systems (P) Ltd., Chennai, India.

First edition: September 2006

10 9 8 7 6 5 4 3 2 1

Printed in the United States of America.

Contents

LIST OF ILLUSTRATIONS

Tables

Maps

PREFACE

As might be expected in a work on one of the world's most perplexing political and humanitarian problems, the final product represents the culmination of many years of research and extensive travel. And as might be hoped, the author ought to undergo a significant change of perspective as the complexities of the area under study become better understood.

I began the project as many in the West would, with an already acquired admiration for the Jewish people's monumental achievement of statehood against what seemed all odds and in the terrible aftermath of the Nazi attempt at genocide. There is, of course, much to be said for the remarkable post-Shoah resurgence of this gifted people. Nevertheless, as my continuing research revealed, their success has come at a terrible price for the similarly gifted Palestinian people displaced during and following the two wars in 1948 and 1967. These massive disruptions of indigenous Palestinian life created the seemingly irresolvable Israeli-Palestinian conflict.

The specific subject matter of this work is but a fragment of the whole that makes up a very complex arena. Jerusalem is a microcosm of the conflict, and the Jerusalem Question rests heavily on all who labor to resolve the broader impasse. Without resolution on the issue of Jerusalem, its holy sites, sovereignty, and municipal government, there can be no peace. The just and equitable peace that all people of rationality and goodwill seek must come through honest and searching dialogue. As this study makes clear, a profound understanding of personal identity, its creation and its malleability, must play a central role in the critically needed realignment of the thinking of Israeli and Palestinian leaders and publics alike.

Experience has also taught me that many readers of the book's findings will struggle to steer a middle course. One well-informed recipient of an earlier version of the manuscript wrote that he agreed with me one hundred percent about the Israeli findings, but disagreed one hundred percent about the Palestinian ones. It was a striking confirmation of how difficult it is to get beyond established identity. He simply could not see the Other's needs. And therein lies the challenge and opportunity of the Jerusalem Question, when seen through the prism of identity and ideology. Read on with the caveat that you may find your own identity challenged, no matter which side of the conflict you occupy.

I would be remiss if I did not thank Laurie Brand, Anne Crigler, Michael Fry, Steven Lamy, and James Rosenau for their support, encouragement, and critical thinking during the process of research and writing. Duane Abler, Jeannette Anderson, and Gina Stepp were my indispensable helpers with cartography, word processing, and proofreading. I also want to thank Farideh Koohi-Kamali, David Pervin, Heather Van Dusen, and Elizabeth Sabo of Palgrave Macmillan for their encouragement and enthusiasm for the project, as well as Maran Elancheran and Bhuvana Venkatesh for their expert help in preparing the typescript for print. My two sons, their wives, and my daughter have had to withstand my frequent digressions into the latest findings, and I thank them for their patience.

By no means least, I thank my wonderful wife Deborah for her continuous support and cheerful spirit as she endured my "absent presence" during months of writing. This book is dedicated to her, and to two other very special people: my late wife Robin, who was there for the beginning, and our new granddaughter, Riley, who is here for the completion. It is for Deborah in gratitude, and for Robin and Riley—as for the Israelis and the Palestinians—in memory and in hope.

A NOTE ON TRANSLITERATION

Though Arabic can be transliterated in more than one way, some names have become best known in a particular form, which I have chosen to follow. But because of the possible variations, a number of inconsistencies will be apparent between the text, the notes, the bibliography, and other sources. Hence Yasser Arafat may appear as Yasir 'Arafat and Ahmad Quray' as Qurei, Korei, or Quri. In some cases, the 'ayn (') and/or hamza (') are retained (as in Abu Ala') and not in others (as in Edward Said, rather than Sa'id).

INTRODUCTION

The Middle East is a region whose enduring and conflicting passions invite the luxury of lazy generalizations. But sooner or later most who study the extraordinary complexity and nuance of its modern history and politics come to the conclusion that its problems are not given to simple solutions. Part of the reason, they learn, is that for thousands of years the people of the Middle East have suffered the almost constant imposition of outside power and outside ideas. Yet within the Gordian knot of alternative histories and contending claims in the broad sweep of its lands from North Africa to Saudi Arabia to Iran, Iraq, and Turkey, there are core issues that may respond to fresh analysis in the search for solutions. For example, the apparent intractability of one of the Middle East's most vexing problems—the Jerusalem Question—may be illuminated when examined through the familiar though underutilized prism of identity studies. Shibley Telhami and Michael Barnett note that "[a]lthough scholars of the region cannot escape the salience of identity, a powerful trend in contemporary international relations theory has proceeded as if identity mattered little for our understanding."[1] Certainly there has been an abundance of work on identity in comparative studies, but Telhami and Barnett imply that much more attention is demanded of international relations specialists. Underlining their view, they state, "No student of Middle Eastern international politics can begin to understand the region without taking into account the ebb and flow of identity politics."

The contemporary heart of the region's great geographic and cultural arc is the center of the more-than-100-year conflict between the Arabs and the Zionists. Henry Kissinger characterized the conflict as an anachronism—a seventeenth-century-style religious war three hundred years too late.[2] Europe's last religious war spanned thirty years (1618–48); though the Arab-Zionist conflict has lasted much longer, its vicious dynamic relies on similar intransigent attitudes and approaches. Palestinian and Israeli identities have the ideology of nationalism as a primary element. At the individual level they may or may not have religious *commitment* as an additional element, but both identities are profoundly affected by religious sentiment.

Nevertheless, the Palestinian and Israeli people of the early twenty-first century are caught up in not so much a *religious war* but more precisely a clash of two personal and collective identities. Albert Einstein saw the clash as between "two rights" and secretly lent his name to efforts to resolve the conflict.[3] In this respect his perspective informs the analysis undertaken here. This is not to imply that there are not also many wrongs on both sides. This has been made abundantly clear by many authors. Asymmetry of power between Palestinians and Israelis is much discussed. While the disparity is acknowledged, this book does not address this asymmetry in further depth, except as it enters into the discussion of alternative explanations for the Jerusalem impasse (see chapter 2) and sometimes plays a role in the stasis-movement dynamic of the Jerusalem Question. For all of its now evident deficiencies, the Oslo process (and its continuation through the Abu Mazen–Beilin proposals, Camp David II, and the final talks at Taba) was based on both sides attempting to realistically move toward equalities from a present position of recognized inequality. As Hanan Ashrawi has observed, while there really is no symmetry or parity at this time, "there can be a *parity of rank* even with an asymmetry of power."[4]

For the purpose of this study the concepts of identity and ideology are deliberately conflated to achieve a new analytic tool. This is in contrast to most scholarly works in the study of international relations, which have concentrated on identity and ideology as separate lines of inquiry. This either-or reductionist approach to identity and ideology invites analysts to miss the richness of a more holistic view of human motivation. The father of modern identity studies, Erik Erikson, conceptualized identity and ideology as interlinked. Since the 1970s the international relations field has expressed growing academic interest in identity as a social construct and has acknowledged some of Erikson's concepts,[5] especially that of "identity crisis,"[6] yet the combined identity-ideology aspect of his conceptualization has been largely overlooked.[7] In the attempt to find more parsimonious explanations, many scholars have failed to mine the richer vein that a combined identity-ideology framework provides. This study extends Erikson's concept of what will be referred to as "the identity-ideology nexus" to the specific case of the protagonists in the debate over the future of Jerusalem. It seeks a richer explanation of the apparent impasse by examining identity and ideology's combined role at times of stasis and momentum with respect to the Jerusalem Question.

Just as the concept of identity has been acknowledged and at the same time overlooked by many, including Middle East area specialists, so also there are problems with the concept of ideology. Political scientists Edward Shils and Raymond Aron announced "the end of ideology" in the 1950s. While Shils and Aron limited ideology's demise to Western industrial society rather than the third world, the realist school took up the notion that ideology was generally in retreat.[8] In 1996 Samuel Huntington advanced another "end of ideology."[9] Like Francis Fukuyama,[10] he proposed the irrelevance of ideology as a factor in world politics, substituting what are by Erikson's definition several elements of ideology. In 2002 Huntington noted, "The century of ideology, the twentieth century, is over, and it seems to me that culture, cultural identity, ethnic, linguistic, traditional, and religious identity—these things now play central roles in global politics."[11] While Huntington defines ideology in terms of the political ideologies that have sprung from Western tradition in the past 200 years (including, no doubt, the totalitarian systems that dominated large parts of the world in the twentieth century), he seems to bypass extant varieties of nationalism. They may be partial rather than total ideologies,[12] but they can empower their adherents to act with equal conviction.

The present study makes use of a specific underutilized typology of ideology, developed by Willard Mullins in the 1970s.[13] The importance of this typology is that it allows examination of Zionism and Palestinian nationalism against five clearly defined parameters. Though the two nationalisms differ in numerous ways—historically, religiously, ethnically, and so on—they nonetheless meet Mullins's strict criteria. They are ideologies that give cause for action and have historical consciousness, unlike the myths, utopias, or philosophies often confused with ideology. These aspects of Mullins's typology differentiate it from other less precise definitions and give the identity-ideology nexus employed here a dynamic quality missing from other explanations. This study, then, overcomes Huntington's circumlocution and retains ideology as a useful concept, and it argues for a conceptualization of identity and ideology that incorporates all of the elements he mentions as central in world politics.

Over the past century, not only Palestinians and Zionists but also Turks, Britons, and Jordanians have fought on Palestine's terrain of battle. Each group of people has had reason within its own identity-ideology nexus to invest itself in the region. Whether it was early-twentieth-century fading Ottoman imperial intent, energetic colonialism in the case of the British Mandate (1922–48), the de facto division of land between Israel and Jordan under their 1949 armistice agreement, or Israeli retention of the territorial spoils of the 1967 war, each people has expressed aspects of its own identity and ideology vis-à-vis Palestine. In 2006 the Palestinians still seek to express their identity by establishing a Palestinian state where international justice, recognition of their historic property claims, and accommodation of some refugees' right of return can be achieved. But with the new century, their conflict with the Israelis has become centered on one essential square kilometer—the Old City of Jerusalem—within which lie the ancient symbols and trophies of these now opposing identities. Reserved for final-status negotiations, Jerusalem, with its core historical and religious elements, constitutes a potential deal-breaker. This study seeks to explain the power of the identity-ideology nexus on the part of the Palestinians and the Israelis with respect to Jerusalem.

Outside the immediate Israeli-Palestinian orbit, the Jerusalem Question is on the lips of, among others, Moroccans, Iraqis, Iranians, and Turks, to say nothing of "the Trio"—Jordan, Egypt, and Saudi Arabia—and "the Quartet"—the United Nations, the United States, the European Union, and Russia. Medieval Christians placed the city at the center of their spiritual lives because the Roman Catholic and Orthodox churches sanctified physical Jerusalem. As a result, and in the absence of geographic knowledge and appropriate technology, their maps showed Jerusalem at the center of the globe.[14] A separate, earlier tradition also named it the *omphalos*, or navel, of the world,[15] and yet another as the birthplace of the cosmos.[16] Mirroring these conceptions in some ways, the modern world seems to have returned to such images, and Jerusalem has become once more the center of the world's attention.[17]

By examining individual and collective Palestinian and Israeli identities in depth, the present work attempts to decipher the conflict over the city of Jerusalem. This is not only because the Jerusalem issue is a microcosm of the larger struggle, but also because its examination may offer insights into those other regions of conflict where cultures, religions and politics, and identities and ideologies intersect. International relations theory has generally focused on structure and system or institutions for explanatory models. Yet the tumultuous and generally unpredicted events of the late twentieth century, especially in Eastern Europe and the former Soviet Union, posed the question of where people and their ideas fit within such increasingly reified theories.

Putting people back into the development of international relations theory is a valid pursuit in the context of the Jerusalem Question. The daily news reports of terror, the televised sound bites from devastated Palestinian towns and villages, Israeli shopping malls, markets, and buses, are about people and the conflict and passion generated by identity and ideology. Thinking about how people's identities and ideologies explain their actions with respect to the impasse over Jerusalem yields some important conclusions about the traditional agent-structure debate. One of the goals of this study is to look again at individuals in leadership and follower roles in the context of their identities and ideologies. What do the Palestinians desire with respect to the city? Why have successive Israeli leaders failed to come to agreement with them over the city's sovereignty? Despite different stated policy positions, why is there so little apparent distinction between the

Israeli Labor, Likud, and Kadima parties when it comes down to the wire regarding the resolution of the problem?

Chapter 1 reviews the difficulty posed by the Jerusalem Question. It is a seemingly insoluble issue, with layers of implacability that transcend millennia. It is the tragic history of how peoples—be they Jewish and Roman, Roman-Christian and Arab, Arab and European Crusader, Ottoman and British, British and Arab, Jewish and British, or Israeli and Palestinian—have never laid aside their differences and shared the city of peace in peace.

Why is the identity-ideology nexus so important with reference to the Jerusalem Question? The answer is that although it is no secret that the issue seems intractable, the underlying identity-ideology dynamic is rarely examined in depth. As a result, the possibilities for political change may remain undiscovered. For example, the degree to which identity is malleable is not always acknowledged, and therein may lie the possibility of negotiated settlement. How identities change is an important aspect of hope for resolution in identity-ideology-based conflicts. Mostly there is stasis over the Jerusalem Question, but at rare moments there is great movement. Understanding the role that the identity-ideology nexus plays in the dynamic also becomes critical in attempts at resolution. The work of a limited number of specialists in the identity-ideology field provides the theoretical backbone of the current investigation.

Chapter 2 considers three alternative categories of explanation for the apparent impasse over the city's sovereignty. Is there a compelling argument for intransigence to be found in the security, economic, or legal facets of the city? Certainly the history of terror in Jerusalem dictates that the Israelis put security issues at the forefront of their concerns in any renewal of the peace process. On the other hand, the imposition of Israeli civil and military strictures around Jerusalem has meant the destruction of the continuity of the Palestinian-populated territory between the northern and southern West Bank. For their own security reasons the Palestinians can sustain the argument that possession of East Jerusalem is essential to their survival. But do security issues prevent compromise on the city's future configuration as capital of both the Israeli and Palestinian states? From an economic point of view, the city has grown to be the largest conurbation in Israel and/or the West Bank. But does its demographic and geographic size equate with economic strength that cannot be shared? The same Israeli civil and military dislocations that have decimated Palestinian life on the West Bank have seriously disrupted its natural commercial activity and economic prospects. On the legal front, arguments have been advanced at the international level in support of the rights of both sides to sovereignty over all or part of the city. Interrelated are the moral arguments centered on the right of return for refugees and the legitimate property rights of the dispossessed. Are any of these arguments compelling enough to preclude negotiated agreement?

Chapter 3 examines the city's reputation as a central focus of religious devotion in the history of three of the world's largest religions: Judaism, Christianity, and Islam. The chapter begins to uncover the significance of individual and collective commitment within these faith traditions to Jerusalem, past, present, and future.

Chapters 4 and 5 concentrate on the biographies of seven Jewish/Israeli leaders and seven Arab/Palestinian leaders, from the inception of Zionism and the awakening of Palestinian nationalism respectively, to the attempts at negotiated peace in the twenty-first century. What are the forces that shaped the identities of these key actors in the conflict, and which ideological concepts became a central part of their identities? Are matters of identity and ideology in combination the real reason for the current impasse over the city? Does the concept of interacting variables, the identity-ideology nexus being one of them, help explain the stasis-momentum dimension in the history of the Jerusalem Question?

The concluding chapter summarizes the findings and puts forward some constructive proposals for the future of what David Lloyd George termed "the most famous city in the world"—a place that is shared by more than 700,000 inhabitants, three dominant faiths, and the world community—a unique place whose permanent peace would reverberate for the good of all.

In conclusion, it should be noted that there is a relative dearth of primary resources on the Palestinian side, and even more so in the English language. Every attempt has been made to find relevant materials. Sometimes it has been necessary to rely on what others record about Arab and Palestinian perspectives, building in the necessary caveats to allow for bias. Zionist and Israeli materials and resources are by contrast quite rich. It is hoped that the disparity in resources is compensated for in part by the inclusion of interviews with and written comments and speeches by Palestinians intimately involved in the Jerusalem Question.

CHAPTER 1
THE JERUSALEM QUESTION

The Pervasive Problem

"The problem of Jerusalem is one of the most emotional and explosive issues in the world," wrote Palestinian international jurist Henry Cattan in 1981.[1] In the same year, prominent Israeli novelist and commentator "Aleph Bet" Yehoshua noted that "in a period of violent religious renaissance [Jerusalem] is a dangerous political explosive which could give rise to an uncontrollable conflagration."[2] Fourteen years later, Palestinian scholar Ghada Karmi commented that "nothing in the history of the Arab-Israeli conflict has been so contentious as the issue of Jerusalem."[3] And in 1999 the Israeli negotiator of the Oslo Agreements, Uri Savir, admitted, "The issue of Jerusalem . . . can easily become a public explosion . . . not just between Palestinians and Israelis, but between the Arab world and Israel, between the Islamic world and the Jewish world."[4]

Explosive, contentious, capable of drawing in much of the world community—this is the pervasive nature of the problem. Yet the danger that the Arab-Israeli conflict, and specifically the Jerusalem Question, poses to the peace of the world in the twenty-first century is not new. What is today Israel and Palestine, on the narrow strip of land between the Mediterranean coast and the Jordan River, was once the crossroads of the ancient civilized world, the bridge between the continents of Africa, Asia, and Europe. As a result, it has been the battleground for imperial powers from ancient times till the present. It has also become, in succession, central to each of three dominant world religions: Judaism, Christianity, and Islam. The area is a magnet for many peoples, many religions, and many political and social persuasions. Because of this conflux of geography, history, and religious and cultural associations, the city at its epicenter is also an enduring lodestone. And like the region of which it is a part, Jerusalem has become a fuse of international conflict. The 2,000-year history of the city alone reveals a complex international web of religious, diplomatic, and political intrigue. Bitter and bloody conflict rent the city several times during the Roman imperial domination of the eastern Mediterranean basin. The Crusader period (1099–1187) saw Jerusalem suffer untold bloodshed in the clash of

Muslim and papal intentions. By the nineteenth century, the city had become the mirror of petty consular rivalries between European nation-states squabbling in the twilight of the Ottoman Empire. The first two decades of the twentieth century found the city of peace at the center of immensely significant geopolitical considerations. The colonial powers of Britain and France vied over regional influence, control of the Suez route to the East, and the railways and pipelines across the Syrian Desert to the oil-rich Persian Gulf.

During the period of the British Mandate (1922–48) Jerusalem was established as the administrative capital of Palestine. Following the declaration of the State of Israel in 1948 and the subsequent Arab-Israeli war, the city was divided de facto between Jordanians and Israelis, crudely partitioned by no-man's-land. The June 1967 occupation of East Jerusalem by the Israel Defense Forces (IDF) and the Knesset's immediate annexation of the eastern side of the city, far from reuniting Jerusalem, created a vexatious problem for Israelis and Palestinians, and for every other nation that became embroiled in it.

Unexpectedly, the early 1990s witnessed the single most dramatic breakthrough in Israeli-Palestinian relations in almost fifty years. The secretly negotiated 1993 Oslo Agreements seemed to hold the promise of resolution to one of the region's most persistent problems and at the same time of bringing peace to Jerusalem. Yet despite thousands of hours of creative negotiations, the Jerusalem Question remained as problematic as ever. As the twentieth century closed, Jerusalem's future was the publicly cited deal-breaker in attempts by the United States to resolve the long-standing Arab-Israeli conflict. The city itself had become the new symbol of the intractability of the more-than-100-year-old Arab-Zionist impasse.

Illustrating this point, in 1999 two of the foremost actors in the Oslo peace process commented on Jerusalem as a final-settlement issue. The Speaker of the Palestinian Legislative Council, Ahmad Quray' (also known as Abu Ala'), explained that

> Jerusalem . . . is the head, the heart of the Palestinian state—the heart of the Palestinian identity. Without Jerusalem, I don't think peace will be achieved. Therefore, this is the most important element of the peace process.[5]

At the same time the Speaker of the Knesset, Shimon Peres, said:

> Jerusalem may be the only issue on the Israeli position which escapes strategy and politics. This is the only place that has the aura of holiness. And the difference between politics and holiness is that when holiness begins, compromise stops.[6]

Both statements reflect the language and underlying strength of the identity-ideology nexus and invite consideration of the dynamic that seems to bring either stasis or momentum over the Jerusalem Question.

The Salience of Identity

The two main contenders over the future of Jerusalem have distinct identities and ideologies. Yet there is little to be found in the literature that links identity, ideology, and the Jerusalem Question in a specific way. Allusions to the role identity may play in the larger conflict are occasionally found in passing observations. For example, the late Edward Said quoted a passage from Erikson's work about Martin Luther as a young man. Erikson wrote that

> only in a crisis, individual or historical, does it become obvious what a sensitive combination of interrelated factors the human personality is—a combination of capacities created in the distant past and of opportunities divined in the present; a combination of totally unconscious preconditions developed in individual growth and of social conditions created and re-created in the precarious interplay of generations.[7]

Though he was speaking of 1967 when a particular crisis for Palestinian identity came to the fore, Said touched on the essence of the present study when he noted Erikson's description of the human personality and the dynamics of its origins, unconscious preconditions, and present opportunities. But like so many other scholars, Said made no comment beyond this general reference. He was intent on establishing a different point and therefore went no further in exploring Erikson's concept. Ironically, the people who stand as the initiators of the Palestinian identity crisis—the Zionists seeking to extend their own national identity and to fulfill their own ideological imperatives—are beset with an identity crisis too. The question of who is a Jew is a continuing debate in Israel (and in Jewish society elsewhere for other reasons), especially in light of post-Zionism and the demographic and social change that is ongoing in Israeli society.

Importantly though, Said noted the usefulness of Erikson's model of identity formation in the Palestinian-Israeli conflict. Erikson himself was not unaware of the broader implications of his work on identity. He felt that "the study of identity would become as strategic in our times as the study of sexuality was in Freud's."[8] This prescient observation has been borne out by many recent references to Erikson's concepts, though as mentioned, with little substantive application. The present study builds on Erikson's concepts and examines in depth the effect of the identity-ideology nexus in Arab and Jewish or Palestinian and Israeli political decision making with respect to Jerusalem.

The Problem with Ideology

Almost from the time of its introduction, the term *ideology* has been subject to contrary passions and conceptual confusion. When A.-L.-C. Destutt de Tracy first used the word during the French Revolution, he intended it to signify the science of ideas. He meant to improve not only human knowledge but also human life on earth. Human beings, he believed, needed to be freed from prejudice and prepared for the rule of reason. At first Napoleon supported the "ideologues," and their proposals for reform of the French education system were accepted. A few years later, however, he blamed them for his military defeats. As a result

> [i]deology was, from this time on, to play this double role of a term both laudatory and abusive not only in French but also in German, English, Italian, and all the other languages of the world into which it was either translated or transliterated.[9]

The conceptual confusion surrounding the term has only grown since then. The later impact of theorists such as Marx and Mannheim relegated ideology to the realms of distorted thought.[10] Over the years, the definition of ideology varied from author to author, sometimes being used synonymously with myth, utopia, or belief system. Ideology was and generally is still considered to be less than rational, and more often than not it is taken for granted. As a result, the concept has not been accorded a meaningful role in mainstream international relations theory, and over the past thirty years a few scholars have pointed out this absence.[11] The realist school, for example, has no room for ideology, supposedly because it does not provide the basis for a rational foreign policy. While the realist acknowledges ideological persuasions, he does not believe that foreign policy flows from ideology but rather that it stems from the underlying quest for power in the national interest.[12] Thus, in the development of realist and neorealist international relations theory, the politics of interest has crowded out the politics of ideology.

In the early 1970s Willard Mullins recognized what others have more recently referenced as the invisibility and lack of systematic analysis of the concept of ideology.[13] He therefore set out to improve the concept's use within political science. He first cleared away the semantic confusion over the use of myth, utopia, and ideology. He did so by extending the work of several others, including McDonald, Halpern, Burke, Geertz, and Friedrich. Ideology is basically a modern invention, introduced with the collapse of the ancien régime. On the other hand, myth and utopia predate the French Revolution. Ideologies certainly have elements of myth and utopia, but it is historical consciousness that distinguishes ideology. An ideology explains its past, acknowledges its present, and visualizes its future. Myth and utopia do not comprehend historical change; they are recurrent and nonhistorical. Accordingly, Mullins devised a five-part typology including historical consciousness. To this he added cognitive power, evaluative power, action-orientation, and logical coherence as essential elements. Unfortunately Mullins did not provide specific cases to illustrate his new definition. Do Zionism and Palestinian nationalism qualify as ideologies? Since the focus of this study is in part the Palestinian nationalist and Zionist positions with respect to Jerusalem, chapters 4 and 5 examine the two perspectives in light of Mullins's five-part definition.

Sasson Sofer offers a reinterpretation of the place and role of ideology in international theory, explaining its value in understanding world politics. Like Mullins, Sofer clarifies terms, noting that "belief system, doctrine and world view, myth, ethos, and utopia have come to be employed interchangeably."[14] Specifically he points out the invisibility of ideology in international relations dialogue. By "invisibility" he means that the concept is either disregarded, rejected, poorly used, or avoided by the substitution of other concepts that do not address the relationship between idea and action. Sofer notes that both sociology of knowledge and political sociology yield concepts that can be joined to improve the use of ideology as an explanatory tool in international relations theory. He shuns the favored status accorded to the politics of interest and argues that ideology is "the overt expression of specific and defined national political goals." As a result, he is able to state:

> Ideology as the major underlying conceptual structure of the political elite is a basis for national decisions and assessments. It could, in certain cases, provide an explanation for why a particular policy achieves legitimation. Not only is the utilitarian basis of policy important, so too is its relationship to the society's central values.

Using Marxism and liberalism as primary examples, Sofer addresses the ideological prisms of the Soviet Union and the United States respectively. The Jerusalem Question lends itself to similar analysis when linked to the "central values" of both Zionism and Palestinian nationalism, which in this study form part of the identity-ideology nexus.

Sofer expands on his 1988 essay with a full-length study of Zionist foreign policy. Emphasizing the salience of ideas in understanding why people act as they do, he writes, "There is no issue more complex or disputed—and which still has to be satisfactorily explained by philosophers and historians— than the place of ideas in history and the extent to which they determine actions."[15] Consistent with Mullins's typology, and demonstrating the potential of the ideological dimensions of the Jerusalem Question, Sofer further comments:

> The basis of a political tradition lies in a permanent outlook that is not affected by each passing event. That constitutes the essence of the historical and ideological heritage that a nation passes on through the generations,

one that is acquired through a long process of trial and error, successes and failures.

Alan Cassels approaches the subject of ideology from the perspective of international history, surveying two hundred years of diplomacy. A historical approach allows him to trace the entry of ideology onto the world stage and to its subsequent spread throughout the international system. While Cassels does not examine specific ideologies in any great detail, he deals with "the more generic phenomenon of ideological thinking, and with how the cast of mind recognizable as ideological has shaped foreign-policy making."[16] Connecting with Mullins, he notes that "ideology and the ideological pattern of thought supply a medium through which foreign policy issues can be transmitted to and perceived by a mass audience." Unfortunately Cassels falls prey to the conceptual looseness to which Mullins objects. Cassels accepts that ideology can be only a blurred concept, that ideologies have "an element of irrationality," may be only "marginally amenable to ratiocination," and are subject to being "taken on trust" or "emotional faith."

Before returning to the development of this study's identity-ideology framework, the discussion turns to several categories of literature specific to the Jerusalem Question.

The Gap in the Literature

Literature multiplies almost daily with attempts to explain and answer the long-standing Jerusalem Question. The growing complexity of the issues has produced over fifty proposals to resolve the problem[17]—most of them since the watershed 1967 Arab-Israeli War. A bibliography of the holy city, published in 2001, lists 563 entries for Jerusalem literature in various languages dating back to 1833.[18] In 2005, a search of a large online bookstore revealed more than 56,000 items on the city. Of necessity, therefore, the literature review undertaken here concentrated on representative materials produced after 1967. In addition, since the focus of this study is the application to the Jerusalem Question of theoretical work in identity and ideology studies and the interplay of the two concepts in forming actors' perceptions and decisions about the city, only literature with relevance to this interest has been considered. Understandably, after the 1967 war there was a substantial increase in material on the Arab-Israeli conflict. However, Jerusalem per se did not feature much in that literature until the 1980s. When the issue of the city's negotiated future came to the fore on the final-status agenda anticipated by the 1993 Oslo Agreements, a rash of new materials emerged.

Inevitably, because the city is a focus of political, legal, cultural, religious, and social crosscurrents, it is a subject of study in various disciplines. The

Jerusalem Question can be viewed from various perspectives: through the lens of narrative history or the pages of documentary and diplomatic history; or via sociological and urban planning studies, legal analysis and/or prescriptive proposals, and foreign policy studies. Authors who deal with the history of the city include Elon (1989), Asali (1990), Gilbert (1996), Benvenisti (1996), Wheatcroft (1996), Armstrong (1997), Coughlin (1997), Wasserstein (2001), Cline (2004), and Goldhill (2005). Among political studies and papers are Musallam (1996), Friedland and Hecht (1996), Sharkansky (1996), Lustick (1996), Dumper (1997), Cheshin, Hutman, and Melamed (1999), Klein (2001), and Breger and Ahimeir (2002). There are legal and prescriptive works from Lapidoth (1994), Hirsch, Housen-Couriel, and Lapidoth (1995), Segal et al. (2000), and Khalidi (2001). Foreign policy studies include Brecher (1972, 1975), Vertzberger (1990), and Sofer (1998). Each body of literature yields its own cache of useful background information and relevant examples for this study, and some authors make general reference to identity or ideological issues, or both.

For example, Amos Elon notes that Jerusalem is a "Capital of Memory. Memory gave them [the Jews] their culture and their identity."[19] He summarizes:

> The twin roots of the renewed strife in her streets are nationalism and faith. It is difficult to say which of these two forces is the more powerful. . . . Each offers the believer an identity and a plan of salvation; each also holds out a system of ultimate ends that embody the meaning of life and are absolute standards by which to judge events.

From time to time Martin Gilbert lends support to the argument for ideology's role in the past, present, and future of Jerusalem. For example, he quotes Russian Zionist Menachem Ussishkin, who on his return from a visit to Jerusalem in 1913 spoke favorably of the city as "the heart of the nation and of the world." With prophetic overtones, Ussishkin argued that "Jerusalem must be surrounded by a ring of Jewish settlements. . . . The shame and reproach must be removed from the holy and hallowed 'Wailing Wall,' which was surrounded by dirt."[20]

Gilbert also alludes to the power of Palestinian ideological feelings for Jerusalem. In an indirect reference, he allows former deputy mayor of Jerusalem Meron Benvenisti to make the point for him:

> I belong to a nation fighting for its soul, and its soul is Jerusalem. I identify with my nation's longing for Jerusalem. I, too, experienced the transcendental experience of our return to the holiest of our places. At the same time, I am a son of this city and know the meaning of a son's love for it. I cannot, and

will not, forget the love, which is as strong as my own, of the Arab residents of Jerusalem for this city.[21]

With respect to Zionist ideological concerns vis-à-vis Jerusalem, Bernard Wasserstein believes that "there was very little demand in Israel or in the Jewish world between 1948 and 1967 for any campaign to liberate Jerusalem or for irredentist capture of the eastern part of the city."[22] He claims that Jerusalem became of ideological interest to the Israelis only after 1967. Thus, following the war, "Ben Gurion's view was . . . that Jerusalem was essential for, as it were, sentimental or ideological nationalist reasons."[23] Whether the evidence supports Wasserstein's belief in the late development of an ideological position on Jerusalem as capital is taken up in chapter 4.

Roger Friedland and Richard Hecht argue that Jerusalem will be "the best battleground" when the antipartitionists on both sides are faced with the negotiated outcome of the peace process. The reason is that "the hard structures of the city are built upon foundations that are more enduring, more materially effective, than stone or concrete. The city is built upon a set of symbols that threaten to tear it apart."[24]

Ian Lustick promotes an idea that runs contrary to one of this study's general findings. He asserts that many key Jewish and Israeli leaders have been against making Jerusalem Israel's capital. Specifically of 1948, he writes that "many of Israel's founding fathers, such as Yosef Sprinzak, Pinhas Lavon, Moshe Shapiro and Eliezer Kaplan, opposed making any part of Jerusalem Israel's capital, not only because of fear of provoking the international community, but because of a disdain for the city itself compared to the comforts and 'appropriate climate' of Tel Aviv."[25] This statement seems too strong with respect to Shapiro (a.k.a. Shapira) and Kaplan. It is true that in late September they had opposed Ben-Gurion's proposed military action against Latrun in order to make Jerusalem Jewish.[26] But earlier in the summer Shapira had told journalist Kenneth Bilby that "big plans were afoot for Jerusalem. He expected the Jewish population to jump another 100,000 within a few years . . . [and claimed that] most of the immigrants who docked at Haifa port expressed a desire to settle in Jerusalem—and *Israel would* funnel them there as fast as the state's resources permitted."[27] In late 1949 Shapira was appointed to a special ministerial committee to oversee the transfer of the government and its ministries to Jerusalem. In a 1968 interview he admitted, "True, we agreed to a state without Jerusalem in 1947; but we merely waited until an opportunity arose to rectify the situation." According to Michael Brecher, "he, like many others, emphasized that Jerusalem had occupied a pivotal position as political and cultural centre of the Yishuv during the Mandate."[28] Further, Brecher's analysis demonstrates that by the time the decision to make Jerusalem the seat of government

(December 11, 1949) was taken, most of the cabinet (including Kaplan and Shapira) supported it. Of the twelve ministers, nine were present for the vote. Levin and Sharett were out of the country, and Shazar was ill. "A few were hesitant (Kaplan, Remez). And one dissented—Sharett."[29] Yet Sharett had told the UN General Assembly's ad hoc Political Committee on November 25, 1949: "Their attachment to Jerusalem led the Jews to form the majority of its inhabitants and to recreate their spiritual, cultural, and political centre in the Holy City," and "Israel's ordeals, sacrifices, and responsibilities, as the sole guardian of Jerusalem's historic values, along with economic and moral considerations, 'have impelled and continue to impel the transfer to it of central institutions such as always have been housed in Jerusalem.' "[30] Lustick claims that the reason for Labor (Mapai) and religious dissenters coming on side was "[p]artisan politics—namely, fear of losing political points to Herut, which was rumored to be ready to propose making Jerusalem Israel's capital if the Mapai government did not do so."[31] Again this seems an overstatement that ignores the "bitter sacrifice" mentioned by so many over internationalization in exchange for an independent state without Jerusalem.[32]

Lustick [33] also puts forward the argument that the Jerusalem Question is not a special case. Just as Israel need not be a special case in comparative studies, so too the issue of Jerusalem may be viewed as a much more normal case of "a political fetish" that has failed to achieve its goal. Lustick sets out to demonstrate that the Israeli leadership has consistently failed in bringing the project of Jerusalem as the "undivided and eternal capital" to hegemonic reality. Therefore, he submits, a resolution to the problem of Jerusalem is less difficult than is often thought. In analyzing the speeches and comments of several Israeli leaders, however, Lustick takes for granted that their positions are post-1967 political constructs and does not consider that they could be evidence of deep-seated identity-ideology issues. Evidence of Jerusalem as a marker of identity for Jewish/Israeli leaders forms the basis of chapter 4 of the present study.

Brecher explores in detail various Israeli foreign policy issues, among them the policy area of Jerusalem. Acknowledging the importance of the Jerusalem Question, he says that it

> dominates the cultural-status area of Israel's foreign policy. Its role as a uniquely unifying symbol of the Jewish People during the past three millennia is universally acknowledged. Its associations—national, religious and cultural—are deeply rooted in the consciousness of Jews everywhere. Thus not without reason was Jerusalem perceived by the Zionists and others as an inseparable part of the revived Jewish State.[34]

Brecher also notes that for the Jewish community in Palestine (the *Yishuv*) in 1947–48, the decision to concede Jerusalem to internationalization in return for establishment of the State of Israel was almost intolerable. But at the time the *Yishuv* felt they had no choice: this was the *temporary* quid pro quo to attain a Jewish national entity.

Yaacov Vertzberger mentions identity and ideology as aspects of belief systems, values and stereotypes. However, his discussion is at a lower level of abstraction than that offered by the identity and ideology perspectives at the center of the present investigation. In passing he makes the following tangential and telling comment: "People tend to adopt beliefs that are compatible with their core needs (Walker, 1983), which are acquired in childhood."[35] Seeking the next level of abstraction, we quickly arrive at the level of identity and ideological issues. With respect to attitudes, Vertzberger himself hints at the need for a higher level of abstraction when he comments, "People adopt attitudes that seem to them congruent with their values, particularly their core values, which are tied to self-expression and self-identity."

Beyond these few references in relevant literature, in-depth material connecting identity, ideology, and the Jerusalem Question remains scarce.

Why Identity, Ideology, and the Jerusalem Question?

While the centrality of identity and ideology to the Israeli-Palestinian impasse over Jerusalem has been largely overlooked in the scholarly literature, significant events on the broader canvas of international affairs and the study of international relations indicate that there is good reason to consider their combined role in human experience. Three apparently unrelated developments demonstrate the heightened interest that has emerged in these subjects since the 1980s. They are the collapse of the Soviet Union, the debate over methodology within the International Relations field, which pits constructivism against rationalism, and the September 11, 2001, terrorist attacks on the World Trade Center and the Pentagon.

Issues of identity and ideology came to the fore in the watershed upheaval in the Soviet bloc in the late 1980s. Writing about the subsequent unification of East and West Germany, Konrad Jarausch notes that

> [identities] serve to impart meaning to the world and offer important clues to the core beliefs of a subject. Second, identities define attitudes towards one's surroundings that operate as important constraints for political decisions [and] also powerfully influence actual behavior, especially in crisis situations that require existential choices based as much on emotion as on reason.[36]

Similarly, Robert English has chronicled the role of ideas in the collapse of Soviet identity and ideology and the emergence from the shadows of a new pro-Western identity—one that had been long in preparation among Russian intellectuals. He writes, "Identity powerfully influences the interplay of deep-rooted cultural and fast-moving material factors in deciding how national interests—and so international behavior—are determined."[37] In the case of the Soviet Union, several new identities were needed to make sense of the failure of the old order in the rapidly changing late-twentieth-century world system. The Soviet Union became, in effect, a shatter zone from which identities and ideologies reemerged.

Almost thirty years earlier, Mullins had written in similar terms about the role of ideology per se:

> In times of historical crisis, when fundamental, time-honored, "self-evident" truths are questioned, ideologies bring the issue of a society's worth to the level of consciousness and guide men's actions over historical terrain that is, looked at in comparison to traditional society, terrifyingly unfamiliar and uncharted. This, I believe, helps to explain why ideologies are rapidly spreading from the West to the societies of the so-called "developing" world, where traditional order is being disrupted and transformed.[38]

For Mullins, historical consciousness was a vital component of ideology and was not limited to tradition but included explanations of the present and visions of the future. Applying Mullins's model to the Soviet Union, the communist empire was the "developing world." Its system had become traditional, and it was overcome by a "new" ideology from the West. Strangely it was an ideology that was at the same time not so new. It had many echoes of Russia's illustrious past—the seventeenth- and eighteenth-century reaching-out-to-the-West of Peter the Great and Catherine the Great, and the pervasive influence of traditional religion in the form of the Russian Orthodox Church. The imperial Russian ideology also allowed for a multiplicity of ethnic identities within the then-Russian sphere. Thus within Mullins's explanation we begin to see the possible conflation of identity and ideology, as articulated separately by Erikson.

The constructivist side of the debate that emerged in international relations theory in the 1990s concerned itself in part with the role of ideas, norms, and values in the construction of social life. The debate has major implications for the two dominant paradigms in international relations theory. As Christopher Hemmer and Peter Katzenstein observe, "To liberalism, constructivism adds consideration of the effects identities have on both formal and informal institutions. To neorealism, it adds consideration of the effects of ideational rather than material structures, specifically the effects of identity on actor interests."[39] Because constructivists deem social objects and practices and even agents constructs rather than preexisting primitives in the explanation of social forms, identity, for example, is to be "denaturalized" in order to be understood.[40] That is, there is nothing primordial about belonging to a particular nationality, say French or English. In such cases, and despite longevity, identity is purely a social construct. Yet from a psychological or psychoanalytic perspective, the constructivist argument comes as no surprise. Robert Wallerstein notes that within the psychoanalytic field in the 1980s and 1990s, the formulation of "a social-constructivist view" provided a "more congenial home [for] many of Erikson's conceptions, particularly his identity concept."[41] Erikson's view was that identity is of necessity a construct. His perspective on human psychosocial development, however, suggests that identity formation results from a process that is in part primordial. Erikson's concept of the development of human personality and identity rests on what he termed the "epigenetic principle," whereby each element in that development "exists in some form before 'its' decisive and critical time normally arrives." His colleague David Rapaport wrote that

> [t]he crucial characteristic of [Erikson's] psychosocial theory of ego development . . . (in contrast to the "culturalist" theories) is that . . . [it traces] the unfolding *of the genetically social character of the human individual* in the course of his encounters with the social environment at each phase of his epigenesis. Thus it is not assumed that societal norms are grafted upon the genetically asocial individual by "disciplines" and "socialization," but that the society into which the individual is born makes him its member by influencing *the manner in which* he solves the tasks posed by each phase of his epigenetic development.[42]

In this Erikson's position is somewhere between the traditional primordial and constructivist perspectives. Recent developments in the cognitive science and neuroscience fields parallel some of his concepts. According to Sandra Blakeslee, "[n]euroscientists are finding that [circuitry in the prefrontal cortex,] *which fully matures in late adolescence*, is an internal guidance system that fills each person's world with values, meaning and emotional tone, taking shape according to a person's culture."[43] Further, the more emotionally charged the experiences in life, the better they are recalled. And while it has long been known that life's experiences are laid down in the brain's neural pathways, it is now suggested that these pathways are subject to modification throughout life. They exhibit the most plasticity in early life, but even adult circuitry is open to some modification. There is also evidence that behavior modification by cognitive-behavior therapy can actually change the structure of the brain at the neural level.[44]

The dramatic and unpredicted change in international alignments following the Islamic fundamentalist terrorist attacks on New York's World Trade Center and the Pentagon in Washington also invited a fresh appraisal of the role of both identity and ideology, especially in the Middle East. The disaster focused attention on the ideology of the previously obscure al-Qa'ida terrorist network and the underlying identity of its leader, Usama bin Ladin, and his followers. What did they believe? Why did they plan and commit such acts? The attacks produced a widening public interest in what was perceived as ideological thinking and the role it plays in individual and collective identity.

But mere interest in identity and ideology does not necessarily translate into satisfactory explanation. Acknowledging the difficulties involved in unraveling the causal relationship between ideas and action, some analysts have become interested in eclectic explanations and the connections between variables and how their interaction may help explain complex events.[45] In this context Peter Gourevitch examines the September 11 attack. Rather than seeking a linear causal relationship, he explores the concept of interacting variables, which allows examination of several variables, one or more of which may grow in strength and so indicate causality. Some may emerge with causal strength only under certain conditions. By definition, then, one or more variables may also demonstrate weakness or even latency. As Gourevitch says, "Many of the quarrels in our field arise out of a desire to assert aggressively the predominance of a particular, favored variable." But because there are many variables at work in complex situations, "taking account of them all is impossible, and even investigating several is messy."[46] Examining the interaction of variables provides a useful approach to learning more about how causality may work in such complex situations.

One model of causality that works with interactions also comes from cognitive studies. "Interactive activation" is a concept that helps explain the way in which the brain processes information according to context. In the particular example that Gourevitch employs, a reader observes a letter and the brain begins the process of deciding what the letter is in its context. First the shape is perceived as being like an *l* or an *I* or a *t*. The brain arrives at meaning by creating hypotheses about the letter and testing them in the context of surrounding letters and already existing concepts such as known printed words. The brain processes this interaction of information and context to arrive at a decision.[47] In other words, context changes the way the information is understood. The variables are interacting, and the observer's understanding is altered as a result. Information is changed by context.

The events of September 11 have a basis in the interaction of certain ideas and conditions: the beliefs of Usama bin Ladin; Wahabism; disputes within Islam; concepts of *jihad*, capitalism, and democratic principles in relation to the international flow of al-Qa'ida funds; Saudi political stability; Taliban extremism; Western strategic interests, and so on. An understanding of what happened is better achieved by examining how the variables interacted. Again Gourevitch is careful to remind the reader that the relationship between idea and action is not straightforward. One Muslim fundamentalist differs from another, as does one Marxist or one Christian from another. It is not the text but the interpretation of it that counts. Nevertheless, tracing the interaction of variables may provide for deeper understanding.

Gourevitch suggests that to gain a better grasp of the events of September 11, researchers should consider the interaction of "the content of the [related] ideas, their guide to behavior, the sociology of belief, and the link to forms of power."[48] All of this is a variation on the theme of the well-known intertwining of international and domestic politics, which is also a case of interactive activation.

In the same way, the parameters of the Jerusalem Question demonstrate complexity and the probability of interactive activation when one considers the number of domestic and international actors, the multiple issues, and the conflicts between the Palestinian and Zionist identity-ideology nexuses, to name only some of the variables. As will be seen, examination of these identity-ideology nexuses and the actions taken in respect of Jerusalem by Jews, Israelis, Arabs and Palestinians yields a more nuanced understanding.

Of course, conflicts where identity and ideology appear to play a role are not new. Yet as noted earlier, some presumed that the end of ideology had arrived with the collapse of the seventy-year-long Cold War ideological conflict. But ideologically rooted conflicts in areas of the world as diverse as the Philippines, Kashmir, the Middle East, Cyprus, Kosovo, North Africa, and Northern Ireland seem to say otherwise. The diversity of identities and ideologies represented by this list suggests that it would be a mistake to dismiss the power of ideological thinking. Similarly, the end of the Cold War did not signal the demise of identity and ideology as potentially useful explanatory concepts in international affairs.[49] In 1988 Sasson Sofer wrote presciently, "The relevance of ideology has not disappeared in the age of the balance of terror, nor is it likely to disappear in the course of future international progress."[50] In 1996 Cassels noted that "the continued prevalence of nationalist attitudes makes nonsense of the claim heard in the West on the downfall of communism that ideological conflict had been extinguished and the end of history reached."[51] Indeed, as mentioned earlier, one result of that collapse was the reemergence of identities and ideologies suppressed by the Soviet system.

Introduction to the Identity-Ideology Framework

There are many works on Jewish/Israeli identity and the genesis of Palestinian identity, but the subject of identity and ideology in combination has yet to be engaged directly with regard to the Jerusalem Question. Rashid Khalidi traces the development of Palestinian identity in terms of the construction of a modern national consciousness, and Jerusalem features as a significant element. He mentions that parochial loyalties "served as the bedrock for an attachment to place, a love of country, and a local patriotism that were crucial elements in the construction of nation-state nationalism."[52]

Attachment to Jerusalem is a powerful example of such loyalty. Khalidi notes that it is equally vital to Palestinians and Israelis as an aspect of identity:

> Most importantly, central though Jerusalem is to the Palestinians and to their self-image, it is also central to the self-image of their Israeli adversaries. For both, it is important today as a space, and historically, over time, as an anchor for modern identity.

Indeed, Jerusalem is the core around which "virtually all narratives about Palestine—religious and secular; Jewish, Christian, and Muslim; Palestinian and Israeli—revolve." Perhaps understandably, in Khalidi's study the city never quite receives the attention such statements seem to promise. Rather, in the impressive textual evidence he brings forward, Jerusalem is the backdrop to his broader concern in establishing the historicity of Palestinian identity. Khalidi attempts to set the record straight with respect to the timing and origins of Palestinian identity. Demonstrating that the antecedents of contemporary Palestinian identity are found in the late nineteenth century at about the same time that Jewish immigration to Palestine began, he repudiates the Zionist canard that Palestinians had no individual identity apart from Arabs, or are at best late arrivals in the region. He charts continued identity development through the waning days of Ottoman power in the pre–First World War period and on into the British Mandate, asserting that by 1923 the essential elements of Palestinian identity were in place. However, due to the catastrophic Palestinian losses in the 1948 war, he sets the mid-1960s as the marker for the reemergence of Palestinian identity.[53]

While Khalidi uses the prism of the literature on national identity,[54] it is the somewhat neglected work of three theorists (Erikson, Mullins, and William Bloom) that gives this study its departure point. Drawing on Erikson and others, Bloom contributes understanding of the intersection of the role of personal and national identity formation and international relations.[55] Mullins provides the basis of a working definition of ideology.[56]

The dynamics of identity formation are crucial to the development of this study's explanatory framework, but the inclusion of ideology *as a function of* individual and collective identity is a key concept. That is to say, identity and ideology are linked in this framework to form what could be a potent motivator of political behavior. The fusion of the approaches of Erikson, Mullins, and Bloom creates an analytical tool that may be particularly useful where the identity-ideology nexus appears to underlie political decision making.

Refining the Concept of Identity

Bloom charts the development of the psychological concept of individual identity through an exegesis of the writings of Freud, Erikson, Mead, Parsons, and Habermas. For the purpose of this study, however, emphasis will be placed mainly on Erikson's writings as the most pertinent for examining the *relationship* between identity and ideology. As Freud's daughter Anna commented, Erikson was the first to extend Freud's conclusions about the centrality of childhood experiences to adult social life.[57] Thomas Fitzgerald explains that Erikson was "the first to use the term *identity* in its presently accepted scientific sense."[58] Philip Gleason notes that the word *identity* is found in the English language from the sixteenth century onward. It was first a narrowly defined term within mathematics, then a philosophical term used by John Locke and David Hume to break down the religious concept of the soul. As to its present analytic application, Gleason asserts that "*identity* is a new term . . . [which] came into use as a popular social-science term only in the 1950s."[59] Erikson's specific interest developed into works on the psychohistory of leading personalities such as Maxim Gorky, Martin Luther, George Bernard Shaw, Mahatma Gandhi, and Thomas Jefferson. The application of Erikson's early work on the connection between the development of ego identity and adult society and the relationship to ideology is apparent in these studies. He writes that his mentor, Sigmund Freud, used the word *identity* only once in his writings, and that was "when he tried to formulate his link to the Jewish people."[60] Freud spoke of "inner identity" not in reference to race or religion but in relation to what Erikson terms the Jewish "readiness to live in opposition." Erikson notes at this point in his discussion of "The Problem of Ego Identity":

> It is this identity of something in the individual's core with an essential aspect of a group's inner coherence which is under consideration here: for the young individual must learn to be most himself where he means most to others—those others, to be sure, who have come to mean most to him. The term "identity" expresses such a mutual relation in that it connotes both a persistent sameness within oneself (selfsameness) and a persistent sharing of some kind of essential character with others.

In other words, an essential part of Freud's continuing identity, forged early in life by the anti-Semitic nature of the world around him, was his "readiness to live in opposition." This trait provided some of the necessary undergirding for a professional and public life marked by considerable animosity.

Erikson also contends that in order to have a vision of the future, as Shaw said, a young person needs something akin to "a religion" and "a clear comprehension of life in the light of an intelligible theory." Erikson names this needed theory an ideology. Finding an ideology, he says, is "a necessity for the growing ego." His more precise definition of ideology is

> a coherent body of shared images, ideas, and ideals which (whether based on a formulated dogma, an implicit *Weltanschauung*, a highly structured world

image, a political creed, or a "way of life") provides for the participants a coherent, if systematically simplified, over-all orientation in space and time, in means and ends.

As will be seen, Erikson's definition is close to the one developed by Mullins, who sought to operationalize "ideology" in a meaningful way for political analysis. Where Erikson focuses on description, Mullins introduces a typology that with "further conceptual refinement" could "be made operational for empirical research."[61] Because Mullins's emphasis is on securing a working definition, he gives no specific examples of ideologies, preferring to leave the development of relevant case histories to others. Erikson delineates the ego's need of ideology in relation to identity, concluding that "group identity harnesses in the service of its ideology the young individual's aggressive and discriminative energies, and encompasses, as it completes it, the individual's identity."[62] This leads him to state that "identity and ideology are two aspects of the same process." He speaks of the "loose ends of identity formation [that are] waiting to be tied together by some ideology."

As a result of his reading of Erikson and others, Bloom has developed the following explanation of why and how identity is formed in the human life cycle, and why it is promoted and defended:

> In order to achieve psychological security, every individual possesses an inherent drive to internalise—to identify with—the behaviour, mores and attitudes of significant figures in his/her social environment; i.e. people actively seek identity.
>
> Moreover, every human being has an inherent drive to enhance and to protect the identifications he or she has made; i.e. people actively seek to enhance and protect identity.[63]

What Bloom sets out here is the dynamic of identification theory. Further, he seeks to explain the role of this personal dynamic in the development of *national* identity. This is his unique contribution to the understanding of how individual and collective identities relate in international relations. He uses psychological and social-psychological theory to answer the following questions:

> Why do individuals and mass national populations give their loyalty to the nation-state? Why are they prepared to die for it? What are the structure and dynamics of their psychological attachment? How is it evoked? How does it affect government decisions and international politics?

As Bloom notes, what is crucial to his application of identification theory to the national level is that "*given the same environmental circumstances* there will be a tendency for a group of individuals to make the same identification, to internalise the same identity." This also applies to the "tendency for a group of individuals to act together to protect and to enhance their shared identity." As will be shown in succeeding chapters, the histories of the Zionist and Palestinian nationalist movements as seen through the prism of individual biographies demonstrate evidence of Bloom's assertions about shared identity.

Bloom also incorporates the work of social theorist Jürgen Habermas, who describes identifications beyond the infant-parent level as "identity-securing interpretive system[s]"[64] (Erikson's "ideologies"). In respect to Zionism and Palestinian nationalism, it could be argued that this phrase describes the two ideologies particularly well. If identity and its ideological components are indeed universal psychological needs, then human political behavior may be affected far more by the unconscious inner life than is generally supposed.

As noted, Bloom's primary emphasis is on the link between personal identity and national identity. And while decision-making elites are not the focus of his attention, he acknowledges that they are "equally subject to identification" and offers the following relevant remark for this study:

> At the micro level, identification theory can say little about how the individual decision-makers will behave. Certainly, a powerful public opinion and a mobilised national identity dynamic must affect the decision-maker, but the actual decisions will depend upon the decision-makers' own degree of identification, peer pressure, group mores, individual psycho-history and so on—a kaleidoscope of elements worthy of substantial research.

The analysis of these elements with respect to Jerusalem, especially the psychohistories and actions of representative decision-making Zionists and Palestinian nationalists, is the heart of this study.

It is important to state at the outset that this enquiry is not an attempt to make a meaningful mosaic from every childhood and adolescent experience of the actors chosen, but rather to search for patterns in their developing identity. Harold Lasswell came to the same general conclusion in 1930 in his work, *Psychopathology and Politics*. He wrote that his purpose was not "to make a hit-and-miss collection of isolated anecdotes about the relation between early experiences and specific political traits and interests" but "to discover what developmental experiences are significant for the political traits and interests of the mature."[65] Erikson delineates "eight stages of man" in the human life cycle (see table 1.1, where the diagonal entries picture "*a gradual unfolding of the personality through phase-specific psychosocial crises*" [Erikson's italics] across the eight stages). The crises are "psychosocial" because they are "precipitated both by the individual's readiness and by society's pressure."[66] Since this chart is focused on identity alone as one of several concepts within the life cycle, many of the boxes remain empty. Column 5 shows,

Table 1.1 Individual identity formation, life cycle stages, and psychosocial crises

	1	2	3	4	5	6	7	8
I Infancy	Trust vs. Mistrust				Unipolarity vs Premature Self-Differentiation			
II Early Childhood		Autonomy vs. Shame, Doubt			Bipolarity vs. Autism			
III Play Age			Initiative vs. Guilt		Play Identification vs. (Oedipal) Fantasy Identities			
IV School Age				Industry vs. Inferiority	Work Identification vs. Identity Foreclosure			
V Adolescence	Time Perspective vs. Time Diffusion	Self-certainty vs. Identity Consciousness	Role Experimentation vs. Negative Identity	Anticipation of Achievement vs. Work Paralysis	Identity vs. Identity Diffusion	Sexual Identity vs. Bisexual Diffusion	Leadership Polarization vs. Authority Diffusion	Ideological Polarization vs. Diffusion of Ideals
VI Young Adult					Solidarity vs. Social Isolation	Intimacy vs. Isolation		
VII Adulthood							Generativity vs. Self-absorption	
VIII Mature Age								Integrity vs. Disgust, Despair

Source: Identity and the Life Cycle by Erik H. Erikson. Copyright © 1980 by W.W. Norton & Company, Inc. Copyright © 1959 by International Universities Press, Inc. Used by permission of W.W. Norton & Company, Inc.

in the terminology of the specific crises, the issues that have been worked out earlier (or not) but that impinge on the next psychosocial crisis—in this case, the identity crisis. It is at the end of the adolescent stage that "identity becomes phase-specific (V, 5), i.e., must find a certain integration as a relatively conflict-free psychosocial arrangement—or remain defective or conflict-laden." The horizontal axis, V, contains the derivatives of earlier crises in the terminology of the impending crisis. Any entries that appear after the crisis on this axis are derived from its resolution and are the precursors of the next crisis. Erikson comments that in this case the final two entries, "Leadership Polarization" and "Ideological Polarization," relate to the ideological component of identity. At this juncture the young person will seek out leaders to follow beyond the family circle, as well as totalizing ideas or ideologies to set the world in an orderly frame. What happens up and through the end of adolescence, then, is central to identity formation. And this integration sets the stage for further modification of identity, as individual readiness and social pressures dictate. Identity is more than a collection of early experiences; it is the ongoing interaction of those experiences and identifications with a changing environment.[67] From Erikson's and Bloom's work it is apparent that the need for a secure sense of personal and collective identity is always present, but that circumstances may require modification of identity at certain breakpoints beyond completion of the adolescent stage. Wallerstein comments that Erikson's concept of

> identity formation, though declared complete with the successful navigation of adolescence, nonetheless extends forward into the next stage, the sixth of the life cycle, the achievement of adult intimacy and solidarity through proper choice of marriage partner and life vocation. . . . Yet clearly the consolidation of ego identity is never achieved easily, or decisively, or for all time.[68]

Erikson's eight-stage model clearly demonstrates a continuity of identity through all stages. He concludes that "identity does not connote a closed inner system impervious to change, but rather a psychosocial process which preserves some essential features in the individual as well as his society."[69]

In his review of the relationship between psychological theory and international relations theory, Bloom argues that in general the intersection of personal and national behaviors has been poorly explained. However, he does make an exception in the case of Daniel Katz, whom he cites for analytical precision. Katz outlines four kinds of latent forces that can be aroused so that the individual assumes his/her national role.[70] With Katz's essay in view, Bloom defines the forces as follows:

1. Emotional and behavioural conditioning to national symbols: those aspects of the political and general socialisation process in which the child

is "trained" to a sentimental attachment to symbols of the nation, such as the flag, national anthem and head of state.

2. The sense of personal identity as a national: those general aspects of socialisation by which an individual comes to perceive her/himself as being of a particular nationality. This is associated with education concerning a common history, fate and culture, and is established in contradistinction to out-groups which display different histories, fates and cultures.

3. Compensatory and defensive identification with militant nationalism: that "type of national identification that is based not so much on the individual's attraction by the advantages of group belongingness as on his attempts to solve his own internal conflicts and insecurities." This involves the mechanisms of displacement and projection. . . .

4. Instrumental involvement in the national structure: this can best be highlighted by appreciating the results of rejection of the national structure which would "vary from imprisonment and exile to virtual ostracism."[71]

National identity (including nationalism) is a part of personal identity, but it is generally latent unless aroused. It may be triggered by awareness of an out-group—the foreigners the individual meets in another country, or when his/her nation is involved in war. Katz explains that in times of war the ordinary citizen is called upon to exhibit aspects of nationalism that are normally subsumed by the concerns of everyday life. Because these aspects of national identity are latent, they are normally inactive. But when a national crisis arises, they are aroused in defense of the nation. The concept of latency in the emergence of behaviors rooted in identity is a significant aspect of the analysis undertaken here, though the concept is applied primarily to personal rather than national identity. But since personal identity, ideology, and national identity are part of the same process, latency in any one element affects the others. In psychological terms latency refers to the apparent inertness of aspects of identity until they are triggered by crisis, whether it is developmental (as in the individual's capacities) or related to specific historical breakpoints in the social milieu. When coupled with the concept of interacting variables, latency becomes a useful concept in explaining why identity-ideology issues seem to emerge with great effect under certain circumstances. Erikson notes the latent aspect in ideology for the majority of people. He writes,

"[I]t is true that the average adult, and in fact, the average community, if not acutely engaged in some ideological polarization, are apt to consign ideology to a well-circumscribed compartment in their lives, *where it remains handy for periodic rituals and rationalizations*, but will do no undue harm to other business at hand."[72]

Bridging Identity and Ideology

In developing identification theory, Erikson created a new, wholly psychological definition of ideology and tied it directly to identity. Thus he provided a bridge between the individual and collective dynamics of identity and the role of ideology. He wrote that identity and ideology, as two aspects of the same process, "provide the necessary condition for further individual maturation and, with it, for the next higher form of identification, namely, the *solidarity linking common identities*"[73] (Erikson's italics).

The underlying interaction of identity and ideology to be used in examining the Jewish/Israeli and Arab/Palestinian positions on Jerusalem is conceptualized as follows:

The inherent need for psychological security causes all people to develop personal identity by adopting "the behavior, mores, and attitudes of significant figures in [the] social environment," and "to enhance and protect [the] identity"[74] thus established. Subsequently, this created identity incorporates ideology—"a logically coherent system of symbols which, within a [particular view] of history, links the cognitive and evaluative perception of one's social condition . . . to a program of collective action for the maintenance, alteration, or transformation of society."[75]

That is, in the case of the Palestinian Arab–Zionist conflict over Jerusalem, in response to their inherent drive for psychological security, individuals on both sides establish identity based on the beliefs and actions of significant players in their early formative environments with regard to the city's significance for their respective people. Once formed in this way, identification with the city and its physical and spiritual properties as specifically Jewish/Israeli or Palestinian will be maintained, protected, and enhanced to meet the demands of the contenders' respective identity and developing ideology.

Since the conceptual framework proposed in this study conflates identity and ideology, there is nothing to hinder the reinforcing effect of identity components on ideological components and vice versa, once the ideological is established. In other words, experiences, ideas, concepts, beliefs, values, worldviews, etc., can "flow" back and forth between identity and ideology, find reinforcement, and consolidate each other. Because identity has its roots in early childhood and adolescence, and because ideology is conceptualized here as an integral part of identity as it continues to develop, the dynamics of the maintenance, defense, and enhancement of identity apply equally to ideology. The linkage between the two concepts means that threats to ideology threaten identity, and enhancements of ideology enhance identity. Further, since elements of early identity find support in subsequent ideological thinking, in the case of the Jerusalem Question identification with the city may become an aspect of identity that is later supported by ideological considerations expressed through association with political youth movements or Zionist/Palestinian nationalist organizations. This dynamic interaction is an essential element of the identity-ideology nexus. Combined in this way, the complementary concepts of identity and ideology take on new significance and strength. Just as "readiness to live in opposition" became a part of Freud's identity, so also Jerusalem's preservation and protection may be a marker of identity for both Zionists and Palestinian nationalists. If this is so and the identities and ideologies underlying the Jerusalem Question are antithetical, then it is small wonder that the issue has thus far defied resolution. The implications of Erikson's and Bloom's work for the formation of identity in individual Zionists and Palestinian nationalists and their acceptance of specific ideological components, as well as the extension of the identity-ideology nexus into group and national identity, may be profound.

By adopting Erikson's proposition that identity formation includes but also transcends the past, Bloom connects with Mullins, who points out that historical consciousness is an operational component of ideology. Changing historical circumstances may affect identity, as they may also affect the formation of aspects of ideology. If possession of Jerusalem is part of Palestinian nationalist identity, then it is part of Palestinian nationalist ideology. Jerusalem as an element in the Palestinian identity-ideology nexus may also be subject to modification over time. And if possession of "undivided Jerusalem" is an aspect of Zionist ideology, then it is also an aspect of Zionist identity, but both may be subject to the effects of historical change.

Another connection between Bloom and Mullins is seen in ideology's action orientation. Of this component Mullins writes: "The significance of ideology in mobilization is . . . that it 'gives one cause for doing.' It provides grounds or warrants for the political activity engaged in."[76] Identification theory gives "cause for doing" through internalization of particular identity components. The application of Bloom's theoretical approach to the "undivided and eternal city" or "Holy Jerusalem" component of Zionism and Palestinian nationalism respectively, suggests that both leaders and followers would demonstrate internalization of this "city component" as part of identity. They would also seek to maintain, defend, and extend the importance of the city as part of that identity.

An essential element in individual and group identification with an ideology seems to be the power of its symbols to give cause for action in the real world in the pursuit of psychological satisfaction. Hence Bloom points out that "political ideologies and ideas of nationalism cannot of themselves evoke identification."[77] What is required is that a political ideology "interprets and provides an appropriate attitude for an *experienced* reality" (Bloom's italics). That is to say, the ideology, or in Habermas's terms, the "identity-securing interpretive system," must work in the real world by providing the tools to interpret what the individual is experiencing, and the means to react against threat. An ideology's symbols are powerless without a related experience. They cannot "secure identity" if they cannot help interpret events in the real world. But when there is a connection with lived experience, they take on meaning for the individual and evoke identification that must be protected against threat. Thus Jerusalem becomes an *empowered* symbol when it is related to the Palestinian or Israeli lived (or even just imagined, in the case of Jerusalem) experience of the city, especially under threat of loss.

In respect of Jerusalem, we could expect that Zionist and Palestinian leaders would make known an official ideological position that provides the general population with the means to benefit psychologically in terms of security of identity. They might encourage the retention of Jerusalem as an appropriate behavior in the name of national identity and in confirmation of personal identification with the city. The theory also invites examination of "how the dynamic of national identity influences, or is manipulated and appropriated by, decision-making."[78] Bloom's work finds "a coherent methodological link between individual and group . . . behavior."[79] It may therefore have relevance to the relationship between Zionist and Palestinian nationalist leadership and their respective publics regarding Jerusalem's future. Perhaps identification issues have primacy in determining public attitudes and approaches to the city.

Summarizing the Framework

The significance of the theoretical framework developed here is that it combines overlooked perspectives in several fields. As noted, some few international relations scholars have observed marked deficiencies in the application of the concept of identity, despite its ready acceptance. Similarly, the conceptual work of Erik Erikson, the recognized architect of identity, has been much undervalued and almost forgotten, even in the field of psychoanalysis. So, too, the concept of ideology has suffered from near "invisibility" within the international relations field. At the same time that these disciplines have overlooked concepts that could have global relevance, the ability to anticipate instability and upheaval in world affairs seems to have diminished. The framework put forward here attempts to redress the situation by drawing on Erikson's dynamic of identity within the human life cycle and combining it with an overlooked typology of ideology, thus creating an analytic tool that is responsive to the human element in international relations. Utilizing the concept of interacting variables, the framework allows examination of the Arab-Zionist and later Palestinian-Israeli conflict with particular reference to the debate over Jerusalem's future. Since the Jerusalem Question has been an element of the history of both peoples to a greater or lesser degree over the past century, it provides fertile ground for the examination of the role of the identity-ideology nexus as a variable in interaction with others. The situation on the ground in Jerusalem has shifted dramatically at times, while at others stasis seems to have set in. Since the concept of latency refers to something hidden, dormant, or quiescent, which may or may not become visible and active, by definition latency in the identity-ideology nexus regarding Jerusalem underlies both stasis and movement. In the case of stasis, latent elements remain unfulfilled and await new opportunities, while in the case of movement they become active and influence progress toward or realization of their goal. Both movement and stasis are also mediated by external events and conditions that constitute interacting variables, favorable or unfavorable to resolution of the Jerusalem Question for one or both parties. Examples of such interacting variables are, among others, overwhelming threat of loss, domestic factors (e.g., elite unity or disunity, and political party stance), inertia or status quo conditions, territorial possession or its lack, preponderance or absence of military strength, and effective or ineffective international involvement. The theoretical framework developed here allows for a unique analysis of the reasons why the Jerusalem Question exhibits a stasis-movement dynamic and what lessons may be learned from the application of the identity-ideology framework in terms of a resolution of the current impasse.

If the identity-ideology nexus also constitutes an interacting variable of Israeli and Palestinian policy formulation and decision making on the Jerusalem Question, then we should expect to find

1. that there is evidence of significant personal identification with Jerusalem during the childhood and subsequent life stages of key Zionist and Palestinian nationalist figures, expressed in adult life as the opportunity arises to confirm that identification;
2. that for both Jews/Israelis and Arabs/Palestinians, a preponderance of unfavorable interacting variables in the form of external events and conditions causes latent forces in the identity-ideology nexus regarding Jerusalem to remain quiescent, resulting in stasis over the Jerusalem Question;
3. that for both Arabs/Palestinians and Jews/Israelis, the triggering effect of favorable interacting variables causes hitherto latent forces in the identity-ideology nexus regarding Jerusalem to become active, resulting in movement on the Jerusalem Question.

Methodology

Getting behind the spoken and written word to the core identity issues and ideological positions is the novel focus of this study on the Jerusalem Question. Accordingly, the methodology adopted is based on a partial application of anamnesis—the clinical case study technique used by medical doctors and psychiatrists in establishing a patient's recalled personal history.[80] As applied here, anamnesis allows analysis of the establishing of identity by reference to life history and charts the acquiring of ideology, paying particular attention to what is said or written (especially in adulthood) that is reflective of earlier stages.

While this methodology would normally include both longitudinal and cross-sectional analysis in building political and personality profiles, here the emphasis is on the longitudinal component, which allows for the development of a psychobiography for each individual. Life history and the attendant psychosocial crises are deemed to be a significant element in personal and political identity formation and may be at the root of identity and ideological positions on Jerusalem. Therefore, cross-sectional analysis of basic personality traits (e.g., affect, drives, interpersonal relationships) is less of an emphasis.

The approach in this study is of necessity qualitative, dependent on biographical research, discourse analysis, and interviews with significant actors mainly in Israel and Palestine.[81] The selection of the fourteen personalities was based on examining the intricate history of the more-than-100-year conflict between the Arabs of Palestine and the Zionists. Thus the biographies are representative of the varied positions on both sides across time. It seemed essential to include key actors in the formation of the Zionist and Palestinian nationalist movements and to continue with the primary leaders who have been at the center of most activity with respect to the Jerusalem issue until the present. Apart from these considerations, the choice of one leader over another was random. It should also be mentioned that the author had no prior knowledge of the wealth of information regarding Jerusalem in each personality's background. The degree of similarity that emerged between the two groups of personalities with respect to elements in their life histories and their feelings about Jerusalem was surprising. Since the development of Palestinian nationalism follows the same general time line as the Zionist endeavor, the interaction between the fourteen leading personalities makes for an effective discussion of their respective identity-ideology nexuses with regard to the Jerusalem Question.

Alternative Explanations

If identity and ideology issues are not the primary reason for the seeming intractability of the modern-day Jerusalem Question, what might be the alternative explanations? Three possibilities emerge: economic considerations, security concerns, and legal issues. Do any of these potential explanations outweigh the significance of the ideology-identity dimension? If any or all three alternative explanations have merit, are they perhaps cumulative in their effect on limiting the ability of either side to come to a negotiated settlement on Jerusalem? These alternatives are now briefly taken up in chapter 2.

CHAPTER 2
ALTERNATIVE EXPLANATIONS

The disparity in military and economic power between Palestinians and Israelis has severely limited the negotiating leverage of the Palestinians. Further exacerbating this disparity is the fact that the Palestinians were not represented by even a quasi government until the mid-1990s. While it could be argued that the Palestinians are intractable on the Jerusalem Question because they have legal rights or economic or security needs on which they will not compromise, the burden of the efforts directed toward resolution must lie with the established nation in power.

In discussing the possibility of alternative explanations for the lack of progress on the Jerusalem Question, it becomes clear that the Palestinians are unlikely to oppose active Israeli steps to end the economic and military stranglehold they maintain over the city. Establishing a joint Jerusalem municipality with appropriate jurisdiction over the city's administrative functions would begin the process of restoring the West Bank's economic life. The closure of Jerusalem to Palestinian nonresidents of the city would cease and the routes from the northern West Bank to the south via East Jerusalem would be opened. Similarly, the removal of the IDF presence in the city and the sharing of police forces for public order would resolve most of the Palestinians' problems on the security issue. The legal issues are more complex, and as several authorities point out in what follows, there is no simple answer to them on either side. However, the baseline for final negotiations with respect to certain key legal issues regarding Jerusalem has been set. In the 1993 Declaration of Principles, both sides agreed to be bound by UN resolutions 242 and 338.

Whether resolution of these economic, security, and legal issues alone would suffice to bring final agreement on Jerusalem is in part the subject of this study. For the above reasons the discussion in this chapter revolves mainly around alternative explanations from the Israeli perspective, with some reference to Palestinian economic, legal, and security issues.

Economic Considerations

Does the Israeli government's failure to come to agreement with the Palestinians on Jerusalem's status rest on the state's overriding economic interests? How does the city compare with major Israeli cities with respect to population, economic diversification, and growth potential? The analysis begins with a brief historical overview of the economy from the Ottoman period onward.

During much of the period of Turkish rule beginning in 1517, the city was an economic backwater. According to several nineteenth-century eyewitness accounts,[1] it was a filthy city—one that had "sunk into the neglected capital of a petty Turkish province."[2] The traveler Edward Robinson continued, "[S]he sits sad and solitary in darkness and in the dust." Moreover, it was poor in natural resources. Records from the early 1800s show that it lacked sufficient water for the dyeing of cloth.[3] At the same time, the city's bazaar traded in produce from the hinterland's sparse agriculture.

In the mid-nineteenth century, both the *sanjaq* and the city of Jerusalem grew in importance. This was in part a protective measure taken by the Ottomans to guard against further Egyptian encroachment, such as that experienced between 1831 and 1840 when Muhammad 'Ali and Ibrahim Pasha controlled Palestine. In the 1850s the expansion of the Christian and Muslim pilgrimage and tourist business began to breathe new life into the city's limited economy. Over the next few decades, European consular offices opened, and hotels, roads, railways, post offices, churches, and religious properties were built. In 1876 Jerusalem's population was 25,000, and by 1910 it had reached almost 70,000 (see table 2.1). But this increase was not primarily due to Jewish immigrants, who first began arriving in 1882 from Eastern Europe and Russia. They did not tend to favor settling in Jerusalem, preferring the coastal plain. During the entire *Yishuv* period (1882–1948) the main Jewish conurbations developed along the coast. Tel Aviv and Haifa grew at the expense of Jerusalem. Under the British Mandate (1922–48), Jerusalem became the administrative capital of Palestine, though its economy remained dependent on tourism and on the services required by the mandatory authorities and the consular corps. By 1946 the city's population had reached only 164,000 despite these developments (see table 2.1).

Following the 1948 war, as a result of the armistice agreement with Jordan, Israeli West Jerusalem was located at the end of a narrow corridor of land. To all intents and purposes, like Jordanian East Jerusalem, the western part was a cul-de-sac. Neither sector prospered for the next nineteen years. Though East Jerusalem was promoted as Jordan's second capital after 1960, it suffered from the Hashemite kingdom's emphasis on the expansion of Amman.[4] West

Table 2.1 Jerusalem's population by religion

Year	Jews	Muslims	Christians	Total
1525	1,194	3,670	714	5,578
1553	1,958	11,912	1,956	15,826
1563	1,434	11,802	1,830	15,066
1800	2,250	4,000	2,750	9,000
1806	2,000	4,000	2,800	8,800
1844	7,120	5,000	3,390	15,510
1850	6,000	5,400	3,600	15,000
1870	11,000	11,000		22,000
1876	12,000	7,560	5,470	25,030
1910	45,000	12,000	12,900	69,900
1913	48,400*	10,050	16,750	75,200
1922	34,100	13,400	14,700	62,200
1931	53,800	19,900	19,300	93,000
1946	99,300	33,700	31,300	164,300
1948	100,000	40,000	25,000	165,000
1967	196,800	58,100	12,900	267,800
1983	306,300	108,500	13,700	428,500
1985	327,700	115,700	14,200	457,600
1990	378,200	131,900	14,400	524,500
1992	401,100	155,500		556,600
1995	420,900	165,800	13,500	602,600** (1)
1996	426,200	170,800	13,600	613,400** (2)
1997	429,100	175,700	13,700	622,000** (3)
1998	433,600	182,000	14,000	633,600** (4)
1999	436,700	189,700	14,100	646,100** (5)
2000	439,600	196,900	14,200	657,400** (6)
2001	444,300	203,500	14,400	669,800** (7)
2002	447,900	209,900	14,400	680,200** (8)
2003	453,700	216,700	14,500	693,200** (9)

Sources: Figures are based on information derived from Sharkansky, *Governing Jerusalem*; Wasserstein, *Divided Jerusalem*; and Choshen and Shahar, *Statistical Yearbook: 1998*; *2000*; and *2002/2003*.

Notes: According to McCarthy, "[t]he population of the cities and towns of Ottoman Palestine is particularly difficult to estimate" (*The Population of Palestine*, 15). Rashid Khalidi notes that the whole Jewish population of Palestine just prior to the First World War was about 60,000 rather than the Zionist figure of 85,000. Of the 60,000, about 10 to 12,000 lived on the land, while the rest lived in Jerusalem, Hebron, Safad, and Tiberias (*Palestinian Identity*, 96).

* Much has been made of Jerusalem having a Jewish majority prior to the First World War, but Ottoman records "indicate no such thing and non-Ottoman sources are dubious at best" (Khalidi, *Palestinian Identity*, 229 n. 88).
** Those of unclassified religion included in total: (1) 2,400; (2) 2,800; (3) 3,500; (4) 4,000; (5) 5,600; (6) 6,700; (7) 7,600; (8) 8,000; (9) 8,200.

Jerusalem remained an economic backwater, even after the transfer of most government ministries and departments from Tel Aviv. Further, its population grew more slowly than that of the rest of Israel, and companies resisted moving to the city for fear of a repeat of the isolation suffered during the war, and because transport costs were higher than on the coastal plain.[5]

After its 1967 annexation of East Jerusalem, the Israeli government financed the construction of buildings for its own use in the expanded city. The Old City's Jewish Quarter, damaged during the 1948 war and poorly maintained under Jordanian rule, was also rebuilt. Next came the housing projects constructed as "facts on the ground," partly with the intention of complicating future Palestinian claims to sovereignty. Along with the housing developments came infrastructure, including new roads to circumvent Palestinian towns and villages and to connect Jerusalem to the coast. The main areas of industrial production, however, have remained outside the Jerusalem sector.[6] The busy daily commute from Jerusalem to Tel Aviv tells the story of where the nation's economic strength is concentrated. In addition, between 1990 and 2002 Jerusalem's population decreased by 81,700 (mostly Jews) as residents left the city proper for locations in metropolitan Jerusalem, the West Bank, and other areas in Israel.[7] By 2005, despite this decrease, the city was the largest conurbation, with a population of 723,700.[8] But as in earlier times, Jerusalem survives largely on government funding, donations from outside the country, and revenues generated by tourism and education, and by servicing the government sector. In 2001–02, 49 percent of Jerusalem's employees worked in the civil service and community service sectors, compared to 27 percent in Tel Aviv–Jaffa, and 33 percent in Israel.[9]

But despite its development as the center of government, over the years the city's limitations have remained the same. With few natural resources, distant from the Lod international airport near Tel Aviv and the ports on the Mediterranean coast, largely cut off from trade with the Arab world, and lacking in overseas investment, Jerusalem continues to struggle with economic weakness. In an effort to ameliorate the situation, Ariel Sharon announced in June 2005 that a $60 million Jerusalem development plan focusing on employment, housing, and revival of the city center would be put before his cabinet that month. Incentives were to be offered to entrepreneurs and workers in the hi-tech and communications fields and for the construction of new factories. The prime minister also initiated a separate program for encouraging young couples to take up residence in Jerusalem.[10]

Even with these factors in mind, economic arguments against sharing Jerusalem with a future Palestinian state appear to have little or no support based on present or foreseeable conditions. There is no threat to the economic growth of the Israeli economy. Rather, as Ira Sharkansky has put it, "the motive forces of Jerusalem policymaking are more likely to be national and religious than a seeking-after economic advantage."[11]

That said, a resolution of the Jerusalem Question could only improve the economic outlook for the city, East and West, considering the influx of international funding that peace would bring, to say nothing of the boom in tourism that would also ensue. Under a permanent-status agreement the annual number of guests in Jerusalem is projected to rise from 1 million to about 2 million, and overnight stays from about 3 million to 5 million.[12] Shimon Peres has argued for many years that an economically prosperous Palestinian entity could only benefit both Palestinians and Israelis.[13]

Israeli Security Concerns

Security is normally defined in terms of external security, internal security, and public order. The latter is usually a matter of police control over crime in the public sphere. However, both external security, in terms of attack from outside Israel, and internal security, in terms of terrorist activity within Israel and the West Bank, are the concern of the IDF. Israel's use of the IDF to counter the First and Second Intifadas has placed the army, rather than the police, at the center of public order issues in and around Jerusalem. Thus one possible explanation for Israeli intransigence over resolving the Jerusalem Question is guaranteeing its external and internal security.

The security of Jerusalem and its environs is a logical concern for all parties involved in the city's daily life. The significance of the Old City as a center of worship for multiple faiths carries security implications because of the possibility of clashes between visitors to the various religious sites. While public order has usually been the issue in such cases, events of the past thirty years have demonstrated the vulnerability and volatility of the area encompassing the Western Wall, the Dome of the Rock, the al-Aqsa Mosque, and the Church of the Holy Sepulchre. Ever since the Israelis took possession of the Old City in 1967, they have often stated that they will provide adequate security and freedom of access to the holy places for adherents of all faiths. The statement is made whenever there is a suggestion that sovereignty over the holy sites should be shared with others. But this response does not appear to be based on security needs.

From the broader perspective, security is a necessary agenda item in any Israeli discussion of peace in the Middle East. Former Knesset and Likud party member Benny Begin expressed this viewpoint when he said, "Israel is a dangerous neighborhood."[14] Israeli government officials on all sides habitually stress security issues whenever they speak of the possibility of an end to hostilities. Security has dominated Israeli thinking since the foundation of the state. Ben-Gurion conceived the milieu as one where there would be hostility for the foreseeable future. The primacy of this view is demonstrated by the fact that for twenty-two years of the State of Israel's fifty-year existence, the defense portfolio was held by the prime minister.[15] Begin argued further that external security is a dominant issue with respect to Jerusalem in that the city is seen as a key link in a chain of strategic locations. As evidence, he quoted a declassified 1967 document from the U.S. Joint Chiefs of Staff. It delineated for the U.S. secretary of defense the "minimum territory in addition to that held on June 4, '67, [that] Israel might be justified in retaining in order to permit a more effective defense against possible conventional Arab attack and terrorist raids."[16] The recommendation of the Joint Chiefs read: "[A]s a minimum, Israel would need a defense line generally along the axis Bardala-Tubas-Nablus-Bira-Jerusalem and then to the northern part of the Dead Sea" (see map 2.1). Expressing his

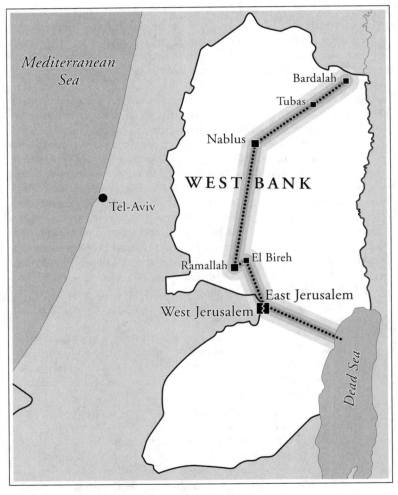

Map 2.1 Proposed minimal Israeli line of defense in the West Bank, 1967.

agreement, Begin pointed out that this line runs along "the backbone of [ancient] Judaea and Samaria" and recalled the Hebrew patriarch Abraham's possession of the same high ground, as recorded in the biblical book of Genesis. The Joint Chiefs' report also concluded that "[t]he envisioned defensive line would run just east of Jerusalem."[17]

Israel's two major political parties, Labor and Likud, demonstrated acceptance of elements of this security line by initiating housing projects on expropriated Palestinian land following the capture of East Jerusalem in 1967. Strategic concerns dictated the Labor government's construction of the neighborhood of Ramot Eshkol in 1968. It was built adjacent to the road to the pre-1967 Jewish enclave on Mount Scopus. The nearby French Hill development was also constructed in 1968 along roads leading to the Old City, Mount Scopus, and Palestinian cities on the West Bank. The same year saw development on Mount Scopus and at Givat Shapira. High-rise apartment blocks, condominiums, and commercial and service buildings in numerous developments created "facts on the ground" in the name of security.

Neither Labor nor Likud showed any inclination to end such development, even following the Oslo Agreements in September 1993. A month later, Labor party deputy defense minister Mordechai Gur spoke of the security needs of Jerusalem in familiar language:

Past experience has proven that in order to defend Jerusalem one must have a strip of defence surrounding it in the North, South, East and West. We shall insist that even though we shall have peace . . . we must take into our calculation the necessity to defend Jerusalem and to build it in such a way that we shall be able to defend it.[18]

In December 1993 prime minister Rabin "approved the creation of a 'municipal continuity' between Jerusalem, Givat Ze'ev, and Ma'ale Adumim, principally through the construction of new roads and tunnels."[19] In June 1967, as chief of staff, he had suggested that Israel apply law to a much greater area around Jerusalem for defense reasons. He later said that if others had not narrowed down his ideas, "there would be no Jerusalem problem today."[20]

Though settlement building and expansion is often associated exclusively with the Likud party, the facts demonstrate that the Labor party played a decisive role in encouraging construction around Jerusalem as early as 1968. Then from 1993 to 2000, while two Labor prime ministers were in office, population in the settlements doubled.[21] According to Peace Now spokesman Didi Remez, the continued appropriation and construction was one reason the Oslo peace process broke down.[22]

Several developments were built strategically so that they commanded the hilltops around Jerusalem to the east.[23] Ma'aleh Adumim lies beyond

East Jerusalem's border, high on a plateau overlooking the descent to the Jordan Valley (see map 2.2). Its history epitomizes the Israeli security argument about Jerusalem. Twenty-three settler families went there in 1975 with the idea of defending Jerusalem.[24] The settlement had the blessing of Labor party leader Yitzhak Rabin, who had proposed that the community be built.[25] According to journalist Gad Nahshon, Rabin "declared the city to be united with Israel forever."[26] It was planned and developed by the subsequent Likud government, led by Menachem Begin, and became the first Israeli city in the West Bank. In 1999 Ma'aleh Adumim's long-serving mayor, Benny Kashriel, explained his view of the

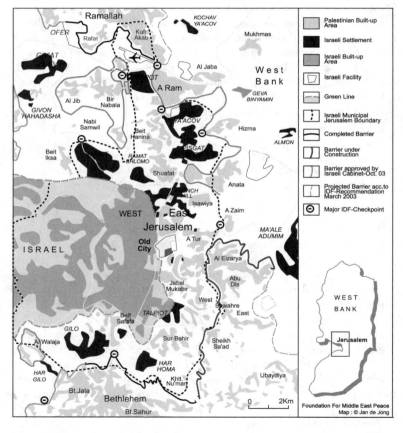

Map 2.2   Jerusalem—November 2003.

city's strategic significance:

> This city is very important to Jerusalem, sitting on the east gate of Jerusalem and protecting the east gate of Jerusalem, going toward the Sea of Galilee, the Jordan border, the Dead Sea, the south of Israel, and the city of Eilat. This was the reason that Ma'aleh Adumim was built at the east gate of Jerusalem. It is a question of security, a strategic point. And this was the reason for Ma'aleh Adumim. This is the reason that we are called Ma'aleh Adumim [Ascent of Adumim]. This is Jerusalem. We are part of the Jerusalem metropolis.[27]

The new city's first phase provided for 20,000 settlers. By mid-2005, the newcomers had reached 31,000 and were able to drive to central parts of Jerusalem in a few minutes through two newly constructed tunnels under Mount Scopus. The next phase of building will add 15,000 residents, with long-term plans for up to 65,000. The city will be larger in area than Tel Aviv and, positioned as it is on the eastern edge of Jerusalem, it is clearly intended as an important security barrier.

Security issues were on the mind of the former chief of the IDF, Ehud Barak, as he prepared for the Israeli election in 1998. Voicing his position on internal security, he said:

> [M]y vision is clear—we have to separate ourselves from the Palestinians, physically separating ourselves with certain security limits, following Robert Frost's, the poet's, suggestion that good fences make good neighbors. . . . And we have to bear in mind our security limits. I'm wishing peace through the need to achieve security for the State of Israel.[28]

Barak also made the commitment to remove Israeli troops from Lebanon if he would be elected as prime minister. It proved to be a winning campaign promise. The two statements were compatible because, in Barak's view, the nature of war and weaponry had changed, making early detection of attack much easier and response much faster. With Israel's sophisticated war footing, it was considered no longer necessary to maintain troops in places unpopular with the Israeli public, nor to fund such operations.

Following his election, Barak made significant changes in Israel's security arrangements. He withdrew all Israeli troops from southern Lebanon in accordance with UN Resolution 425 (1978). He further entertained the possibility of a peace treaty with Syria and the return of part of the Golan Heights, taken in the 1967 war. Barak also reneged on a part of the Wye Agreement signed by his predecessor, Benjamin Netanyahu, and Yasser Arafat in November 1998. Arrangements for a Palestinian-controlled nature reserve in the northern Judean Desert were canceled. Barak decided against "any withdrawal from the Judean Desert for security reasons involving the future protection of the capital, Jerusalem."[29]

Further, at the final talks of the Oslo peace process at Taba in January 2001, Barak instructed negotiator Gilad Sher to change the terms of a proposed land swap. He did so in order to connect Ma'aleh Adumim and Givat Ze'ev, east and north of Jerusalem, by gaining a swath of Palestinian territory that would affect a "fairly large Palestinian population and East Jerusalem's most important land reserves."[30] Once the Palestinians understood the implications of the move, they withdrew their offer to exchange territory for Ma'aleh Adumim and Givat Ze'ev. Like Yitzhak Rabin, Barak felt strongly about the strategic significance of Jerusalem's eastern border. In order to come to terms on Jerusalem's future, he tried to preserve the security advantage that the eastern and northern settlement had given. But security issues were not the fundamental reason for lack of progress in the talks. According to the notes taken by Miguel Moratinos, special envoy of the European Union to the Middle East, the Taba talks were suspended because of the political timetable imposed by impending Israeli elections.[31] It was said that the two sides had never been closer to an agreement. Interestingly, after the meeting Sher admitted that "the status of Jerusalem's holy sites—always a potential deal-breaker—was barely touched."[32]

Following the election of Ariel Sharon in February 2001, the security situation in Jerusalem deteriorated significantly, with a sharp increase in the number of terrorist attacks in the city. In 2002 the severity of suicide bombings in Jerusalem[33] and other cities prompted the Israeli government to order the IDF into the West Bank and Gaza on short missions in an effort to disrupt the attacks. In April the government approved construction of a 350-kilometer (220-mile) electronic security fence to run approximately along the 1948 Green Line (see map 2.2). Even before the outbreak of the al-Aqsa Intifada in September 2000, Barak had proposed a literal wall in the form of a security fence separating the Palestinian West Bank from Israel.[34] Fifty kilometers (thirty miles) of the new fence was to surround Jerusalem on the three sides that bordered the West Bank: north, south, and east.[35] Work on the Jerusalem section was begun in May and accelerated a month later in response to more suicide bombings in the city.[36] Defense minister Binyamin Ben-Eliezer commented that the purpose of the initial few kilometers of fence in southern Jerusalem was to protect the settlement of Gilo, "preventing any possibility of penetration through Bethlehem, Beit Jala and Beit Sahur."[37] In July 2005, the Israeli government gave approval for an extended 680-kilometer (425-mile) barrier. The final route around Jerusalem would leave four Palestinian areas of the city beyond the wall and disrupt the lives of 55,000 people.[38]

Sharon had made clear his own view of security in general and of Jerusalem's future at the swearing in of his new government in February 2003. He mentioned that any agreement with the Palestinians would have to include "security and buffer zones" and "preserve the unity of the Capital of Israel—Jerusalem."[39] The zones were part of his thinking as foreign minister in 1999. He had called for the creation of two such areas: an eastern zone, nine to twelve miles wide in the Jordan Valley; and a western zone, three to six miles wide along the heights of the West Bank overlooking the coastal plain.[40] This thinking explains the rationale for the Sharon government's building of the separation fence in the West Bank and around Jerusalem.

To summarize the security situation with respect to negotiations on Jerusalem's future, there are security issues to resolve and stakes to preserve. It is clear, however, that the overwhelming military power of the IDF and the strategic placement of Israeli developments around Jerusalem ought to make it easier for Israel to agree to the capital of the Palestinian state in East Jerusalem. Even the construction of a security fence around the city does not militate against a resolution. In reality the fence becomes one more "fact on the ground" to be negotiated in a final settlement, though most of it may become the location of the future border with the Palestinian state. As a dimension of final-status discussions on Jerusalem, security does not appear to be a deal-breaker. Former Israeli ambassador and Sharon advisor Dore Gold concludes that

> [s]trictly speaking Jerusalem is not a strategic issue. For Israel, the Palestinian Arabs, and the Arab/Islamic world it is a national-religious question. . . . Thus, Israel's position in Jerusalem is not an instrument for obtaining other national objectives like security, but rather is a central value in its own right.[41]

An argument for intractability on the part of Israel based on security concerns therefore appears to have little merit. As the single most powerful entity in the Middle East, supported by the United States, Israel is fully capable of defending herself from attack within Jerusalem's present or foreseeable boundaries.

Legal Issues

If legal reasons exist for failure to come to an agreement on the future status of Jerusalem, they rest in part on Israeli perceptions of rights in international law to those parts of Jerusalem taken in the wake of the 1948 and 1967 wars. If such rights exist, there could be intransigence on legal grounds. Do legal rights account for Israel's stance? What is Israel's legal argument? According to Hebrew University law professor Ruth Lapidoth,

> Israel's claim to Jerusalem is based on the following idea: When Britain left [in 1948], the area was left without a sovereign, which means there was a

vacuum, an emptiness of sovereignty. This could be filled lawfully only by a state that acted lawfully. The Jordanians tried to take West Jerusalem. They took East Jerusalem by illegal acts; therefore they did not have the right to any claim to sovereignty. They did not have the right to fill this vacuum that was created by the departure of the British people. On the other hand, the Israelis took West Jerusalem in 1948 and East Jerusalem in 1967 by acts of self-defense, which are lawful; therefore they had the right to fill this vacuum of sovereignty and become the sovereign of Jerusalem.[42]

In 1979, Crown Prince Hassan of Jordan issued a detailed rebuttal of the Israeli position, referencing the 1907 Hague Regulations and the 1949 Geneva Conventions. He noted that "Jordan did not acquire sovereignty in East Jerusalem between 1948 and 1967" but was simply a military occupier. Similarly Israel did not acquire sovereignty in 1967 but rather imposed occupation. Therefore sovereignty "remains suspended."[43]

Rodman Bundy, an international lawyer specializing in territorial disputes, argues that the Israeli position is unsustainable, apart from any questions of factuality as expressed in Lapidoth's delineation of the standard Israeli view. From a legal standpoint, filling a sovereignty vacuum "is not sufficient under international law to found a legitimate claim of title or to acquire territory. This is the fundamental flaw in Israel's legal argument."[44]

Nevertheless, the question of where sovereignty is vested with respect to Jerusalem is complex. It may be that the city is a special case, judicially unique. According to law professor Ian Brownlie, "[s]tate succession arises when there is a definitive replacement of one state by another in respect of sovereignty over a given territory in conformity with international law."[45] The reason that Jerusalem's sovereignty is a complex question revolves around the circumstances following the collapse of the Ottoman Empire. In respect of Palestine, there was no clear state succession. Turkey, the successor power to the remains of the Ottoman Empire, "relinquished sovereignty over Palestine" by signing the Treaty of Lausanne in 1923.[46] The League of Nations created the British Mandate for Palestine, but, as mandatory power, Britain did not assume sovereignty over Palestine or Jerusalem. Neither did the League of Nations act as the sovereign power. Ultimately the League of Nations was dissolved and the United Nations took its place. In 1947 the UN called for the partition of Palestine into two states, Israel and Palestine, and for the establishment of Jerusalem as a *corpus separatum* to be administered by a UN-appointed governor. In the wake of the 1948 Arab-Israeli war, this resolution was never carried out.

Further, international law does not give right of sovereignty over land acquired and held under belligerent occupation.[47] The UN Charter states that territory taken during hostilities is to be returned and is therefore not subject to any intervening changes in its legal status. Israel has consistently said that Jerusalem is beyond the scope of UN resolutions that prevent Israel from having free course in the city, both East and West.

The official UN position on Jerusalem remains that it should become a *corpus separatum*. However, it is unlikely that the UN will ever press for such an outcome. In practical terms, the UN's view is that two states should exist side by side, with a negotiated settlement between the two parties over Jerusalem, and with special provision for the holy sites in the Old City.

In 1975, Judge Arnold McNair argued in the case of the South-West Africa Mandate that "[s]overeignty over a mandated territory is in abeyance; if and when the inhabitants of the Territory obtain recognition as an independent state . . . sovereignty will revive and rest in the new state."[48] This led Bundy to argue that

> [i]n the light of Jerusalem's peculiar historical background, it is very difficult for either the Palestinians or Israel to rest their claims to Jerusalem on the principle of state succession. If sovereignty is to "revive and rest" in a new state, which is it to be?[49]

Nevertheless, according to John Quigley, with respect to territorial right as defined in international law, "Palestine has a valid claim to Jerusalem."[50] Palestinian scholar and PLO official Sami Musallam notes, "It is . . . clear that international legitimacy favours the Palestinian side on the issue of East Jerusalem."[51]

What is the Palestinian claim? If it rests on prior occupation, then international law will not allow such a claim for the Palestinians any more than for the Israelis. If it rests on tradition, in that the Palestinians have lived in the area for hundreds of years, the Israelis can make the same claim for the Jewish people, using the biblical record. Complicating the issue is that Israel is recognized as a state under international law. To act toward Israel as if this were not the case would be inconsistent with generally accepted legal principles. Even if Israel's claim to part of Jerusalem could be defeated, the case for Palestinian sovereignty would not automatically follow. The fact that one state does not have a claim does not mean that another does. It seems that a solution to the question of Jerusalem cannot rest on legal grounds alone. Uri Savir, Israeli chief negotiator of the Oslo Agreements, said of the Jerusalem Question and legal considerations:

> Anybody who is going to try to resolve Jerusalem according to international law is going to fall into five different interpretations. I can give you all of them. If you want Israel's line on international law, you can get Israel's line. If you want the Arab line, you can get the Arab line. There is no objective international law regarding a conflict related to Jerusalem.[52]

With these thoughts in mind, it seems that an appeal to an argument from international law to explain Israeli intransigence over the final status of Jerusalem is insufficient. And therefore, as Bundy concludes, "the matter is more likely to require a creative diplomatic solution freed from the strict constraints of law."[53]

Economic issues, security considerations, and legal concerns all remain unconvincing alternatives in the search for an explanation for Israeli and Palestinian intransigence over the Jerusalem Question. Consideration of the cumulative effect of these alternative explanations does not appear warranted either. While there may be a case for Israeli reluctance to negotiate because of security concerns—especially, for example, when there is an increase in suicide attacks focused on Jerusalem—and for Palestinian refusal to negotiate because of military and economic oppression, security issues do not explain the longevity of the impasse. After all, there have been many periods when security concerns have not been so evident. The analysis suggests that a more convincing explanation must lie elsewhere. Indeed, four authorities on the Jerusalem Question concede as much. Arguing for contextualization of legal issues within the broader history of the conflict, law professor Ruth Lapidoth noted:

> As far as I know, neither economic nor strategic questions are important in the case of Jerusalem. What is important is the symbolic value of Jerusalem. It is a symbol for many people, and it has strong religious aspects.[54]

Historian Bernard Wasserstein, commenting on resolution of the Jerusalem Question and its centrality to settlement of the Palestinian-Israeli conflict, said:

> It is not primarily a security issue, it is not primarily an issue other than one of symbols, and the symbolic issue, like most symbolic issues, is one that is even more difficult to solve than some of the other issues.[55]

Savir, having already dismissed legal considerations as a fruitful way forward, summarized the possibility of alternative explanations as follows:

> I don't think it is economics. [And] security with the Palestinians is a function of the quality of relations. There will be two states, and these two states need to cooperate on security. . . . We need to prevent an Arab army west of the Jordan River. But by and large, it is not that much of a territorial issue. Jerusalem has its importance mainly as an identity issue, a religious issue, an issue that is really related to our very being.[56]

For his part, Ahmad Quray' noted that there are many aspects of the Jerusalem Question that can be successfully negotiated, but there is one that cannot: sovereignty. Significantly, Quray' ties sovereignty to issues of ideology and identity and emphasizes that negotiators must give attention to this matter if a solution is to be found:

> The nonnegotiable issue in the conflict over Jerusalem is sovereignty. Sovereignty is not negotiable. Modalities can be negotiated: what kind of security, how to reach the religious places, transportation, taxes—even municipal wards can be negotiated. But the matter of sovereignty is nonnegotiable. We have an ideological solution for that: When I, as a Palestinian, take my car and can go all over Jerusalem—East and West—and feel that it is my city, and the Israeli can take his car and go wherever—East and West—and feel it is his city, and *you* come from Europe, the United States or any other place and feel that there is a special status to this city and that you are at home—I think *then* we can have a permanent solution to Jerusalem. Otherwise it will be a time bomb. It can be quiet today, but nobody can guarantee that after some days or some years it will remain that way. This is what the negotiators and the decision makers should take into consideration if they want to find a real solution.[57]

The desire of today's Palestinians and Israelis to travel freely throughout Jerusalem is rooted in their long-standing associations with the city. In chapter 3 the study turns to the historical aspects of the underlying identity-ideology nexus of both peoples with respect to Jerusalem. Each has a rich tradition nationally, religiously, and culturally.

THE MEANING AND SIGNIFICANCE OF JERUSALEM TO THE JEWISH, ISRAELI, ARAB, AND PALESTINIAN PEOPLES

The Jewish and Israeli Perspective

The emergence of Zionism in all of its facets—religious, political, socialist, synthetic, and revisionist—was the outgrowth of a long historical process. Understanding the centrality of Jerusalem as an aspect of identity and ideology in Jewish and Israeli thought necessitates consideration of religious, political, and cultural aspects. It is a story that stretches across millennia and continents, and across ancient and modern empires as the Hebrew people and their Jewish descendants were settled and exiled, enslaved and freed, persecuted and rescued time after time. An enduring aspect of their journey is their religious heritage, no less the symbols of their faith, including an attachment to the land of ancient Israel and its primary religious and political center, Jerusalem.

For 2,500 years, since the Babylonian captivity (605–459 B.C.E.), Jewish sentiment has been stirred by the exiles' oath: "If I forget you, O Jerusalem, let my right hand forget its skill! If I do not remember you, let my tongue cling to the roof of my mouth—if I do not exalt Jerusalem above my chief joy."[1] Each year since the Roman destruction of Herodian Jerusalem and its temple in 70 C.E., the Jewish community in the Diaspora has repeated to itself "Next year in Jerusalem" at two of Judaism's annual religious convocations: Pesach (the Passover) and Yom Kippur (the Day of Atonement). What has become the State of Israel's national anthem, "Hatikvah" (The Hope), composed circa 1878, was inspired by the founder-settlers of Petah Tikvah, near Tel Aviv. It, too, speaks the language of redemptive return to Jerusalem and the land of Zion:

As long as deep in the heart,
The soul of a Jew yearns,
And towards the East

An eye looks to Zion,
Our hope is not yet lost,
The hope of two thousand years,
To be a people free in our land,
The land of Zion and Jerusalem.[2]

The longing for a return to Zion/Jerusalem has haunted the Jewish imagination across many generations. This was and is a community with a particular land perpetually in view. In precise physical terms, return to Zion centered ultimately on the area now within the Old City and bounded by the Herodian platform built to support the Second Temple of Zerubbabel. It is this temple, or rather the memory of it, that sanctifies Jerusalem in the Jewish mind. However, more recently Jewish religious authorities have claimed that any part of Jerusalem, even within its current expanded boundaries, is holy. According to Zwi Werblowsky, former professor of comparative religion and history of Jewish thought at Hebrew University, "[f]or the Jewish people Jerusalem is not a city containing holy places or commemorating holy events. The city as such is holy."[3] In spiritual terms the return to Zion means a recommitment to the values of the God of the Hebrew people, which in turn means the worship of that God in the location where He has placed His name. Hence Zion is "the city of the great King."[4] According to Martin Buber, "[w]hen the Jewish people adopted this name for their national concept, all these associations were contained in it."[5]

Jewish legend names the rocky outcrop on the Temple Mount, covered since 692 by the Dome of the Rock, the "Stone of Foundation."[6] It is said that here the universe began and Adam was created. Abraham is believed to have attempted the sacrifice of his son Isaac at the same location. The rock could be the threshing floor that King David bought from Araunah the Jebusite, thus creating a Jewish claim to ownership superseding any Arab claim.[7] It is also believed to be on the site of the First Temple of King Solomon (the central rock serving as the altar), or perhaps the location of the sanctuary of the Holy of Holies within that temple. It is generally accepted that the Second Temple also stood in the same location. Following the Roman destruction of this temple, all that remained were the great platform and the outer retaining wall.

Banned from setting foot within the city during the reign of Emperor Hadrian, Jewish worshipers could only bewail the Second Temple's destruction from the nearby Mount of Olives. Succeeding generations were limited in their access, first by the Roman Christian rulers' antipathy for the "murderers of Christ," and later by Muslim control of the city. However, since at least the twelfth century, Jews have come to a portion of the retaining wall, known as the Western or Wailing Wall (ha-Kotel ha-Ma'aravi), to pray three times a day. There they beseech God, "Return in mercy to your city

Jerusalem and dwell in it as you have promised; rebuild it soon, in our own days. Praised are you, O Lord, builder of Jerusalem."[8] Jerusalem was there every day, every Sabbath, every holy day, in prayers over meals, at marriages, births, comings of age, and deaths. Elon notes, "Nothing remotely like this sentiment surfaced among any other exiled people or lasted so long." Further, Zion was a future image. In the Hebrew Scriptures, the book of Isaiah—"the templocentric book *par excellence* in the corpus of Israelite prophecy"—brought back together land and people in a vision of a future world where Zion would be the center of the redeemed world and the throne of its king.[9]

Efforts by the Jewish community in Palestine to improve the circumstances surrounding worship at the Western Wall were made in the 1830s. The Egyptian occupation of Palestine (1831–40) brought a more tolerant regime as far as Jews and Christians were concerned. As a result, there were attempts to construct a new synagogue and to gain rights over Muslim property. These approaches were rebuffed, however, because of Ottoman restrictions on foreign Jews buying property in and around Jerusalem.

In 1838 the British government opened the first European consulate in Jerusalem, and the following year the consulate took on the task of helping Jews.[10] In one instance the consul approached Ibrahim Pasha, the son of Egypt's viceroy, on behalf of a British Jew who had made an offering to fund the paving of the street in front of the Wailing Wall. The whole area was a Muslim *waqf*, a religious endowment made by the son of Salah al-Din in the thirteenth century. It had been protected for six centuries under the auspices of the North African shaykhs of Jerusalem's Maghribi district. According to A.L. Tibawi, this was a cunning attempt "to acquire a vested interest in the Wailing Place."[11] Ibrahim Pasha agreed to the request, only to have his committee in Jerusalem, with the firm support of the local shaykh, turn it down.

In 1852 various international governments and religious bodies accepted status quo arrangements governing the holy sites in Palestine. These arrangements allowed the several religious faiths limited access and freedom of worship at the sites. In the case of the Jews, they were permitted to worship at the Wall without specific rights. Efforts to buy the Wall itself were made without success in the 1850s. At the same time, the British consul continued to make attempts on behalf of both Christians and Jews to allow construction of religious buildings in Jerusalem.

When the Balfour Declaration was signed in 1917, the Zionists attempted once more to improve the Jews' limited access to the Wall. The inclusion of the declaration in the League of Nations Mandate, by which Britain governed Palestine, encouraged the Zionists to press for unlimited rights of worship at the holy site. Zionist activities at the Wall in 1918 elicited Arab fears that the Jews were attempting to create an outdoor synagogue. Further conflict over the use of the site in 1928–29, in which 133 Jews and 116 Arabs were killed, resulted in a reaffirmation of the status quo by the British authorities, following the report by the government's 1930 Shaw Commission and the associated International Wailing Wall Commission of the League of Nations. The surrender of the Jewish Quarter and the capture of the Old City by Jordan in the 1948 war prevented access to the Wall by Jewish worshipers for the next nineteen years.

When Israel came into possession of the Western Wall in the 1967 war, Jewish identification with Jerusalem was expressed even more openly. Suddenly the Wall became "a monument in the domain of memory and of faith."[12] Within the State of Israel, the capture of the Temple Mount catalyzed the desire to make something profoundly religious out of the otherwise political. The nonreligious became religious that day. Israeli defense minister and avowed secularist Moshe Dayan announced, "We have returned to all that is holy in our land. We have returned never to be parted from it again."[13] Dayan also spoke at the funeral for the 1948 war dead on the Mount of Olives after the 1967 war and said, "We have returned to the mountain, to the cradle of our people, to the inheritance of the Patriarchs, the land of the Judges and the fortress of the Kingdom of the House of David."[14] The power of historical identity motivated many. In the words of Jerusalem's former deputy mayor Meron Benvenisti, "[We felt] that we were joining hands with our ancestors."[15] Colonel Mordechai "Motta" Gur told the soldiers who had gathered at the Wall, "It is impossible to express what we feel in words. We have been waiting for this moment for so many years."[16] Gur had been born in the Old City and led the paratroopers who were the first soldiers to arrive at the Temple Mount. When he finally went to the Western Wall that day, he connected with his own past. He wrote:

> Despite the great congregation, I had to undergo my own private experience. I did not listen to the prayers, but raised my eyes to the stones. . . .
>
> I remembered our family visits at the wall. Twenty-five years ago, as a child, I had walked through the narrow alleys and markets. The impression made on me by the praying at the wall never left me. My memories blended in with the pictures that I had seen at a later age of Jews, with long white beards, wearing frock coats and black hats. They and the wall were one.

On June 12 he assembled with his paratroopers on the Temple Mount and spoke to them even more pointedly in the language of identity:

> [Y]ou restored the Mount to the bosom of the nation. The Western Wall— the heartbeat of every Jew, the place to which every Jewish heart yearns—is once more in our hands. . . .

During the War of Liberation, mighty efforts were made to recover for the nation its heart—the Old City, the Western Wall. These efforts failed.

The great privilege of finishing the circle at long last, of giving back to the nation its capital, its center of sanctity, has been given to you.

Another of the first Israelis to reach the Temple Mount in 1967 was the military chaplain, General Shlomo Goren, who two years later became Israel's chief rabbi (1969–79). He blew the shofar and prayed intensely that day. He also suggested to Major General Uzi Narkiss that the latter could go down in history by taking a hundred kilos of explosive and destroying the Muslim Dome of the Rock. This was revealed thirty years later when Narkiss was dying and told a newspaper reporter the story.[17] The power of identity and the power of the historic moment possessed Goren. He said to Narkiss: "You don't grasp the immense meaning of this. This is an opportunity that can be exploited now, this minute. Tomorrow it will be impossible."[18] It was Goren's conviction that the Jewish temple should be rebuilt. In this he was supported by the minister of religious affairs, Zerach Warhaftig, who held that the Jews own the Temple Mount as a result of the Israelite King David's purchase from Araunah the Jebusite.[19]

The capture of the Old City set in motion many radical changes to meet the Israelis' newly released latent identification with their holy places. Using the language of latency and identification, A.B. Yehoshua wrote of the 1967 conflict, "The Six Day War was labeled 'the Jewish War,' and with good reason, for the old Jewish spirit within us was roused like a ghost."[20] Moshe Dayan gave immediate orders for the clearing of Arab houses adjacent to the Western Wall. The work was accomplished in twenty-four hours. In the process, the Israeli government and the Jerusalem administration of mayor Teddy Kollek destroyed more than 135 houses and dispossessed almost 1,000 people. At the same time, they also drove out the Palestinian residents of the Old City's Jewish Quarter who had taken refuge there after the loss of their homes in West Jerusalem in 1948. It is estimated that as a result, an additional five to six hundred Palestinians lost their homes.[21] Dayan announced that he would like to go further and bulldoze a road through the hills, wide enough to allow "every Jew in the world to reach the Western Wall."[22] The Wall suddenly meant more to Dayan than ever before.

On June 19, Israeli foreign minister Abba Eban addressed the UN General Assembly. He spoke in detail about the origins of the war and its outcome. With respect to Jerusalem he said:

In our nation's long history there have been few hours more intensely moving than the hour of our reunion with the Western Wall. A people had come back to the cradle of its birth. It has renewed its link with the mystery of its origin and continuity. How long and deep are the memories which that reunion evokes.[23]

As noted in chapter 1, aspects of identity may be latent, quiescent, called forth only when the critical moment arises, when the variables interact to produce an unexpected outcome. With respect to the Israelis, the capture of the Old City is the most obvious twentieth-century example of momentum through interactive activation of variables regarding the Jerusalem Question. Here latent Jewish and Israeli identity and ideological factors intersected with unanticipated shifts that advantaged the Israeli battalions surrounding the city on June 5–6. As noted, evidence of the power of identity and ideological elements when they reemerge after long periods is found in the reactions of many Israelis who visited the Wall soon after its capture. Arthur Hertzberg writes:

> Within hours of the conquest of the Old City, generals who had seldom, if ever, been to synagogue were disregarding snipers' bullets and walking toward the Western Wall. They were not embarrassed to follow the time-honored custom of writing prayers on chits of paper and pushing them into the crevices of the Western Wall or of kissing its stones.[24]

Since 1967 the Wall has become a national icon for most Israelis, the location of civil and national ceremonies, concerts, and the swearing in of elite army units. Revering the Wall, the Temple Mount, and historic Jerusalem is for most not a matter of practicing the Jewish religion but rather an essential aspect of national identity rooted in the history and religious tradition of the Jewish people.

The Muslim Arab Perspective

The centrality of Jerusalem/Bayt al-Maqdis/al-Quds/al-Quds al-Sharif in Muslim Arab tradition begins at the earliest point in the development of Islam. A verse in the Qur'an dated to 620 concerns the *Isra*, Muhammad's night journey from al-Masjid al-Haram (the Sanctuary Mosque at Mecca) to al-Masjid al-Aqsa (the Distant Mosque).[25] That date is variously calculated to be about a year to eighteen months before the prophet Muhammad's flight from Mecca to Medina, when he and his followers were driven out and left the persecution and corruption of the capital city behind.[26] Al-Aqsa (distant or remote) is thought to be a reference to Bayt al-Maqdis (the Holy House)—Jerusalem—or al-Haram al-Sharif (the Noble Sanctuary) in Jerusalem.[27] According to the Qur'an, the angel Gabriel initiated Muhammad's night journey to Jerusalem on the mystical winged horse Buraq. On arrival, the horse was tethered in the southwest corner of the Western Wall of the Haram. Muhammad then ascended through seven heavens to God's throne by climbing a ladder above the great rock at the center of the Herodian platform.

He was said to have experienced the Beatific Vision (direct knowledge of God) and to have returned home to Mecca before dawn.

Jerusalem is also considered the first direction of prayer *(qibla)* established by Muhammad.[28] For the first eighteen months in Medina, his followers prayed toward Bayt al-Maqdis in reverence for its Jewish and Christian connection with God. Once the Jews and Christians rejected Muhammad as the new prophet, his followers were required to pray toward Mecca. But Jerusalem was still reckoned among Islam's three holiest sites. A well-known Islamic *hadith*, or saying of the Prophet, instructs followers, "[Y]ou shall only set out to three mosques, the Haram mosque [Mecca], my mosque [Medina], and the Aqsa mosque."[29] These three locations were considered of "equal merit" for prayer and pilgrimage.[30]

In 637/38[31] the forces of Omar, the second caliph after the death of Muhammad, captured Jerusalem. Omar traveled to the city from Syria, accepted its surrender, and signed a pact with the inhabitants assuring them of religious freedom in return for a poll tax. He found the Temple Mount desecrated and in ruins. It had remained so during the entire Byzantine period. The Christians saw no religious value in the site of the Jewish temple, despising it so much that they used it as a refuse dump. Omar and his Muslim troops were shocked by the Christians' treatment of the revered place. They cleared the temple platform and the area around the Rock (which was found under a dunghill), and cleansed the place with rose water. Omar is said to have marked out a niche for the direction of prayer, prayed to the south of the Rock, and built a rudimentary mosque there.

The Muslim capture of Jerusalem is an early example of momentum on the Jerusalem issue for one of the parties. In the case of the caliph Omar and his leaders, there is evidence of the interactive activation of the variables in such a way that the latent aspects of identity and ideology regarding Jerusalem in Muslim thought were released. Sabri Jarrar comments that the taking of the city was "the ultimate reward" in a campaign "launched by a community ideologically committed to the hegemony of Islam."[32] He adds, "For the Companions of Muhammad who led the first campaign, such as Abu 'Ubayda and Khalid ibn al-Walid, the capture of Jerusalem must have seemed like part of the fulfillment of the prophetic promise that Islam would prevail."[33] According to one account, when Omar arrived in the city, he immediately sought out the "holy place" by consulting with the Greek Patriarch Sophronius, who at first assumed it was the Christian Church of the Holy Sepulchre that Omar was seeking. Eventually the caliph was taken to the Temple Mount. Once there, he looked for the Rock where Abraham was believed to have attempted the sacrifice of his son in the ultimate act of submission to God's will *(islam)*.

There is evidence that several of the "Companions of the Prophet," eyewitnesses to his life, visited Jerusalem out of religious devotion.[34] Some spent their last days there, including 'Ubada b. al-Samit (d. 654/55), Fairuz al-Dailami (d. 672/73), Shaddad b. Aws (d. 677/78) and Wathila b. al-Aqsa (d. 704/05). The first Umayyad caliph, Mu'awiya (661–80), "linked his own personal identity with Jerusalem, calling himself caliph of Beit al-Maqdis. Thus, it is part of the Islamic faith."[35] Mu'awiya is reputed to have spoken at the first mosque on the site and announced, "The area between the two walls of this mosque is dearer to God than the rest of the earth."[36]

A Christian pilgrim from Gaul, the bishop Arculf, who visited the site around 670, commented on the mosque and described it as a wooden oblong building that would accommodate 3,000 people. The nearby Rock became a place where oaths of allegiance were sworn, not dissimilar to today's Israeli use of the Western Wall plaza for certain civil and elite military ceremonies.

While Jerusalem was not an Arab administrative center in the early Islamic period, the sanctity of the Haram was certainly recognized. From 687 to 692, the second ruler of the Umayyad dynasty, Abd al-Malik, built the Dome of the Rock *(Qubbat al-Sakhra)*, believing the Rock to be the place from which Muhammad had made his ascent to heaven. It seems that Abd al-Malik and/or his son, al-Walid, also built the al-Aqsa Mosque in 708–09 in the place where today's reconstruction stands. The original has undergone significant rebuilding and renovation over the centuries.

The reason for the construction of the Dome of the Rock is debated. In the ninth century it was asserted by an anti-Umayyad author that it was an attempt to displace Mecca in people's affections and that its octagonal shape provided an alternative to the annual pilgrimage *tawaf* (seven circumambulations of the cubic shrine, the Ka'bah) in Mecca. But according to Karen Armstrong, "[i]t is more likely that the Dome of the Rock was an assertion of Muslim identity than that it was designed to deflect the *hajj* from Mecca."[37] In other words, providing pilgrims with an alternative to Mecca was probably not the intention of the builders.

The Dome of the Rock soon inspired other Muslim shrines. The dome-shaped roof became a familiar part of Muslim architecture, its blue and gold symbolizing eternity and knowledge—the beginning of the understanding of God.

In Muslim thought, Jerusalem replicates Mecca in certain ways. As with the Ka'bah, the Rock is associated with Adam, the Garden of Eden, Abraham and Isaac, the center of the world, and fertility. Through contact with Jewish and Christian thought, Muslim teaching assimilated certain ideas about future events and connected them with Jerusalem: the defeat of

Gog and Magog, the Resurrection, and the Last Judgment would take place in the city; the Mahdi (Savior) would come to al-Haram al-Sharif. Perhaps this was why Muhammad's friends were said to have requested that his body be taken there for burial.

In the beginning of the Abbasid period in the eighth century, earthquakes destroyed the al-Aqsa Mosque twice. It was rebuilt and officially named al-Masjid al-Aqsa, and associated with the Qur'anic allusion to Muhammad's night journey. However, the first complete account of the journey was not available until Muhammad ibn Ishaq's biography, written about 100 years after the death of the Prophet. Jerusalem had by then become identified with Muhammad's travel to the Distant Mosque, even though the building was not in place at the time of the mystical journey.

As a result of other building projects, shrines multiplied within the walls of the Haram in the eighth and ninth centuries, several of them commemorating events based on Jewish and Christian Scripture or tradition. In 832 the caliph al-Ma'mun ordered a restoration of the Dome of the Rock and minted coins on which Jerusalem became al-Quds (the Holy), the name used by Palestinians today.

Around the year 1000, the Muslim scholar al-Wasiti published an anthology of various traditions in praise of Jerusalem. These sayings were already well known in the Muslim world at the time. Al-Wasiti attributed the following saying to Muhammad:

> Mecca is the city Allah exalted or sanctified, created and surrounded by angels a thousand years before creating anything else on earth. Then He joined it with Medina and united Medina to Jerusalem, and only a thousand years later created the [rest of the] world in a single act.[38]

It may be that the universality of Jerusalem expressed in these published traditions reflected a more tolerant atmosphere in the city than it had witnessed for some time. But whatever the purpose behind the anthology, the importance of Jerusalem in Muslim tradition is clear.

The al-Aqsa Mosque had also become a seat of learning. A native of al-Quds, the geographer al-Muqaddasi (d. 1000), wrote that the city had "all manner of learned men."[39] In 1095 the Persian scholar and Sufi mystic al-Ghazali (1058–1111) began his most famous work, "The Revival of the Religious Sciences," at al-Aqsa. According to Tibawi, it was to Islam what Thomas Aquinas's "Summa Theologiae" would become to Christianity. Al-Ghazali also wrote "The Jerusalem Tract," a concise explanation of Muslim belief, in response to requests from worshipers at the al-Aqsa Mosque.[40]

A more troubled period in the Islamic history of Jerusalem followed the arrival of the Crusaders in 1099. Present in the city and its environs until 1187, the Crusaders changed the use of many of the city's religious buildings, including the al-Aqsa Mosque and the Dome of the Rock. The founder of the Ayyubid dynasty, Salah al-Din, besieged the city in 1187 and restored al-Aqsa to Muslim hands after eighty-eight years. On the first Friday after the Crusaders were ousted, the cleric's sermon in the mosque focused on Salah al-Din's view of the city and its Islamic significance. It aptly summarizes the importance of the Haram:

> It was the dwelling-place of your father Abraham; the spot from which your blessed Prophet Muhammad mounted to heaven; the *qibla* toward which you turned to pray at the commencement of Islamism [*sic*], the abode of the prophets; and the place visited by the saints; the cemetery of the apostles; the spot where the divine revelation descended, and to which the orders to command and prohibitions were sent down: it is the country where mankind will be assembled for judgement, the ground where resurrection will take place; the holy land whereof God hath spoken in his perspicuous book; it is the mosque wherein the Apostle of God offered up his prayer and saluted the angels admitted nearest to God's presence; it is the town to which God sent his servant and apostle, and the Word which he caused to descend on Mary and his spirit Jesus, whom he honoured with that mission and ennobled with the gift of prophesy [*sic*] without removing him from the rank he held as one of his creatures. . . . This temple is the first of the two *qiblas*, the second of the two sacred Mosques, the third after the two holy cities (Mekka and Medina).[41]

Salah al-Din restored Jerusalem's buildings and Islamic institutions of law and learning. Since its inception as a Muslim center, Bayt al-Maqdis had attracted scholars and Sufi mystics. The Sufis had established themselves there at an early point and were encouraged to return by Salah al-Din. It became clear, however, that al-Quds was not so important politically when its rulers located themselves in Syria or Egypt following Salah al-Din's death in 1193. As in later times, Jerusalem suffered from the dominant power's absence.

The Ayyubids gave way to the Mamluks in 1260 when the latter defeated the Mongols, who had invaded Syria and encroached on Galilee. The battle at 'Ayn Jalut in the Jezreel Valley near Nazareth was decisively won by a Turkish slave army from Egypt, setting the stage for Mamluk domination of Palestine.[42] Ruling the territory for 250 years, the mostly Turkish Mamluk sultans brought stability after the chaos of the Crusader period. Jerusalem, however, was once more isolated from the center of administrative power in Syria. It became a gathering place for exiled Mamluk leaders, scholars, and wealthy patrons of the religious sites. Christians and Jews were allowed rights in the city, where major renovation and new construction were extensive during the period.

The Ottoman Turks defeated their Mamluk relatives, conquering Jerusalem in 1516. Sultan Selim I visited the city immediately and received the keys to the al-Aqsa Mosque and the Dome of the Rock. He and his son Suleiman venerated Jerusalem and resumed the building programs of the Ayyubids, restoring the Dome of the Rock and rebuilding the city walls as they are seen today, after 300 years of ruin and disrepair. Under the Ottomans, Jerusalem, Hebron, and the surrounding villages comprised a district *(sanjaq)* in the larger province *(wilayet)* of Damascus. Aside from the military and civil authorities, the Ottomans appointed three Jerusalemites as religious and social leaders: the *mufti*, the *naqib al-ashraf*, and the *shaykh al-Haram*.[43] The mufti was responsible for interpreting Islamic law *(shari'a)* and handing down nonbinding opinions; the naqib al-ashraf "for protecting the rights of descendants of the Prophet"; and the shaykh al-Haram for administering the two religious sites on al-Haram al-Sharif.

As Ottoman central control diminished over the course of the next two hundred years, local notable families rose to power in religious and social leadership roles. In the eighteenth century these notables gained in strength and ability to represent the people to the Turkish authorities, and to maintain the status quo on behalf of the Ottomans. What are now familiar names in Jerusalem's Palestinian community—Husayni, Khalidi, Abu 'l-Lutf, Dajani—began to appear in the roles of mufti and naqib and in other leadership positions.

It was in nineteenth-century Jerusalem that the outlines of the present debate over the city took on a more familiar form. As the city developed into the administrative capital of Ottoman Palestine, the contours of the future political entity began to be apparent. Two initiatives brought about the diminishing of the port city of Acre and the rise of Jerusalem. First the Ottomans attempted to bring the three Palestinian *sanjaqs* of Jerusalem, Nablus, and Acre into one unit under a single governor. The second initiative was to promote the special status of the city and *sanjaq* of Jerusalem.[44]

In 1830, in an attempt to thwart the ambitions of their viceroy of Egypt (Muhammad Ali) for power over Syria and Palestine, the Ottomans amalgamated the three *sanjaqs* under the governor of Acre. But the growing weakness of the empire led in 1832 to the capture of Syria and Jerusalem by the viceroy's son, Ibrahim Pasha. The new ruler encouraged openness toward the European powers, which one by one established consulates in the city, ostensibly to protect the religious interests of their citizens. As noted earlier, in 1838 the British consulate was the first to open its doors. Others quickly followed: "Prussian (1842), Sardinian (1843), French (1843), Austrian (1847), Spanish (1854), American (1856), and Russian (1857)."

In 1840 Ibrahim Pasha was expelled from Syria, and Jerusalem became the subject of internationalization for the first time. In 1840–41 a Christian administration under European control was proposed for the city, but the returning Ottomans did nothing to bring it about. Instead they promoted

Jerusalem over Nablus and Acre and made it the capital of central and southern Palestine. Even though they were back in control, the Ottomans did not change Ibrahim Pasha's policy of religious toleration, especially during their self-declared *tanzimat,* which signified the *reordering* of Ottoman society with the sultan remaining as final arbiter.[45]

By special decree, or *firman,* of the sultan, Jerusalem was allowed to establish a municipal council in 1863. In 1872 the three *sanjaqs* were united again, with Jerusalem as capital. It was a short-lived arrangement. The Ottomans, fearing growing European involvement in the area, promptly overturned the union, and in 1874 Jerusalem's governor was made directly responsible to the central government in Istanbul. An administrative council was formed next, and Jerusalem was represented as a city and district in the Ottoman Parliament of 1877–78. The effect of the establishment of limited democracy in Jerusalem was that local notables became eligible for central and local government office, and the *sanjaq* of Jerusalem grew in political importance. Four notable families—the Khalidis, the al-Husaynis, the 'Alamis, and the Dajanis—dominated the municipal council by supplying "nearly all the mayors" of Jerusalem until 1914.[46] Other notables included the Jarallah and Nashashibi families.

The late nineteenth century (1882) had seen the establishment of the British as colonial power in Egypt and the first pre-Zionist immigrants to Palestine. These two developments set the scene for the next phase in the significance of Jerusalem in Arab and Palestinian thought, which is taken up in chapter 5 in the biographies of seven key Palestinians and their relation to the Jerusalem Question.

The Christian Arab Perspective

New Testament teaching and Christian tradition link the founding of the Christian Church to the day of Pentecost in Jerusalem in 30/31. Among the crowd at the Church's founding on Pentecost were "devout men, from every nation under heaven," including Egyptians, Libyans, and Arabians.[47] Early Christians remained in Jerusalem until 66, when they fled en masse across the Jordan to Pella to escape the Roman legions of Titus. The Roman campaign resulted in the destruction of Jerusalem in 70.

Slowly some Christians returned to the city. In 132 the Jewish zealot Bar Kochba led a revolt against the Romans, and three years later the Emperor Hadrian razed Jerusalem, rebuilding it as Aelia Capitolina. Jews were forbidden to enter the city on penalty of death. Christians were permitted to remain, but they did not attach special significance to Jerusalem itself in the way that later adherents did. For the early Christians, the concept of holy sites had no meaning. According to Peter Nathan, "the New Testament nowhere indicates any interest on the part of early Christians in the place of the death and burial of Jesus Christ. The only site in Jerusalem that appears to have been significant to them was the Jewish temple on Mount Moriah."[48] It was not until the fourth century that such sites in Palestine became of interest to the Christian world.

In 312 the Roman emperor Constantine had what he claimed was a conversion experience. Shortly afterward he created a tolerant atmosphere for Christianity throughout the empire. Constantine soon promulgated laws curtailing pagan worship and, according to Eusebius, bishop of Caesarea, gave instructions that attention be paid to "the buildings of the [Christian] churches, and either to repair or enlarge those which at present exist, or, in cases of necessity, to erect new ones."[49] This seems to have been the reason for his responsiveness to the suggestion of Macarius, Bishop of Jerusalem, to demolish a Roman temple covering what was believed to be Christ's tomb. Constantine instructed Macarius "to build a church in that city to honor the death of Jesus Christ."[50] It mattered little that the place had been a pagan site since Hadrian's time—dedicated either to Jupiter, Venus, or Tyche. The emperor simply told Macarius to destroy the temple, purge the land around it by removing everything to the bedrock, and build the church there.[51]

In 327, as the temple was under demolition, Constantine's mother Helena Augusta arrived in the city with her entourage on a "pilgrimage." Constantine's new religion was about to restore the earthly Jerusalem to Christians, who had until then focused only on the city's heavenly manifestation. It was also the beginning of modern-day political posturing over the city's religious sites. After all, Helena's tour of the eastern Roman provinces was not so much a pilgrimage as a publicity tour for her son's new Christian Rome. As events transpired, she may have been in Jerusalem when the demolition workers discovered what they believed to be Golgotha, the site of Christ's crucifixion, and the much-anticipated tomb itself. Her fame was only augmented by her supposed discovery of the wooden stake of Christ's crucifixion.

While she was in the Jerusalem area, it is thought that Eusebius persuaded the dowager to order the building of additional churches to commemorate the place of Christ's birth in Bethlehem and his ascension from the Mount of Olives. Together with the Martyrium—later named the Church of the Holy Sepulchre and declared the official tomb of Christ—and the site of His resurrection, these churches became the focus of Christian devotion.

One of the results of Helena's visit was the beginning of the pilgrimage business. Until her journey, no pilgrims are known to have visited the city. From the Christian point of view, it was only after these events surrounding Constantine and his mother that Jerusalem became known as a holy city.

Over the years that followed, various other sites were developed and added to the roster of protected holy sites. In an interesting development, certain events associated with the Temple Mount were transferred gradually to the Church of the Holy Sepulchre. Now Abraham had attempted to sacrifice Isaac near Golgotha, and the prophet Zechariah was killed not in the Temple but in Constantine's Martyrium.

The first period of Christian Jerusalem came to an end in 637 when the friends and followers of the prophet Muhammad arrived outside the walls of the city. The Caliph Omar's forces captured the city, and for most of the next 1,300 years, except for the Crusader period (1099–1187), Muslim powers ruled Jerusalem. The brutal clash of the Crusaders and Muslims set in motion several more centuries of religious antagonism over the city and its politicization. As noted, in the mid-nineteenth century, in late Ottoman times, several European powers became involved in Jerusalem, ostensibly on behalf of their Christian constituencies there. When Edmund Allenby led British forces into the city in December 1917, Christian rule of Jerusalem's holy sites was renewed, but it was carried out according to the status quo rules devised by Sultan Abd al-Majid and established by Ottoman *firmans* in 1852 and 1853. The 1852 *firman* defines the following Christian holy places in Jerusalem: "the Church of the Holy Sepulchre and its dependencies (Old City); the convent of Dayr al-Sultan (Old City); the Sanctuary of the Ascension (on the Mount of Olives); and . . . the tomb of the Virgin Mary (in Gethsemane)."[52] The rules governed rights of access to the holy sites by the various religious communities and prescribed relations between them. The same rules continue to apply today, with the exception that post-1967, Jews were allowed access to the Temple Mount in theory and open access to the Western Wall in practice.

Modern Palestinian Christianity is an outgrowth of this long process. More than ten Christian denominations are represented in Jerusalem. Because of the difficult political situation, the percentage of Christians within the Arab population of Jerusalem has been in general decline since 1922.[53] In recent years the outflow has increased. Fifty-five percent of Palestinian Christians are found in the Old City's Christian and Armenian Quarters, with a few families living in the Muslim Quarter.[54] Most Christians live around the Christian holy sites and work in the pilgrimage and tourist business. The Christians who live outside the Old City are located to the north in the Arab neighborhoods of Shu'fat and Beit Hanina. The significance of Jerusalem for the Christian community lies predominantly with the institutions of which the Palestinian Christians are a part. For example, the Roman Catholic Church came to an agreement with the State of Israel in which the church attempted to protect its future interests following the Oslo Agreements. The Vatican had long held that internationalization of the city was the preferred solution, guaranteeing access to the holy sites under UN governorship. In December 1993 the two parties signed the "Fundamental Agreement Between the Holy See and the State of Israel." In addition to the Vatican's recognition of the State of Israel, the accord spelled out arrangements for the administration of the Christian holy places, pilgrimage, education, welfare, and media issues. The Vatican agreed to a "continuing commitment to respect the aforementioned 'Status quo' and the said rights."[55] It did not, however, acknowledge the claims of either Israel or the Palestinians to the city as their capital.

Another predominant Christian denomination in Jerusalem is the Greek Orthodox Church. As the primary religious property holder in the Old City and possessor of the *praedominium* (access and custodianship) in the Church of the Holy Sepulchre, the Greek Orthodox Church expects to continue to play a significant role in discussions of Jerusalem's future. In November 1994 it joined with the other established churches in the publication of a memorandum providing "the definitive reference point" on the future of Jerusalem from their perspective.[56] It recognized the equal importance of the city for Jews and Muslims, and reconfirmed a commitment to the status quo arrangements.

In many ways the significance of the Palestinian Christian churches may seem out of proportion to their numbers and role in the day-to-day Israeli-Palestinian conflict, which is generalized by some as a Jewish-Muslim impasse. Their presence at the center of the debate, however, highlights the heightened role of identity and ideology issues. As Michael Dumper points out, the crux of the conflict has come down to the powerful ideas that dominate one square kilometer in the heart of Jerusalem.[57] That is where the final resolution still remains elusive.

CHAPTER 4
JEWISH AND ISRAELI PERSONALITIES

The purpose of the following detailed examination is to pursue the propositions outlined in chapter 1, which address the Jewish and Israeli identity-ideology nexus, the concept of latency, the effect of interacting variables, and the resulting stasis or momentum with respect to the Jerusalem Question. The research in this chapter surrounds seven representative actors in the Zionist enterprise spanning more than a century. The evidence is allowed to unfold in the detailed biographies of three founding fathers of Zionism and four prime ministers of the State of Israel. Each of the seven biographies addresses the primary identity and ideological characteristics of its subject, with special emphasis on the individual's relation to Jerusalem, and each is followed by a short summary. Since the concept of ideology is one of the main aspects of the study undertaken here, Mullins's five-part typology (historical consciousness, cognitive power, evaluative power, action orientation, and logical coherence) is first applied to Zionism.

Zionism and Ideology

How does Zionism hold up against Mullins's five-part typology? Zionism may be said to have

1. Historical consciousness: Zionists appeal to the history of the Israelite tribes, and specifically to Judah's role in preserving the identity of ancient Israel across the centuries. They do so particularly in reference to Jerusalem as the Jewish king David's capital established 3,000 years ago. Zionism also has a present orientation and the vision of a future. In discussing the future aspects of ideology, Mullins distinguishes them from utopian formulations. Ideological futures are based on "concrete programs and strategies having immediate social relevance"[1] rather than imagined utopian perfection in "sometime" and "nowhere."[2] Because of this broadened definition of historical consciousness, it can be said that Zionism as an ideology "informs political action" and "tends to explicate the significance of events, situations and possible courses of human action."[3]

2. Cognitive power: To qualify in this category, Zionism must provide its adherents with the necessary filters to abstract meaning from the welter of events. In this case ideology operates to provide logically coherent constraints between aspects of the belief system. As a result, it ought to be possible to say, for example, that a Zionist who believes that Palestine is the Jewish homeland by tradition and historical right also believes that Jewish possession of land should not be opposed by an international body such as the UN.

3. Evaluative power: Zionism allows its adherents to make judgments about what should and should not be done in its name, what support it can and cannot give. Thus the beliefs of some political Zionists allowed them to evaluate the arguments of other Zionists regarding the long-term consequences of specific actions for the establishment of the Jewish homeland. See, for example, this chapter's biographical study of Jabotinsky and his objection to the 1937 Peel Commission Report.

4. Action orientation: It is not so much that ideology causes people to do, but rather that it gives cause for doing. This mobilizing aspect of ideology arises from a combination of its elements: "cognitions, evaluations, ideals, and purposes." Zionism has a long history of mobilizing the return of Jewish people from the Diaspora to the ancestral land, of making *aliya* (going up) to the land of ancient Israel. An essential element in the eventual creation of the State of Israel was immigration, cast in terms of redemption and duty.

5. Logical coherence: An ideology must not be formless or chaotic. While it is not required to adhere strictly to the rules of formal logic, it cannot be logically absurd. It must make sufficient internal sense to separate it from propaganda and ambiguities such as *Zeitgeister* and *Weltanschauungen*. In this regard, Zionism has for over a century demonstrated the necessary "conceptions, reasons, and justifications" that count within its milieu.

Of course, as shown in chapter 3, Zionism also has a powerful religious aspect. This is especially so in respect of the Old City. It is axiomatic that religious commitment to Judaism will influence one's view of Jerusalem's significance, though not necessarily one's view of the locus of the city's sovereignty. Because several of the founding fathers of Zionism were secularists and without apparent religious attachment to the city, some even inimical to it, a case is often made that their interest in the city was dispassionate, pragmatic, and mainly political. But as will be seen, this is far from the truth. Neither is it true of the subsequent Zionist leadership of the State of Israel. Being a secular or nonreligious Jew or Israeli does not necessarily obviate the gravitational pull of religion-based Jewish identity and its associated ideological components.

The Founders and Foundations of Zionist Thinking

Broadly speaking, Israeli political philosophy follows two main schools of thought: (a) the political Zionism of Theodor Herzl, and subsequently the synthesis of the political and practical-socialist Zionism of Chaim Weizmann and David Ben-Gurion; and (b) the revisionist Zionism of Vladimir Ze'ev Jabotinsky. They are represented today in Israel's main political parties, Labor, Likud, and Kadima, Likud's recently formed centrist offshoot. The roots of the two streams of thought go back to the beginnings of the Zionist movement in the late 1800s. The history of each school of thought concerning the Jerusalem Question provides some important background for an examination of the identity-ideology nexus with respect to key leaders and their associates and successors.

An early forerunner of the Zionist endeavor was a society called Hibbat Zion (Love of Zion), from *Zion*, one of the biblical names for Jerusalem. Its members were known as Hovevei Zion (Lovers of Zion). They were at work in the early 1880s promoting settlement of Palestine to Jews in Russia, where persecution had recently taken the form of state-abetted pogroms. This violent development was a major catalyst in the demand for a homeland where Jews could normalize their status among the peoples of the world. A leading member of Hibbat Zion, Moshe Leib Lilienblum, suggested that anti-Semitism was the result of Jewish alienation that could only be overcome by return to the land of Israel. Jewish medical doctor Leo Pinsker had written "Auto-Emancipation: An Appeal to His People by a Russian Jew" (1882), in which he provided the ideological underpinnings for Jewish nationalism. In 1884 he became the leader of Hibbat Zion, whose first meeting inspired the young Chaim Weizmann.

The word *Zionism* was first used in 1885 by the Viennese Jewish author Nathan Birnbaum. He coined the term to describe the movement created to resolve "The Jewish Question"—the problem of persecution of Jewish communities, especially in Eastern Europe. According to his view, other attempts to solve the problem, including emancipation and assimilation into the various cultures and nations of Europe, had not been successful. Nationalism had become the preferred solution for other peoples, went the argument, so why not for the Jews? Despite the religious and historical background of the Jewish people, Zionism was at this stage a secular, political, and incipient national force. The later usage of "Zionism" raises a problem: the application of the term to what developed in Palestine over the next century was not what Birnbaum had in mind. Though he preceded Herzl in suggesting return to Palestine as the answer to the Jewish Question and supported Herzl's efforts by attending the First Zionist Congress (1897), the two men soon disagreed over the aims of political Zionism. Preferring to emphasize national-cultural aspects of Zionism in the Diaspora, Birnbaum left the Zionist movement in 1898. Only later in life did he again promote return of Jews to Palestine, but even then it was to be out of love for the land and without political intentions.[4]

Theodor Herzl

Identity and Ideology

Theodor Herzl (1860–1904) was born in Pest, Hungary, into a wealthy conservative Jewish family. He attended Jewish elementary school and public high school. Following the death of his only sister in 1878, he and his parents moved to Vienna, where he entered law school. In 1882 he engaged in protest after he read an anti-Semitic work. In 1883 he resigned from a student society over its anti-Semitic attitude. Although he qualified as a lawyer in 1884, he soon took up writing as a profession. After some success as an author of short stories, he became the Paris correspondent of a liberal Viennese daily in 1891, writing about French life. Anti-Semitism soon became a theme again, and Herzl proposed answers to the Jewish Question in terms of assimilation, religious conversion, and socialism.

In 1894 he rejected these solutions when he came face-to-face with French anti-Semitism in the celebrated Dreyfus affair, centered on an assimilated Jewish military officer who had been falsely accused of treason. Herzl's experience of attending the trial as a journalist confirmed for him the belief and experience of many Jews that it did not matter how assimilated or how loyal to their adopted nations they were; they would always be undervalued and persecuted. This was the turning point for Herzl. He concluded that the only solution to the Jewish Question was emigration to a land set apart as a Jewish enclave.

In 1896 he published *The Jewish State (Der Judenstaat)*, the basis for his reputation as the father of political Zionism. Herzl's solution was a national home for the Jews achieved by diplomacy among "the civilized nations of the world in council."[5] Interestingly, despite his willingness to consider several possibilities besides Palestine, he wrote, "All through the long night of their history the Jews have not ceased to dream this royal dream: 'Next year in Jerusalem!' is our age-old watchword. Now it is a matter of showing that the dream can be transformed into an idea that is as clear as day."

Convening the first Zionist Congress[6] in 1897 in Basel, Switzerland (the Jews of Munich having refused to host the meeting), Herzl persuaded the delegates to accept his formulation: "The aim of Zionism is to create for the Jewish people a home in Palestine secured by public law."[7] Confirming his commitment to more than a national home, however, Herzl wrote in his diary, "At Basel I founded the Jewish State."[8] He was to preside over the World Zionist Organization until his death.

A few years later fierce debate erupted within the new movement when Herzl announced his support for a British government proposal that the Jews establish a homeland in British East Africa. Erroneously referred to by his British interlocutors as an offer of land in Uganda (the location was actually in what became Kenya), the proposal became immediately significant to Herzl in the wake of a new pogrom in Bessarabia. He was careful to make clear that he continued to support Palestine as the preferred solution, and was working to that end. But the circumstances of the moment compelled him to consider other options, especially if they put him into a positive relationship with a great power such as Britain. He also considered the pressure such a move might put on the Ottoman authorities to grant Jewish rights in Palestine rather than lose Jewish investments. At the Sixth Zionist Congress in 1903, the delegates voted in favor of sending a commission to Africa to investigate. The Russian Zionists, however, led by Menachem Ussishkin, were united in their opposition and insisted that the homeland could be in Palestine alone. After a bitter and lengthy public debate, Herzl was reconciled to his colleagues. Weakened over the years by a heart ailment, he died of pneumonia in 1904 at the age of 44.

The following year the Zionist Congress officially adopted Palestine as the only territorial goal for which it would strive.[9] Clearly the power of memory and symbol was too great to overcome. As Baruch Kimmerling notes:

> It became apparent that only Eretz Israel could serve as a powerful enough symbol to recruit significant numbers of the Jewish people throughout the world for collective political, social, and economic activity, either as actual participants in immigration and the building of a new society, or as moral and/or material supporters of the movement.[10]

Despite Herzl's death, two of his perspectives continued to be promoted by many in the Zionist leadership. He had minimized the role of the Palestinian Arab population, treating them as if they did not exist, and had sought great-power involvement in the creation and support of the new Jewish entity.[11] These principles were to dominate the Zionist movement for years to come.

Herzl and Jerusalem

Herzl discussed the Old City and the holy sites with Sultan Abd al-Hamid II in May 1896. The sultan said that the Ottomans would never give up Jerusalem, insisting that the Dome of the Rock must remain in Muslim hands forever. Herzl replied:

> We could get around that difficulty. We shall extraterritorialize Jerusalem, which will then belong to nobody and yet to everybody—the holy place which will become the joint possession of all believers—the great *condominium* of culture and morality.[12]

When he visited the city for the first time in 1898, he was stunned by the filth and shocked by "[t]he musty deposits of two thousand years of

inhumanity, intolerance, and uncleanliness . . . in the foul-smelling alleys."
He wanted to build the Jewish capital on Mount Carmel near the coastal
city of Haifa.[13] Still, he did not rule out Jerusalem completely:

> If we ever get Jerusalem and if I am still able to do anything actively at that
> time, I would begin by cleaning it up.
> I would clear out everything that is not something sacred, set up workers'
> homes outside the city, empty the nests of filth and tear them down, burn the
> secular ruins, and transfer the bazaars elsewhere. Then, retaining the old
> architectural style as much as possible, I would build around the Holy Places
> a comfortable, airy new city with proper sanitation.[14]

Herzl's first visits to the Wailing Wall produced no deep emotion in him.
"[It] refuses to come," he said, "because that place is pervaded by a hideous,
wretched, speculative beggary. At least, this is the way it was when we were
there, yesterday evening and this morning." The reason for his lack of emotion
was not disgust at religion or lack of association with the ancient place, but
rather the constant begging.

Writing in his diary a few days later, Herzl proposed that he would build
a new city outside the Old City walls, leaving only "houses of worship and
philanthropic institutions" within. He spoke of "the wide ring of hillsides
all around, which would turn green under our hands, [and] would be the
location of a glorious New Jerusalem." Herzl's vision of the future Jerusalem
was anything but antagonistic to the city. He continued in his diary:

> The most discriminating from every part of the world would travel the road up
> to the Mount of Olives. Tender care can turn Jerusalem into a jewel. Include
> everything sacred within the old walls, spread everything new round about it.

In a novel published in 1902, titled *Altneuland* (*Old New Land*), Herzl
described his image of a renewed Jerusalem. The novel's purpose was to
awaken the Diaspora to the possibilities of a Jewish state and to stimulate
their enthusiasm for it. In his imagination, Haifa had become a modern
port, Tiberias a renowned spa resort, the Old City a museum, and Jerusalem
as a whole "was risen in splendor, youthful, alert, risen from death to life."[15]
Two of the characters in the novel gazed on a panorama of the old and the
new Jerusalem and saw that

> [t]he Holy Sepulchre, the Mosque of Omar, and other domes and towers had
> remained the same; but many splendid new structures had been added. That
> magnificent new edifice was the Peace Palace. A vast calm brooded over the
> Old City.
> Outside the walls the picture was altogether different. Modern sections
> intersected by electric street railways; wide, tree-bordered streets; homes,

gardens, boulevards, parks; schools, hospitals, government buildings, pleasure resorts. . . . Jerusalem was now a twentieth century metropolis.[16]

The image of Jerusalem set out here meshes with the observation of one of Zionism's foremost scholars regarding Herzl's true feelings about the city. Arthur Hertzberg concluded that "when talking to himself, at his most private, Herzl did dream of possessing Jerusalem."[17]

Summary: Theodor Herzl

Theodor Herzl was not deeply entrenched in Jewish tradition, nor did he speak Hebrew. He was the product of the late-nineteenth-century German-Jewish enlightenment (*haskalah*). His perspective was shaped by his secular heritage, and of the leaders at Zionism's birth he was one of the most assimilated. However, his family background and early Jewish education allowed him to express identification with his roots sufficiently to protest strongly the fin-de-siècle anti-Semitism of European society. He was already writing with passion about solving the Jewish Question when he was challenged by the Dreyfus affair. His zeal for resolving the alienation of his cultural heritage brought on a life of continual travel as he searched for allies and supporters of his Zionist mission to create the structure of a Jewish polity and the means to transfer a population to Palestine. His early death was attributed to overwork, critical opposition, and a weakened heart. By the end of his life he had used all of his personal resources in pursuit of the Zionist cause, leaving his wife and children without inheritance.

The facts of his adult career indicate strong identification with his Jewish heritage, demonstrated by maintenance, protection, and enhancement of that identification in the form of the developing ideological components of Zionism. His devotion to founding a new society in the old land, and his incessant search for the financial and legal means to make a reality of what he called the "royal dream" of "Next year in Jerusalem!" exemplified his ideological fervor. Herzl's diary entries in 1898 during his visit to Jerusalem reveal a great desire to clean and renovate the city and preserve the sacred while revitalizing its surroundings. Herzl's commitment to Zionism was the basis for much of his written work, which provided the prime documentary sources during Zionism's foundational years and inspired the goals of the World Zionist Organization.

At the time of Herzl's involvement in the Zionist cause, any resolution of the Jerusalem Question was still very much constrained by Ottoman domination of Palestine and Jewish inability to do anything other than seek a homeland by diplomatic means. In other words, stasis on the Jerusalem issue was the prevalent condition mainly due to the preponderance of Ottoman power. Herzl's background and preferences regarding Jerusalem were expressed in his Zionist endeavors and his later fiction and nonfiction writings. He was convinced of the importance of the city to the future Jewish national entity. But a discussion with the sultan as early as 1896 about the Old City and the holy places brought only a stern refusal to give them up. In the circumstances, Herzl's latent identification with the city could find no outlet other than to propose to extraterritorialize the Old City for the good of humanity. The presence of Christian and Muslim sites in his imaginary Jerusalem, fictionalized six years later in *Altneuland*, further demonstrates his recognition of the constraints. The interacting variable of Ottoman imperial possession and control precluded any other conclusion on Herzl's part. In other words, Herzl's reaction was confirmation of his latent identification with the city as a function of his Jewish upbringing. But without the possibility of taking that identification to the conclusion Herzl would prefer (he dreamed of "possessing Jerusalem"), the only option for improved Jewish access to the city was to *propose* extraterritorialization. And in the circumstances, even that proposal had virtually no possibility of success.

Chaim Weizmann

Identity and Ideology

Chaim Weizmann (1874–1952) was the second major force in Zionism's development. Born in western Russia near the Polish border, in the area known as the Pale of Settlement, he came from a family of rabbis dating back for several generations on his father's side. The fourth of fifteen children, Weizmann had a traditional Jewish education. Learning focused on religion, Bible, Talmud, and Mishnah. According to biographer Jehuda Reinharz, "Chaim Weizmann's lifelong and deep sense of Jewishness, his attachment to Jewish folkways, was cradled and formed in this intense Jewish environment."[18] Generally the answer to the difficulties of life was to wait for the Messiah to return the Jews in exile to Zion.

Weizmann's father, however, was a seeker of new ways of thinking, a reader of the daily press, and influenced by *haskalah*. He was associated with Hibbat Zion, which had its first congress in 1884. The society became very active in Pinsk, where Weizmann went to secondary school. The rabbi at the synagogue he attended there, David Friedman (Dovidel Karliner), was an active supporter of Hibbat Zion's program for settlement of Palestine. In Pinsk

> Weizmann's early notions and sympathies were beginning to crystallize into an ideology. . . . Perhaps it was Rabbi Friedman who first anchored Chaim's emotional attachments to Zion and helped harness them in the cause of Zionism. . . . Chaim . . . became imbued with his rabbi's attitudes.[19]

Several families from Pinsk who were members of Hibbat Zion settled in Palestine during Weizmann's youth. His own family's strong attachment to the movement was attested to by the fact that eventually nine of the twelve surviving Weizmann children went to live in Palestine. As Reinharz concludes, "[a]ll evidence points to the fact that the combined influences of his home in Motol and his milieu in Pinsk directed the adolescent, almost inevitably, into the nascent Zionist groups." Weizmann himself wrote, "I am in the Zionist movement since I was 15."[20]

Weizmann and Jerusalem

In 1885, at the age of 11, Weizmann wrote a significant letter to his teacher as he left to go to secondary school. In it he mentioned the first meeting of the Lovers of Zion movement in November 1884. He wrote: "I am sending you one of my ideas for you to see, *and that concerns Hevrat Hovevei Zion and Jerusalem which is in our land.* . . . Because by this we can rescue our exiled, oppressed brethren who are scattered in all corners of the world" (Weizmann's emphasis).[21]

With his strong religious background, Weizmann was more likely to have a deep-seated emotional tie to Jerusalem. However, when he visited the city for the first time in 1907, he was not impressed. Reflecting on that visit much later, he wrote:

My most unhappy experience during the . . . tour of the country . . . was Jerusalem. . . . Jerusalem was the city of the *Challukkah*, a city living on charity, on begging letters, on collections. . . . From the Jewish point of view it was a miserable ghetto, derelict and without dignity. All the grand places belonged to others. There were innumerable churches, of every sect and nationality. We had not a decent building of our own. All the world had a foothold in Jerusalem—except the Jews. The hotel to which we were directed was a dilapidated and verminous ruin, with nondescript people pouring in and out all day long, and all of them engaged apparently in wasting their own and each other's time. It depressed me beyond words. . . . I remained prejudiced against the city for many years, and even now I still feel ill at ease in it, preferring Rehovoth to the capital.[22]

During his 1907 visit, it also came to his mind that one day there could be a new structure in Jerusalem to represent the Jewish community. In his autobiography he continues, after his negative remarks about the city's conditions:

But I was struck, as everyone must be, by the glorious surroundings of Jerusalem; and I thought then that there was only one place where, in time to come, we might erect some building worthy of the Jewish community; there was one hill still uncrowned by monastery or Church—the Scopus, on which stood then only the small villa of Lady Grey Hill, and on which now stands the Hebrew University.[23]

Weizmann's education had taken him to university in Berlin and Geneva, and eventually he accepted a post in Britain as professor of chemistry at Manchester University. His work on acetone synthesis was of great value to the British government in the manufacture of cordite for artillery shells during the First World War. In London during this period, he cultivated contacts at the highest levels, promoting the case for a Jewish homeland. The British government's 1917 Balfour Declaration in support of the establishment in Palestine of a national home for the Jewish people was to a large degree the result of his persistent efforts.

In 1918 the British Foreign Office in London gave permission for the Zionist Organization to set up the Zionist Commission to facilitate relations between the British military administration in Palestine and the Jewish community there. Weizmann was made chairman and led a visit to Jerusalem in April that year. While there, he offered the Moroccan shaykhs of the Old City's Maghribi section £70,000 for the Wailing Wall and surrounding property, via the British military governor Ronald Storrs. His hope was that the Jews could worship at the Wall without harassment. The negotiations failed in early May when the Muslim authorities heard about the offer and objected. Weizmann did not let the matter rest. Requesting "your authority to deal with this question as soon as possible," he wrote in unequivocal terms to Lord Balfour on May 30:

THE HANDING OVER OF THE WAILING WALL TO THE JEWS. We Jews have many holy places in Palestine, but the Wailing Wall—believed to be a part of the old Temple Wall—is the only one which is in some sense left to us. All the others are in the hands of Christians or Moslems. And even the Wailing Wall is not really ours. It is surrounded by a group of miserable, dirty cottages and derelict buildings, which make the whole place from the hygienic point of view a positive danger, and from the sentimental point of view a source of constant humiliation to the Jews of the world. Our most sacred monument, in our most sacred city, is in the hands of some doubtful Moghreb religious community, which keeps these cottages as a source of income. We are willing to compensate this community very liberally, but we should like the place to be cleaned up; we should like to give it a dignified and respectable appearance.[24]

Despite his personal prejudices against Jerusalem, which is nevertheless "our most sacred city," Weizmann was also willing to lend his energetic support to the establishment of the Hebrew University in Jerusalem, and in the same letter sought Balfour's support. The idea of an institution of higher learning had been proposed before, as early as 1882, then at the First Zionist Congress in 1897, and again in 1901 at the Fifth Congress. According to

Reinharz, since the beginning "the Jewish university had been an entirely Zionist affair. The idea was born out of Zionist impulses and would be realized by Zionists."[25]

In 1913 the idea had resurfaced at an opportune time for Weizmann, who had just had a setback in his university career in Britain. Now he threw himself into the new task with zeal. He wrote to his wife, "To my way of thinking, this is the one slogan that can evoke a response just now—the Hebrew University. *Die Zionsuniversität auf dem Berge Zion* [Zion University on Mount Zion]! The Third Temple!"[26] Weizmann saw the establishment of the university as central to the cultural and spiritual rebirth of Zionism, and as a political statement about the Zionists' seriousness in settling the land permanently.[27]

That same year Weizmann persuaded Baron Edmond de Rothschild to help finance the educational effort, though the baron agreed only to a research institute, not a university. Weizmann went to the meeting willing to compromise on anything except that the teaching had to be conducted in Hebrew and the new institution had to be located in Jerusalem.[28] Plans were already afoot to purchase land on the Mount Scopus–Mount of Olives ridge overlooking the Old City from the east.

On a visit to Jerusalem in July 1918, Weizmann was able to participate in the laying of the foundation stones for the Hebrew University. Evidently he was impressed by the surroundings. He later wrote:

The physical setting of the ceremony was of unforgettable and sublime beauty. The declining sun flooded the hills of Judea and Moab with golden light, and it seemed to me, too, that the transfigured heights were watching, wondering, dimly aware perhaps that this was the beginning of the return of their own people after many days. Below us lay Jerusalem, gleaming like a jewel.[29]

Thirty years later in March 1948, as the UN engaged in discussions concerning the imminent departure of the British from Palestine, it was suggested that a UN trusteeship be set up and Jerusalem internationalized. Subsequently Weizmann commented to the press, making the following remark about the reasons for Jewish acceptance of internationalization of the city:

[The Jews] were called upon to co-operate in a settlement for Jerusalem which set that city's international associations above its predominantly Jewish character. We accepted these limitations only because they were decreed by the supreme authority of international judgment, and because in the small area allotted to us we would be free to bring in our people, and enjoy the indispensable boon of sovereignty.[30]

Notable was his opinion that Jerusalem's character was predominantly Jewish, and that if it were not for the UN's judgment, the city would have remained Jewish territory—clearly his preference.

When the State of Israel was founded in May 1948, Weizmann was asked to serve as its first president, which he did from 1949 until his death in 1952. On his return to Israel at the end of November 1948, he told the crowds who welcomed him, "Do not worry because part of Jerusalem is not now within the State. All will come to pass in peace."[31] It is an intriguing comment against the backdrop of the times, when Ben-Gurion had seemingly just given up on the whole of Jerusalem as Israel's capital in favor of *partition of the city*— a condition he preferred over internationalization. Weizmann's mood is summed up by Nasser Eddin Nashashibi, who wrote that on December 2, 1948, "Weizmann lamented the fact that Jerusalem had been excluded from the state of Israel and asserted that Jerusalem belonged to the Jews."[32]

Summary: Chaim Weizmann

Weizmann's early life has all the hallmarks of a very strong Jewish identity cluster. He was born into an observant family with a long line of rabbis in his ancestry. He had a traditional Jewish upbringing—education centered on Bible, Talmud, and Mishnah. As far as the components of Zionist ideology are concerned, Weizmann was focused on the return to Zion by his bold and free-thinking father, who was an early participant in the pre-Zionist movement, Lovers of Zion. Conviction about the need for *aliya*, immigration to Palestine, was cultivated in the family: nine of the twelve surviving children in his family made the journey. Weizmann declared that he was a Zionist from the age of fifteen, a formative period for the further embedding of identity. As Erikson pointed out, in adolescence the need arises to create a new identity on the foundations of that provided by early parental influence and environment.

From an ideological perspective, Weizmann showed a lifelong commitment to the land, to immigration and to the State. His tireless efforts to find a great power that would recognize the need for a Jewish homeland demonstrate his drive to see the dream become reality—to enhance the identification. With respect to Jerusalem, at eleven years of age Weizmann wrote about the Lovers of Zion and the society's relation to "Jerusalem which is in our land." Weizmann was obviously influenced by his father's circle, which thought only of immigration to the land of Palestine. Logically, Weizmann emphasized Jerusalem in his concept of the land he sought. His adult interest in establishing a university there was long lasting and again a strong indication of his identification with the city as a center of Jewish culture and spirituality. His comment upon his arrival to assume the presidency of the State, to the effect that Jerusalem would eventually rest in Jewish hands, also speaks to his expectation of Zionist possession of all of Jerusalem.

Latency is apparent in Weizmann's relationship to Jerusalem. He was raised with a traditional understanding of the centrality of the city to the Jewish identity. The constraints relating to achieving Jewish hegemony over the city varied throughout his lifetime. A contemporary and disciple of Herzl, he experienced the same limitations as his leader regarding goals for Jerusalem while Ottoman rule was still in force. Thereafter Weizmann was engaged in the higher priority of establishing the Jewish homeland in the aftermath of the Balfour Declaration. Any attention he could give to Jerusalem was ancillary to this overall goal. However, identification with the city continued to be expressed in terms of building the Hebrew University, which the academic in Weizmann conceptualized as a secular "Third Temple on Mount Zion." When he arrived in Israel to take up the presidency of the newly declared state, Weizmann asked his audience not to despair that all of Jerusalem was not in Israeli hands, adding, in anticipation of fulfilling a personal goal, that all would come to pass in its time. The immediate constraint was the de facto division of the city with Jordan, the result of the 1948 war. The interacting variable of the war's incomplete outcome from the Israeli perspective meant that Weizmann's identification with the city as wholly Jewish could not come to fruition. The refusal of the Palestinians to accept the terms of the UN partition resolution had led to war and its outcome. There had been movement toward resolving the Jerusalem Question from the Israeli perspective in that the western part of the city was secured, but once more stasis had set in. With respect to the Old City and the eastern half of the city, further Israeli access was held in check by her war-induced fatigue and depletion, the armistice with Jordan, and the United Nations' tacit acceptance of the status quo in the divided city.

Vladimir Ze'ev Jabotinsky

Identity and Ideology

Vladimir Ze'ev Jabotinsky (1880–1940) was the creator of Revisionist Zionism, the right wing of *Yishuv* and Israeli politics. His perspective continues to inspire and inform the Likud party to this day. Jabotinsky was born in Odessa into a Russian Jewish family. The death of his father when he was six years old put great stress on the family. His mother, however, was intent on providing for her children's education. Jabotinsky later recalled an influential comment made to him by his mother at this age. He asked her, "Will we Jews ever have a kingdom of our own?" She replied, "Of course we will, you silly boy."[33] He apparently never doubted her, arranging in the late 1930s, in the event of his death, for his body to be taken to Palestine when the Jewish state was formed. At age eighteen he was able to go to Switzerland, then on to Italy to study law. He became a journalist first in Switzerland and later worked in Vienna and Rome, espousing socialist and Zionist ideas. The 1903 pogrom in

Kishinev induced him to greater interest in Jewish self-defense,[34] a theme that was to emerge very strongly later. At the Sixth Zionist Congress in 1903 he was deeply impressed by Herzl, and it was there that he decided to learn Hebrew. Subsequently familiar with twenty languages and fluent in seven, Jabotinsky was recognized as an outstanding Russian writer and orator. He served as an officer in the Jewish Legion on the side of the British in Egypt during the First World War, having successfully campaigned for volunteer Jewish units within the British army. He was decorated for leading the first company across the Jordan in 1917 as part of Allenby's advance on Jerusalem.

In 1921 Jabotinsky joined the Zionist Executive[35] as a Palestine resident and was reelected at the Twelfth Zionist Congress later that year. This put him in a position to oppose Weizmann directly, which he did not fail to do. Jabotinsky was a maximalist when it came to plans for Jewish expansion in Palestine. His approach to the British mandatory authorities was very different from the gradualist approach of the urbane, pro-British Weizmann.

Though both men were followers of Herzl, Jabotinsky did not view Zionism in terms of a return to the land of the Jewish fathers. Zionism was rather the imposition of Western civilization in the East by means of Jewish colonists. He believed that the Western colonial powers should support the Jewish entity against the Arab world. He also promoted the immediate declaration of Jewish sovereignty over the original League of Nations–mandated territory. Jabotinsky's concept of Jewish territory included both sides of the River Jordan. As a result, he voted against acquiescence in the 1922 White Paper, by which Britain sought to mollify Arab feelings about the Balfour Declaration and its consequences. He resigned from the Zionist Executive in 1923 when it became clear that there would be little official Zionist resistance to what he perceived to be the growing anti-Zionist position of the British.[36]

In 1923 Jabotinsky formed the Revisionist youth movement, Betar, and in 1925 the World Union of Zionist Revisionists. He returned to Jerusalem in 1927 and lived there for two years. But in 1929 the British government canceled his reentry visa while he was overseas on a speaking tour, and he lived in exile from then on. In 1935 he and his followers separated from the official Zionist body, forming the London-based New Zionist Organization, of which he was president. Events in Palestine heightened his growing sense that military response to the Arabs was necessary. Accordingly, following the first period of the Arab Revolt in December 1936, he accepted executive control of the dissident Jewish military underground organization, the Irgun.

In July 1937 the Royal Commission, chaired by Lord Peel, issued its report on the causes of the Arab Revolt. It recommended the partition of Palestine into a large Arab state and a small Jewish state with an enclave from Jerusalem to Jaffa under permanent British mandatory control (see map 4.1). As a result, Jabotinsky was further convinced of the need to oppose British rule.

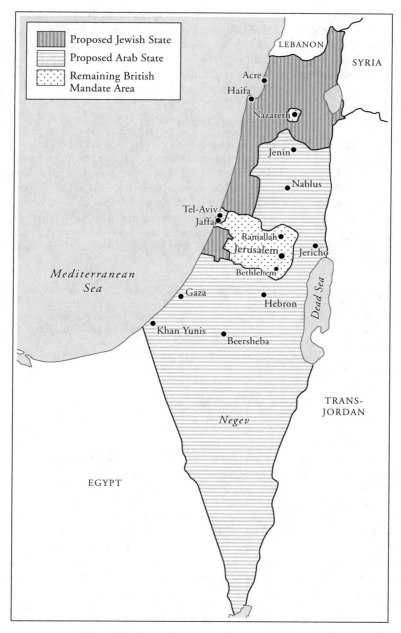

Map 4.1 The Peel Commission Partition Plan, July 1937.

For him, partition was out of the question as he believed that the 1917 Balfour Declaration included both sides of the Jordan as the territory of the intended Jewish homeland. In Jabotinsky's view, Transjordan was already an illegal entity. His opposition to the report was to be short-lived, however. In 1940 he died of a heart ailment while on a visit to the United States to organize Jewish support for the Allied war effort.

Jabotinsky and Jerusalem

Jabotinsky's son, Eri, wrote about his father's view of Jerusalem. He prefaced it by speaking of his own attachment to the city, which arose from relocating there with his parents in the fall of 1919. Eri says that he himself fell in love with Jerusalem from the start and "was ever after seized with awe at the very sight of the city." When he wasn't there, he always felt that he was in exile. He could not explain the emotion, but he wondered whether his feelings were the result of "Zionist indoctrination," or "maybe I inherited this emotion for Jerusalem from my father?" When it came to Vladimir's opinion of the city, Eri observed:

> He did not write much about Jerusalem. A few fragments have remained here and there and one small map, drawn by himself and marked by notes relating to plans for the defense of the city. Nor did he speak much about the city, at any rate not with me. But I know the reason: it was something self-understood: this is our city, here we shall remain forever.
> Did my father love Jerusalem? . . . [I]n Jerusalem, everything was clear and self-evident, without need of words.[37]

The elder Jabotinsky did express himself negatively at times about the parochial nature of Jerusalem. He was there alone on a visit in 1928 and found the atmosphere so much to his dislike that he spent as much time as he could in Tel Aviv. "Jerusalem is still a miserable provincial town, without cultural life or inner cohesion," he wrote.[38] But this did not prevent him from arguing on behalf of the protection of Jewish interests at the Western Wall following the Yom Kippur disturbances that year. At a meeting with the *Yishuv*'s Va'ad Leumi (National Council), Jabotinsky upbraided the members for their lack of urgency. He saw British interference with worship at the Wall as "the last ditch" and asked what the council intended to do. His account reads, "There were some that said: 'What are we defending?— the Wall, symbol of the past?' They were right. But I regret to tell you: it is also the symbol of the present."[39] According to Shmuel Katz, "It had been suggested [by Ben-Gurion] that the Jews should approach the Arabs and assure them that they had no designs either on the Wall or on Eretz Israel altogether [as symbolized by the Wall]."[40] Jabotinsky's response was

Who would believe you? Who will swear to it? I will not. I shall not mortgage the dream of our land. And if I said this, who would believe me? Where will you find the fool who will believe that the Jewish people, which makes so much noise, sends pioneers, goes down with fever, dies, does not come here with the intention of becoming a majority? You cannot make a compromise between two truths. Our truth is deep, so is theirs.[41]

Taken together, these comments highlight three points: first, the frustration on the part of an urbane and cultivated Russian writer trapped in a cultural backwater; second, the passion and disappointment on the part of a committed fighter in the face of a passive *Yishuv* leadership; and third, an ideological resolve in respect of the city that represented the heart and core of the Revisionist Zionist goal—a deep truth. According to Hertzberg, "Jabotinsky and his followers had no doubt that the capital of the restored Jewish state would be Jerusalem."[42]

The Revisionists had their political base in the cities and preferred to work there rather than in the rural areas where the Labor Zionists held sway. According to Friedland and Hecht, "Jabotinsky believed the Jewish race would be reborn in Palestine's cities, not its countryside. Jerusalem was Zionism's symbolic center and namesake."[43]

Following the publication of the Royal Commission's 1937 report, Jabotinsky issued a proclamation in which he spoke of the centrality of Jerusalem to the Jewish community. He wrote, "From the spiritual standpoint, the National Home without its capital [Jerusalem]—its symbol of sublime prophecy, would turn the entire Zionist ideal into something to be ridiculed."[44]

In August he attended the Zionist Convention in Zurich, where the partition plan was accepted. He spoke out in 1938 about the capitulation he believed had occurred at Zurich, berating the Zionist organization for its willingness to give up 96 percent of its heritage in the name of partition. Specifically he made the argument that the preamble to the British Mandate had included a reference to the Jews' historic links to Palestine. He noted that the connections were found in the Bible—in place names such as Hebron, Shechem, Gilead, and "the Holy City, Jerusalem."

Summary: Vladimir Jabotinsky

Jabotinsky was raised in a Jewish home with expectations that there would be a Jewish state. His Russian and European education produced a poet, a writer, a militarist, a visionary, a brilliant speechmaker, and a Zionist of the most fundamental kind. His identity was firmly tied to the creation of a home for the Jewish people, but not for sentimental or religious reasons. His view was intellectually based and rational. Making a homeland in

Palestine was a matter of harsh struggle—the Jews needed the land and the Arabs were to be resisted with an iron wall of Jewish bayonets until they came to accept that the Jews had won by conquest.[45] The need for Jewish military force was a key concept in his realist analysis of what it would take to establish a state. While Jabotinsky did not say much about the centrality of Jerusalem to Zionism—as his son said, it was "self-understood"—when he did speak with conviction about the city, it was to defend its significance in the face of Jewish passivity. When he once scribbled a map of the city, it was to chart its future military defense.

Regarding stasis or movement on the Jerusalem Question, Jabotinsky lived at a time when the constraints were such that his strong personal identification with the city was impossible to realize in terms of Jewish territorial possession. In the 1920s and 1930s the *Yishuv* leadership still chose to work in the diplomatic sphere to achieve their ends. Weizmann favored cooperation with the British, while Ben-Gurion, though disillusioned with the British, espoused a gradualist approach. Jabotinsky was also constrained by his own brand of militant Zionism, which remained less popular than Weizmann's or Ben-Gurion's version and thus had less leverage. These interacting variables prevented Jabotinsky from experiencing the resolution of the Jerusalem Question in his preferred maximalist terms, with the whole city under Jewish control and as capital of the new Jewish state on both banks of the Jordan.

Four Zionist Prime Ministers and Jerusalem

The foregoing political and philosophical antecedents in the history of Zionism provide the context for an examination of the administrations of four Israeli prime ministers. They are David Ben-Gurion, Menachem Begin, Yitzhak Rabin, and Shimon Peres. The identity and ideological foundation of each are examined with emphasis on their perspectives on the Jerusalem Question. By looking at different periods in Israeli history, it is possible to study the effect of Zionist identity and ideology issues across time and political persuasion. There are certainly differences among Zionist leaders in each period; yet, with regard to the issue of Jerusalem, there are also some remarkable similarities.

David Ben-Gurion

Identity and Ideology

David Ben-Gurion (1886–1973) was born David Green (Gruen/Gryn) in Plonsk, Russian Poland, the fourth child of Avigdor and Sheindel Green. His father was a lawyer, a prominent member of the Jewish community, and the founder of a school for modern Hebrew. The young Ben-Gurion was introduced to Hebrew by his grandfather beginning in his third year. Avigdor Green was an early member of Hibbat Zion. His regular meetings with the local members meant that the "Land of Israel" was a constant topic of conversation in the Green household. As Ben-Gurion said,

> I can hardly remember a time when the idea of building what we used to call "Eretz Israel", or the Land of Israel, wasn't the guiding factor of my life. It is no exaggeration to say that at three I had daydreams of coming to Palestine. And certainly from my tenth year on, I never thought of spending my life anywhere else.
> The events of my childhood influenced me very naturally in this direction.[46]

At one point in his early years he came in contact with Herzl, who made a visit to Plonsk. Welcomed by many Jews at the time as a messiah-like figure, Herzl made a strong impression on Ben-Gurion: "One glimpse of him and I was ready to follow him then and there to the land of my ancestors."

When he was eleven years old, his "deeply observant" mother died. Understandably Ben-Gurion suffered the loss greatly, saying later that life seemed meaningless at that time and that he was obsessed by feelings of human frailty. But after some years there was improvement: "[W]hen I was fourteen, I suddenly emerged from this tunnel to throw myself heart and soul into the Zionist movement." Accordingly he and two friends founded a Zionist youth group to teach modern Hebrew. They named it the Ezra Society, for "the great teacher who returned to Jerusalem from Babylon to rebuild the Temple." Ben-Gurion explained, "There seemed to us marked affinity between Ezra's mission and time and our own newly born hopes for Palestine."

Atypically among those who have written about Ben-Gurion, biographer Shabtai Teveth makes an observation about the centrality of Ben Gurion's early years to his later psychology. It is one that has significance for the interrelation of identity formation, ideology, and subsequent adult action. Teveth writes:

> For Ben-Gurion, the first things were also the final ones, and what filled his early years occupied his world forever. The foundation for his life's work was his formidable personality, composed of the virtues and failings with which he was born plus gifts from his mother that lasted his long journey through life: currents of tenderness and love, confidence in his singularity, and the glimmerings of a dream of the rebirth of Israel all combined in a mixture miraculously suited to his mission. So it seemed that when his mother died, her creation, so to speak, was complete.[47]

At the age of eighteen Ben-Gurion went to Warsaw and joined Po'ale Zion (Workers of Zion), a movement devoted to melding Herzl's political

Zionism and socialist Zionism via the interests of the Jewish proletariat. At the time, Ben-Gurion was active in opposition to Herzl's "Uganda" proposal, supporting Eretz Israel as the only option for a homeland. As a direct result he immigrated to Palestine in 1906, taking up work as a farm laborer for the next four years.

In 1910 he moved to Jerusalem to work for a friend who published a Zionist journal. It was at this time that, like many other Po'ale Zion members, he adopted a new surname. He became Ben-Gurion ("son of a lion cub"), after Joseph Ben-Gurion, a first-century democratic leader of the Jews, whom zealots killed for his moderation in the uprising against the Romans in 66 C.E. David Ben-Gurion's middle name was Joseph. Thus his new name was appropriate in more ways than one: just as Joseph Ben-Gurion had been a military leader in first-century Jerusalem, so also David Joseph Ben-Gurion aspired to be a military leader in the twentieth-century city.

Apart from visits home and an interlude in Istanbul to study law, Ben-Gurion stayed in Jerusalem until deported to Egypt in 1915 by the Ottoman authorities, who were allied with Germany in the First World War. While he awaited deportation, Ben-Gurion met a Jerusalemite Arab, Yahia, with whom he had studied in Istanbul. In his mind they were close friends. For years to come he told the story of one of their conversations,[48] and it provides an important insight into his thinking about the Arabs. In simple terms it defined Ben-Gurion's lifelong view. "Asked what he was doing in prison, Ben-Gurion told Yahia about the deportation order. 'As your friend I'm sorry,' Yahia replied. 'As an Arab I am glad.' " According to Teveth,

> [t]his experience laid the foundation of all his political thinking, the princi-
> ple that as long as the Jews were in the minority in Palestine, they must be
> allied with the ruling power in the region, to enable them to stand up to the
> Arabs; this was more important to him than dialogue and understanding
> with the Arabs.

Ben-Gurion's position with regard to the Palestinian Arabs was solidified in his mind by the Arab Revolt of 1936. He came to believe more firmly that war was the only way to achieve the aims of the *Yishuv*. Peace agreements with the Arab population were only a means to an end. Since both peoples wanted Palestine, he believed that there could only be conflict until one side won decisively. On June 9, 1936, he wrote to the Jewish Agency Executive:

> Peace is indeed a vital matter for us. It is impossible to build a country in a
> permanent state of war, but peace for us is a means. The end is the complete
> and full realization of Zionism. Only for that do we need an agreement.[49]

This unfolding perspective is noteworthy because Ben-Gurion's view of *Arab* Jerusalem played a significant role in his plans for the city during the first Arab-Israeli war.

At the 1937 Zionist Congress, Ben-Gurion was reelected chairman of the Jewish Agency Executive. At the same time the delegates accepted the Royal Commission's report and supported his proposal that the Jewish Agency Executive explore the possibilities of partition with the British government. Both Ben-Gurion and Weizmann favored partition, though for differing reasons. The pro-British Weizmann believed it best not to counter the mandatory power. Ben-Gurion, on the other hand, had lost faith in the British, but his pragmatism led him to believe that a Jewish state of any size could become a power base for Zionist goals. His gradualist inclinations also separated him from the Revisionists,[50] though the ultimate goal was the same.

This pragmatic stance was a matter of Ben-Gurion's mind and heart. He made this clear in October 1937 when he wrote to his son Amos from London: "I am certain we will be able to settle in all the other parts of the country, whether through agreement and mutual understanding with our Arab neighbours or in another way." Ending his letter, he wrote, "Erect a Jewish State at once, even if it is not in the whole land. The rest will come in the course of time. It must come."[51] He displayed this conviction even in the face of the proposal to partition Palestine, which he accepted in principle at the time. By 1939 the British had retreated from the Royal Commission's recommendations and, in need of Arab support in the war, proposed that an Arab state be set up in Palestine with Jews as a minority population.

The Second World War saw international opinion swing back in favor of the Jews and a homeland, especially when the full horror of the Holocaust became known. Ben-Gurion had become more convinced that whatever form the Jewish entity would take, the Jews were alone as a people. The hardening of anti-British sentiment within the Jewish community in Palestine led to increasing Jewish terrorist activity, with two underground paramilitary groups, the Haganah and the Irgun, working in cooperation. A split in the Irgun allowed the terrorist Stern Gang (Lehi) to emerge. In July 1946 the Irgun, under Menachem Begin's command, dynamited the King David Hotel, which housed the British administration in Jerusalem. Ninety-one people were killed. Ben-Gurion was outraged.

Ben-Gurion and Jerusalem

Describing an event during Ben-Gurion's earliest years in Palestine, Teveth writes, "Before the end of February [1909] he paid his first visit to Jerusalem, where the sight of the Western Wall brought on such extreme emotional agitation that he remained in the city for a week."[52] Teveth mentions this psychic disturbance only in passing. In e-mail correspondence, Teveth wrote further of this event using a metaphor related to identity. He said, "Think of it [his first visit to the Wall] as a son meeting a father after a very long separation."[53] Ben-Gurion was adept at covering up his emotions,[54] believing that their open expression was a weakness. The emotional impact of the Western Wall is all the more significant in light of this proclivity. By his own admission, Ben-Gurion was irreligious, even atheistic as a youth.[55] In his later years he demonstrated no great sympathy for the elements of traditional Judaism[56] (though he quoted the Bible extensively in his speeches and writings—more than any other Jewish politician then or since). Yet a first visit to the Western Wall, one of "the major primordial symbols of Jewish collectivity,"[57] produced such an emotional effect that he was compelled to rest for a week. According to Teveth, at the time there were two parts to Zion/Jerusalem for Ben-Gurion:

> the site itself, and the place in the heart (High Zion). The first was not much different from what he saw in Plonsk, and perhaps worse (Jews living on Haluka), the majority of whom were anti-Zionists. The latter was something to hope for, cherish and work hard to make true.[58]

Following this emotional experience, Ben-Gurion returned to live in Jerusalem in 1910. Teveth noted that the young man had now decided to try to win over the Orthodox in the city and accepted an invitation to become a member of the editorial board of the Labor Zionist journal *Ha-Ahdut (Unity)*. "Once [Ben-Gurion] moved to Old Zion, something resonated in his heart and connected New Zion (Judah [Petah Tikvah] and Galilee [Menhamia and Sejera], where the new proletariat was) to the old one. . . . [T]he site has magic powers of its own."[59] Writing of this period, Ben-Gurion gives a hint that mentally, he had already accepted Jerusalem as the capital. Of his decision to take up the new post, he says:

> I somewhat reluctantly agreed to become a journalist. Perhaps one of the minor points influencing my decision was that the nub of Zionist activity in the country had moved from Jaffa to Jerusalem, in symbolic emphasis of our affinity with the city which had always been and was to become once more our capital.[60]

Years later in the wake of the 1936 Arab Revolt and the ensuing recommendations on partition, Ben-Gurion was faced with the question of the future Jewish state's proposed capital in a direct way. A pragmatist, he knew that the constraints against full possession of Jerusalem were great. Indeed he had even proposed ceding the entire city, until his colleagues opposed him fiercely.[61] He then proposed an adaptation of the partition plan. Motti Golani asserts that elements of the British proposal became the model for all future Israeli positions on Jerusalem until 1967. He focuses on Ben-Gurion's practical approach, which said that part of Jerusalem is better than none, since according to Ben-Gurion, "the name Jerusalem means everything" to the millions of Jews in the Diaspora. Thus West Jerusalem would become the capital of the Jewish state, with the Old City ruled by the British mandatory authority or an international equivalent (not Arab). This degree of compromise is not surprising given the political constraints of the period. But it should not be confused with a lack of commitment to the city on Ben-Gurion's part. His Jewish identity-ideology nexus indicates otherwise. As even Golani admits, "I found no prominent Israeli statement, in the years covered by this paper [1948–67], questioning the ideological, cultural, and religious Jewish-Israeli affinity for Jerusalem."[62] The interacting political variables simply prevented full realization of Jewish yearnings for the city. The outbreak of war following the British retreat in 1939 from the Royal Commission's proposals set the discussion back several years.

In April 1947 Britain requested the transfer of its Mandate responsibilities to the United Nations, and Jerusalem was to become once more a central issue for Ben-Gurion. In November the UN passed Resolution 181 advocating the partition of Palestine, and the future of the city was again in the balance. The resolution called for establishing an Arab and a Jewish state with mutual economic interests, and for the internationalization of Jerusalem (see map 4.2). There was a provision in the resolution that after ten years a nonbinding referendum would take place among the residents regarding the city's future. For his part, Ben-Gurion was happy to agree to this in the hope that after a decade the Jews would find it easier to possess the city, even though the projected demographics of the area were not to the Jewish advantage at that point. Despite the apparent unevenness of other terms of the resolution (there would be 500,000 Jews and 400,000 Palestinian Arabs in the Jewish state), the Jewish community in Palestine would have a legitimacy it had never had before, in the form of its own independent state. The Jewish Agency accepted partition, though agreement to the internationalization of Jerusalem was a bitter pill. But it was once again a matter of pragmatism: a state without Jerusalem was better than no state at all. For its part, the Arab League rejected the plan on behalf of the Palestinians.

Even before the British formally asked the UN to take over the Mandate, Ben-Gurion had concluded that an armed conflict with the Arabs was inevitable. He had held the defense portfolio from 1946 and had already begun an arms buildup. In November 1947, just before the UN partition resolution was passed, Golda (Meyerson) Meir met secretly with King

Map 4.2   The United Nations Partition Plan, 1947.

Abdullah on behalf of the Jewish Agency. They agreed that, during a very likely conflict between the *Yishuv* and its Arab enemies, the Jews would take the areas designated for them in the UN plan, Transjordan would take Arab Palestine, and the two sides would make peace. However, the fate of Jerusalem was never mentioned.

Immediately following the passage of the UN resolution, Palestinian Arabs attacked the Jewish community. The Jewish forces retaliated, and by mid-January 1948 Palestinians in sections of West Jerusalem were fleeing. In February Ben-Gurion gave orders to the Haganah to take possession of more Palestinian areas in West Jerusalem and to populate them with Jews. In March the Haganah agreed on offensive actions (Plan D[alet]) against the Palestinians, including the expulsion of the population of entire villages.

On April 1 Ben-Gurion met with Haganah leaders and ordered an attack on the Arab village of Qastel, which overlooked the Tel Aviv–Jerusalem road. Thus several weeks before the official British withdrawal, Plan D became operational, with a view "to open a corridor from the coast up to Jerusalem [Operation Nachshon] and to annex as much of the city as possible to the Jewish state."[63]

Ben-Gurion later claimed that the Negev was his first priority,[64] but based on interviews with Yigal Allon, Yigael Yadin, and Ben-Gurion himself, foreign correspondent Dan Kurzman wrote:

> The full impact of his lifelong obsession with the Bible struck with blistering force when it appeared that Jerusalem would fall to the Arabs and perhaps be lost forever to the Jewish state. Whatever happened to any other Jewish areas, the Holy City must be saved. It was the soul of the Jewish people, the fount of the light to be cast unto the nations. He had agreed that it be internationalized as a *temporary* concession. But an Arab flag over Jerusalem? Not for one minute![65]

Two critical events led to the subsequent Zionist capture of significant parts of the city. First, on April 8, was the death of Palestinian leader Abd al-Qadir al-Husayni in the fighting at Qastel. Second, just one day later, was the infamous attack by the Irgun and the Stern Gang, in which 254 Palestinian civilians were killed at Deir Yassin on the western edge of Jerusalem.

Conditions inside Jerusalem had been deteriorating for several months. The Jewish Quarter of the Old City was under siege from Palestinian Arabs. On April 10 Ben-Gurion called an emergency meeting to find a way to alleviate the city's food shortage. Three convoys got through and the problem was lessened. On May 11 Golda Meir secretly visited King Abdullah again to try to persuade him not to attack Israel in the coming days. He said that the situation had changed and he could no longer keep his earlier agreement.

On May 14 Ben-Gurion proclaimed the State of Israel. According to the Arab Legion commander Sir John Glubb, on May 17 King Abdullah ordered the Arab Legion to defend the Old City in response to a Jewish offensive launched a few days earlier.[66] On May 19 the Jordanians arrived on the north side of the city and prevented further advances by the Jewish forces.

Revisionist historians note that the conventional "War of Independence" account pits an Israeli David against an Arab Goliath. But the supposedly numerically outmatched Israelis in fact always had superiority, more so as the war continued. Subsequently released documents also show that various Arab armies were each interested in Palestine for reasons other than just to help the Palestinians. The notion of a collusive Arab front does not stand up. King Abdullah certainly had a different agenda. Significant for this study is that Ben-Gurion met his general staff on May 24 and listed his priorities. First, Jerusalem, the Galilee, and the Negev. Second, offense and not defense. Third, defeat one party at a time. Fourth, force the hand of the Arab Legion.[67] On May 28, however, with the help of career British officers, the Arab Legion brought the Jewish Quarter to the point of surrender.

A general cease-fire came into effect on June 11, 1948. West Jerusalem, including Palestinian areas where the population had been driven out, remained Jewish. East Jerusalem and the Old City were to stay in Jordanian hands. On September 26 Ben-Gurion put a new plan before the cabinet. He proposed launching an attack to take the whole city, but the vote went against him. He suppressed publication of the proposal, not wanting to embarrass those who had voted against it.[68] For some time afterward he blamed the cabinet and excused himself over what he called the "loss" of East Jerusalem, which he said would be a cause for "lamentation for generations."[69] Further, both he and General Moshe Dayan, who became influential in the first few years of the State, believed that the 1948 war should have ended differently. They felt that Israel should have occupied "the whole country, from the Jordan to the Mediterranean, and that a great opportunity had been lost to redeem the 'Land of Israel' up to its natural frontiers."[70] Once more the depth of Ben-Gurion's convictions about the need to have the whole of Jerusalem in Israeli hands is obvious.

Did the Jordanians sense that Ben-Gurion wanted the city in toto? There are some indications of this. The first one concerns the economic under-development of East Jerusalem by the Jordanians. For twenty years under Jordanian rule, Amman and the East Bank were emphasized and the economic growth of the West Bank was neglected. The reason was not just preference for the Hashemite capital of Amman. According to Hudson, investment in East Jerusalem was pointless, since "the Jordanian authorities feared that sooner or later Israel would strike again."[71]

A second indication of Jordanian understanding of Ben-Gurion's perspective on the city comes from Glubb. In his memoirs he wrote that in 1948, weeks before the end of the Mandate, a Haganah officer had mentioned to an Arab Legion officer that the Jews knew what the Legion was about to do in Arab Palestine. He then said that the Jews did not mind as long as the Legion did not interfere with Zionist forces in Jerusalem. When asked what would happen if they did, the Haganah officer replied, "You will only enter Jerusalem over our dead bodies." Glubb surmised, "Perhaps the Jews had long beforehand determined to seize the whole of Jerusalem."[72]

A separate indication of Ben-Gurion's passion for capturing the entirety of Jerusalem at the time is found in his own response to later criticism by Knesset members that he had abandoned Jerusalem in his role as minister of defense. He replied:

> The fate of Jerusalem was decided by the military, economic and settlement activities that began on November 30, 1947, and have continued until this very day. . . .
> The struggle for Jerusalem is not only political. . . . There are two elements—political and spiritual—in the struggle for Jerusalem. . . .
> Our struggle for Jerusalem did not begin in the UN General Assembly, but encompassed a constructive effort extending over many decades.[73]

With respect to the second phase of the war (May 1948–January 1949), Ben-Gurion also wrote to Charles de Gaulle years later about Israel's intentions:

> If we could expand our borders and liberate Jerusalem in the war that the Arab peoples were launching against us, we would liberate Jerusalem and western Galilee and they would become part of the State.[74]

Having signed armistice agreements in early 1949, Ben-Gurion explained to the cabinet on May 29 why he did not rush into peace treaties. He believed that Israel had time on its side in all the major issues—borders, refugees, and Jerusalem. On the latter, he felt that the idea of internationalization was fading as people grew accustomed to the status quo.[75] It was a perspective that matched his long-term vision that eventually the Zionist goal would be fully achieved, including repossession of all of Jerusalem. As long as practicalities demanded a different situation, then he could rationalize less-than-complete outcomes. However, his overall goals remained intact.

On December 5, 1949, in response to a renewed debate in the UN over Jerusalem and the holy places, Ben-Gurion announced in the Knesset that Jerusalem was an inseparable part of the State of Israel, and its eternal capital. In this case the primary trigger for Israeli momentum on Jerusalem was institutional opposition from the UN. Ben-Gurion's address was couched in powerfully emotive terms, filled with references to the history and longing of the Jewish people over millennia, appealing to the core identity of the first Jews to become Israelis. In this speech Jerusalem is Jewish, redeemed, holy, sovereign, worth dying for, and inseparable from the state. It is the heart of the state, the eternal capital.

> [W]e regard it as incumbent to declare that Jewish Jerusalem is an organic and inseparable part of the State of Israel—just as it is an integral part of the history of Israel, of its faith and of the spirit of our people. Jerusalem is the very heart of the State of Israel. . . .
>   . . . [I]t is inconceivable that the U.N. should attempt to sever Jerusalem from the State of Israel or to infringe the sovereignty of Israel over its eternal capital.
>   . . . Our links with Jerusalem at the present day are no less intense than they were in the days of Nebuchadnezzer and Titus Flavius; and when Jerusalem was attacked after the 14th May, 1948, our heroic youth were capable of laying down their lives for our holy capital city, no less than our forefathers did in the days of the First and Second Temples.
>   . . . [W]e declare that Israel will never abandon Jerusalem of its own volition, in the same way as we have not for thousands of years given up our faith, our national character and our hope of return to Jerusalem and Zion—despite persecutions unparalleled in history.
>   A people which for two thousand five hundred years has steadfastly observed the oath which the first exiles swore on the rivers of Babylon not to forget Jerusalem will never acquiesce in separation from Jerusalem. And Jewish Jerusalem will never accept foreign rule, after thousands of its sons and daughters have for the third time liberated their historic homeland and redeemed Jerusalem from destruction and ruin.[76]

Exactly what Ben-Gurion meant by "Jewish Jerusalem" is a subject of debate. It is claimed that he never intended to take the whole of Jerusalem, East and West—that he was satisfied to have a part of the city. Yet, as we have seen, a number of his statements and actions belie that conclusion and add weight to the argument that the whole of Jerusalem was his ultimate objective, an objective based in core identity and ideology. The language in his address speaks to more than West Jerusalem. His Jerusalem is "an integral part of the history of Israel, of its faith and of the spirit of [the Jewish] people," "eternal," "the holy capital city" of Babylonian and Roman times, "Zion," and "redeemed" along with the "historic homeland." This cannot be only West Jerusalem of 1948. A claim is being staked here for the whole. This is the language of identity and ideology.

On December 10, 1949, the UN General Assembly voted by a large majority (38–14, with 7 abstentions) to uphold its previous resolution of November 29, 1947. Jerusalem was to come under a special international regime as a *corpus separatum*, to be administered by the UN through its Trusteeship Council and governed by its own appointee.

On December 13 Ben-Gurion reaffirmed what he had said about Jerusalem a week earlier. Nothing had changed. He added, "We cannot assist in the forcible separation of Jerusalem, which would unnecessarily and unjustifiably violate the historical and natural rights of the Jewish people." He also noted that "the State of Israel has had, and will always have, only one capital—eternal Jerusalem. This was so three thousand years ago and so it will be, we believe, to the end of time."[77] At the end of the speech, on the prime minister's recommendation, the Knesset voted to transfer itself and the government of Israel to Jerusalem. Over the next several months government departments were moved from Tel Aviv, though the present Knesset building did not open until July 1966.

Early in 1950 Ben-Gurion sent Moshe Dayan to conduct secret negotiations with King Abdullah with a view to a territorial exchange. The prime minister proposed giving up certain portions of West Jerusalem that were formerly Palestinian, as well as the Jerusalem-Bethlehem road in Israeli territory. In return he requested Israeli sovereignty over the Jewish Quarter and the Western Wall, and safe passage to Mount Scopus, with its university and hospital, and to the Jewish cemetery on the Mount of Olives. Despite cordiality, the negotiations were unsuccessful.[78] Once again the importance of the issue of Jerusalem in Ben-Gurion's mind came to the fore, with attempts to acquire significant territory and access through secrecy.

Ben-Gurion retired from politics for two short periods, from December 1953 to February 1955, and again in June 1963. He was reelected to the Knesset in 1965 as the head of a new party (Rafi) formed with his protégé Shimon Peres and Moshe Dayan. But his days as leader were over. In December 1967 the party would vote to disband and rejoin Mapai, leaving Ben-Gurion as the only Rafi member in the Knesset.

The day after Israel's capture of the Old City in 1967, Ben-Gurion visited the Western Wall accompanied by Peres. He noticed a tile sign in front of the Wall, which read "Al-Burak Road" in English and Arabic but not in Hebrew. It was a reminder of the prophet Muhammad's legendary horse, Buraq, left tethered by the Wall as the prophet took his journey to heaven from the famous rock above. Ben-Gurion looked at the sign with disapproval and asked if anyone had a hammer. A soldier tried to pry off the tile with a bayonet, but Ben-Gurion was concerned about damage to the stone. An axe was produced and the name on the tile carefully removed. The symbolism of expunging Arabic from the redeemed Jewish holy site was not lost on the surrounding crowd, or on Ben-Gurion. They cheered, and Ben-Gurion exclaimed, "This is the greatest moment of my life since I came to Israel."[79]

The next day he went further and proposed "the demolition of the walls of Jerusalem because they are not Jewish."[80] Ben-Gurion believed that this would indicate continuity of Jewish control of the areas inside and outside the walls. He went on to suggest the building of "thousands of huts" all over the captured city to create "facts" on the ground. Subsequent debate within Israeli circles about what to do with the captured West Bank found Ben-Gurion recommending its return. He saw no possibility of maintaining a demographic edge by incorporating so many Palestinians into Israel.[81] However, when it came to the Golan Heights and Jerusalem, he stated that they should be kept.[82]

On June 17, following the war, the General Assembly of the United Nations passed a resolution (by a 99–0 vote, with 18 abstentions) with respect to the Israeli capture of Jerusalem. The resolution required that Israel abstain from making any change in the status of the city. Ben-Gurion later commented:

> We had reason to expect that this resolution would suffer the same fate as that which had called for the internationalization of Jerusalem nineteen years earlier, provided the Israeli Government and people quickly ensured a large Jewish population not only in the Old City but in the surrounding areas as well.[83]

In the Knesset at the end of July, Ben-Gurion expressed himself with exuberance about the IDF victory, especially in respect of Jerusalem. He spoke of the captured city in terms of a cherished treasure and the redemption longed for through the centuries:

> There is no doubt that the most important and dearest of all the territories which the valor of the IDF has restored to our control is the Old City of Jerusalem and its surrounding area, to which the eyes of the entire world and especially world Jewry are turned.

He was concerned, however, that the present government was not taking advantage of the situation expeditiously enough to resolve the long-standing question of the city's future. Convinced that military control alone could not change reality, he proposed:

> There is only one way to ensure for all eternity the Jewishness and Israeliness of Jerusalem and the surrounding area to the foot of Mount Scopus in the east, to beyond the airfield at Atarot in the north, and to Rahel's Tomb in the south—and not by the removal of non-Jews from this area, not a single one. On the contrary, all that is and will be required of us is to improve the economic and social conditions of the present inhabitants. But as soon as possible we must also settle, rebuild, and populate the Jewish Quarter in the Old City that was destroyed by the Arabs twenty years ago and all the empty and unpopulated areas to the east, north, and south of the city, with thousands

and tens of thousands of Jewish families from the New City and from other parts of Israel and with Jewish volunteers from the Diaspora.

Only such an irrevocable fact of renewal and completion will provide final and unquestionable permanence to the redeeming work of our glorious Army in the Six-Day War and put a stop to the debate going on in the UN since November 29, 1947, on the character, image, and regime of Jerusalem, capital of the Eternal People from the time of King David and to the end of time, if there will be such an end.

The first task, he believed, was to renew the Mount Scopus campus of the Hebrew University, the opening of which he had attended with Chaim Weizmann and Lord Balfour forty-two years earlier. But beyond that he painted the picture of a Jerusalem reminiscent of Herzl's renewed city in *Altneuland*.

We must not content ourselves merely with renewal of the university on Mount Scopus. We must enlarge the airport at Atarot to enable it to handle the largest, fastest, and most modern aircraft, so that pilgrims, immigrants, and tourists will be able to come from all parts of the world straight to the Eternal Capital of Israel. Nor is that all. We must plan, design, and erect Jewish settlements to the north, east, and south of Jerusalem—naturally only on empty land without prejudicing present inhabitants one iota.

Outside the Jewish Quarter of the Old City, Jewish settlements will be created which will live by industry and crafts, transportation and commerce, and as far as possible, agriculture as well. Not only many of the present inhabitants of Israel but large numbers of Jews from the lands of prosperity—people with capital, initiative, vision, resourcefulness, wisdom, and know-how—will come to settle in the environs of east Jerusalem without displacing the present inhabitants, Arabs or others. On the contrary, nothing will so raise the economic and cultural level of the local Arab and other inhabitants as a modern Jewish community with a high level of culture and creative enterprise.

Only such settlement work within and around the Old City will restore Jerusalem for all eternity to the nation that created eternal value in it and made the city the joy of the world, even its ruins and poverty. We can enhance its reputation and honor by making it blossom as one of the greatest and most important spiritual and scientific centers in a world that is renewing and uplifting itself. Maybe in our day the prophecy will come true that "out of Zion shall go forth the law and the word of the Lord from Jerusalem."

David Ben-Gurion finally retired in 1970 and died in 1973.

Summary: David Ben-Gurion

From his earliest days David Ben-Gurion was shaped by traditional Jewish influences and the first stirrings of Zionist ideas. Core identity is formed early and maintained, protected, and enhanced. Ben-Gurion learned Hebrew from his grandfather and father from the age of three. By his own admission, he envisaged living in the land of ancient Israel from the same age. His father was a founding member of the Lovers of Zion and held meetings in the family home, where "Eretz Israel" was a frequent topic of conversation. The experience of meeting Herzl at an early age was another powerful influence on Ben-Gurion's future. By the age of fourteen he claimed that he was a committed Zionist, teaching Hebrew to others in preparation for immigration to Palestine.

There can be little doubt that Zionist ideology formed the core of his identity. The centrality of his view of the importance of settlement in the land was illustrated in 1918 by his departure from his pregnant wife, whom he left behind in New York until she could later join him. His collection of family correspondence, *Letters to Paula*, reveals a one-dimensional mind. The Zionist cause overwhelmed everything else in his life. He wrote, "The main thread running through these letters is a reaction to the pangs of loneliness of a young, pregnant woman who shortly after her marriage in America was left alone—because her husband was a Zionist, and the implementation of Zionism was more important to him than anything else."[84] The guilt he expressed about leaving his wife behind is an indication of the priority he placed on establishing the Jewish homeland, and the time and energy he devoted to the task.

The degree to which his perspective on Jerusalem's importance for Zionism played into his attitudes and actions is again evident from an early point in his career. His emotional response to a first visit to the Western Wall found its echo at the end of his life when he stood before the newly captured Wall in 1967 and declared it to be "the greatest moment of my life since I came to Israel." In other words, the icon that Jerusalem and its historico-religious sites had become for him lay not far beneath the surface.

Despite his professed agnosticism and/or atheism, that symbol continued to influence his thinking and actions throughout life. In terms of stasis or movement over the Jerusalem Question, its effect on his policy making and political actions was profound. However, being a pragmatist whose strict priorities included settlement of the land by immigration and "pioneering," and then the creation and recognition of the state, he believed that the establishment of Jerusalem as a unified Jewish entity could wait. In other words, the constraints on full realization of his preferences for Jerusalem were sometimes self-imposed by his priorities for establishing the state. They were also forced upon him at times by the differentials in power between the *Yishuv*/State and the international actors involved, especially the British mandatory authorities and the UN. But throughout the 1948 war and afterward he demonstrated his conviction that the city must become a Jewish possession sooner or later.

In response to changing conditions, he was willing to delay possession of the city under the 1947 UN partition plan, if agreeing to internationalization—with a clause for a referendum on final status after ten years—meant that the State of Israel could become a reality. Thus, as with his Zionist predecessors, his opportunities for realizing possession of Jerusalem were limited by the interacting variables of outside power and his own priorities for the establishment of the state. However, once those priorities were met, Ben-Gurion responded to the slightest chance of taking the city in part or whole with great energy, courage, and boldness. Whenever the conditions allowed expression of identification with Jerusalem via concrete actions, it became very apparent where he stood. For example, he was prepared to fight for the city once the Arab world rejected the 1947 partition resolution. Significant movement on the Jerusalem Question came for the Zionists in 1948–49, once the state had been declared, the armistice agreement had been signed with Jordan, and de facto possession of the Western half of the city had been achieved. Under these conditions, the renewed UN push for internationalization in the November 1949 General Assembly debate triggered Ben-Gurion's decisive declaration of West Jerusalem's annexation and its establishment as Israel's capital and seat of government. Further, he continued to strive for more of the city by opening discussions with Jordan in the early 1950s. Ben-Gurion sent Moshe Dayan to negotiate for Israeli sovereignty over the Jewish Quarter and the Western Wall, and for access to Mount Scopus and the Mount of Olives' Jewish cemetery, in exchange for former Palestinian territory in West Jerusalem and the Jerusalem-Bethlehem road. While the discussions came to naught, they demonstrated Ben-Gurion's continued attempt to fulfill what amounted to his personal ideological imperative to resolve the Jerusalem Question in favor of Israel.

Menachem Begin

Identity and Ideology

Menachem Begin (1913–92) was born in Brest-Litovsk, Poland, the third and last child of Ze'ev Dov and Hassia (Korsovski) Begin. A border town at the convergence of Lithuania, Germany, and Poland, Brest was 70 percent Jewish during Begin's childhood. His father worked in the timber business and was an early activist pioneer of the Zionist movement, along with a colleague, Mordechai Sheinerman, grandfather of Ariel Sharon. Sheinerman's wife was the midwife who delivered Menachem.

The First World War was a time of privation for the family, with scarce food and several temporary homes. Ze'ev Dov Begin spoke four languages and, being pro-German, found some work translating into that language. Linguistic ability passed on to the children, with Menachem outdoing his father by learning to speak nine languages. But when asked their primary language on official forms, the Begin children would always write, "Hebrew."

Ze'ev Dov was also an observant Jew, though capable of some flexibility in his religious outlook. In adult life Menachem Begin remained Orthodox, though not strictly observant. He would eat only kosher food but would not attend synagogue every day or even every Sabbath. However, his father taught the children pride in their identity: "For him, Jewish tradition and Jewish nationalism were as one."[85]

In his schooling Begin showed himself an ardent student, excelling in the humanities. At the age of ten, along with his siblings, he became a member of Hashomer Hatza'ir (Young Guard), the Jewish scouting movement. Three years later, as the movement became Marxist in orientation and with their father's encouragement, the children left. At the age of fifteen, Begin joined Jabotinsky's youth movement, Betar, whose members wore military-style uniforms, drilled, and learned to use firearms. Of this period he wrote:

> I was fascinated by the total Zionism of Betar, the ideal of *Eretz Yisrael* as a Jewish State in our time. All those elements which, from reading and listening to others, I accepted as true found expression in Betar, and I had no doubt whatsoever that this was the movement in which I would want to serve the Jewish people all my life.[86]

The young Begin first heard Jabotinsky speak in 1930 and was captivated. The Revisionist leader became his idol, his master, and the world figure whose ideas would provide him with his road map.[87] As Begin later said,

> The greatest influence in my life I attribute to Jabotinsky. I was won over by his ideas, and I learned the doctrine of Zionism from him. My entire life has been influenced by him, both in the underground and in politics: the willingness to fight for the liberation of the homeland, and the logical analysis of facts in political matters.[88]

It was Jabotinsky's all-round intellectual and practical abilities that impressed Begin. The leader was

> a speaker, a writer, a philosopher, a statesman, a soldier, a linguist. . . . But to those of us who were his pupils, he was not only their teacher, but also the bearer of their hope.[89]

In addition, Jabotinsky was impatient with conventional Zionism's gradualist approach. He wanted an immediate Jewish state comprising land on both sides of the River Jordan. The 1917 Balfour Declaration had not specified the country of Transjordan, he said, but a national home for the Jewish people in the whole of Palestine. When the British subsequently created a kingdom for Abdullah, Jabotinsky rejected the concept. Here lie the origins of Begin's own maximalist views on *Eretz Israel*, even to the point of refusing to meet privately with Jordan's King Husayn in later years.

In the 1930s, having studied law at Warsaw University, Begin became Betar's chief organizer in Poland and recruited all over the country. He spent many hours listening to and studying Jabotinsky at close quarters, later mimicking his speaking style and dress. Begin's father's influence should not be dismissed, however. While Begin adopted his mature political views from Jabotinsky, Ze'ev Dov may be credited with other important aspects of his character and personality. Bravery was one of Dov's distinguishing traits according to Begin's sister, and to Begin himself:

> I have never known a man braver than him. Perhaps it has been decreed by fate, but throughout my life I have worked with courageous people. Yet I shall never forget how my father fought to defend Jewish honour.[90]

This characteristic was to stand Begin in good stead in the difficult years immediately ahead. In May 1939 he married Aliza Arnold, also a Betar member. Jabotinsky came by train from Paris to Warsaw for the wedding. But by early September the Second World War had begun and German bombs were falling on Warsaw. This conflict was very different from the 1914–18 war for the Begin family. All but Menachem and his sister and their spouses died in the Nazi era. Early in the war, Aliza Begin was able to travel to Palestine via Lithuania. Menachem was less fortunate: as a Zionist activist he was imprisoned for two years by the Russians, first in Lithuania, then in Siberia. His experience in surviving almost impossible hardships—prison, the gulag, interrogations; deprived of food, water, sleep, and human contact; and relentlessly holding to his convictions despite it all—demonstrated the intermixture of his father's independence and bravery, and the asceticism of Jabotinsky's way.

Eventually Begin was freed, became a Polish army private, and made his way to Jerusalem, where he was reunited with his wife in 1942. The following year he became leader of the Irgun and worked actively against the British, selecting nonmilitary targets for bombing until the war was over. In July 1946 he received Haganah approval for the bombing of the King David Hotel, which housed the headquarters of the British civil and military administration in Jerusalem. In the attack, ninety-one people died, including forty-one Arabs and seventeen Jews. Warning phone calls were made to the hotel but not acted upon. The Haganah later withdrew support of the bombing following an appeal by Weizmann.[91] In the months that followed, the Irgun and the Stern Gang escalated their attacks on the British, trading whipping for whipping, hanging for hanging. After he became prime minister in 1977, Begin wrote into his will that he and his wife should be buried next to two of the "martyrs" from the Irgun and the Stern Gang, men who had committed suicide in prison in 1947. Begin never forgot his fighters for the cause and, in his second term as prime minister, even issued a set of postage stamps bearing the faces of several such "martyrs."[92]

Begin and Jerusalem

As the British Mandate came to an end, Ben-Gurion worked to bring the Jewish military elements into one cohesive force. The Irgun agreed to join with the Haganah, the Palmach and the Stern Gang to form the IDF. Begin and the Irgun agreed to do so "within the boundaries of the Hebrew independent State."[93] According to Shmuel Katz, a Revisionist propagandist and member of the Irgun in Europe at the time, this clause excluded Jerusalem, which was understood to be on the path to internationalization with Ben-Gurion's support. Katz wrote:

> We would not disband entirely. We never forgot Jerusalem, where the Israeli Government refused to claim sovereignty, where the Old City had fallen and the New was in danger. There the Irgun would have to continue its independent existence to struggle for the inclusion of the whole city in the Jewish State. Until then, a remnant of the Irgun abroad had to be kept in being.[94]

In opposition to Ben-Gurion, Begin attempted in June 1948 to claim part of an intercepted Irgun arms shipment on board the *Altalena* (Jabotinsky's pen name) for his Jerusalem contingent. Ben-Gurion was determined not to allow the Irgun or Begin to be a divisive element within the new state. The *Altalena* was shelled from the Tel Aviv foreshore and set on fire. Begin capitulated.

After the establishment of the state, and with the formation of a parliamentary system, Begin became leader of the Herut party, following the political philosophy of Jabotinsky. He had forsaken armed opposition but not his perspective on *Eretz Israel* or Jerusalem. In a Herut press conference on September 19, 1948, he noted that the provisional government of Israel could not be "entirely exempt from indirect responsibility for the Jerusalem tragedy because of its own policy."[95] The failure of Israeli forces to capture the Old City was, in Begin's words, a tragedy.

Early in the first Knesset in 1949 he raised Jabotinsky's "two banks of the Jordan" image, saying, "There will be no peace for our State, and there will be no peace for our people, if we do not liberate that part of our homeland from the invading troops."[96] The invaders were the Jordanians and their British military advisors. In April 1949 he asked parliamentary members of the Religious Front why they were not ashamed of "the abandonment of the Jordan—the whole Jordan" to the Hashemites. "How is it that your hand did not shake in officially recognizing the control of Abdullah in the Old City of Jerusalem?" He pressed for a "united Jerusalem" rather than West Jerusalem as the capital, saying:

> Don't tell us that there is no value to declarations. The foreign nations must know that Jerusalem is ours, it is all ours—the Temple Mount, the Western Wall—and Jerusalem on both sides of the wall is our capital, not only in theory but practice.[97]

Consistently losing to Ben-Gurion and other Labor party leaders in the 1950s and early 1960s, Begin did accept a role in the National Unity Government formed by Levi Eshkol just prior to the 1967 war. Begin had suggested in the face of the growing threat from Egypt that the opposition parties join the government in a grand coalition and that Moshe Dayan be named minister of defense. On the way to the Knesset to take up his position as minister without portfolio, Begin paid a visit to Jabotinsky's grave on Mount Herzl in Jerusalem. His bones had been brought to Israel three years earlier and reinterred in accordance with his will.

The 1967 war gave Begin an unusual opportunity to affect the struggle for Jerusalem. On June 5 it became clear that King Husayn was intent on joining the war on the side of Egypt. At the prime minister's Tel Aviv office, Begin and the minister of labor, Yigal Allon, pressured Eshkol for the reunification of Jerusalem. Years later Yitzhak Rabin publicly confirmed their crucial involvement: "We also recall today the memories of ministers Yigal Allon and Menachem Begin of blessed memory who took a major part in the decision to liberate Jerusalem."[98]

Arriving in Jerusalem from Tel Aviv to the sound of Jordanian shells and mortars landing near the Knesset, Begin now urged an emergency cabinet meeting on the prime minister. The cabinet voted in favor of taking the Old City. To avoid damage to the holy sites, the army was told to do nothing more than surround the city in the hope that the Jordanians would surrender. After midnight on June 7, however, Begin heard on radio that the UN was about to order a cease-fire on all fronts. The Old City was encircled but not captured. Fearing the loss of the city as in 1948, Begin called Eshkol at 4 a.m. and suggested that the IDF enter the Old City without delay. Eshkol asked Begin to phone defense minister Moshe Dayan, who agreed that the pending UN call for a cease-fire changed the picture. Begin now became the go-between. Dayan asked Begin to call Eshkol and get a decision to enter the Old City. Eshkol consulted with his cabinet and gave the order for the Old City to be taken. By 10:15 a.m. the battle was over. Begin's passion for reuniting the city had kept the issue of Jerusalem on the front burner and contributed to its capture. Three weeks later, along with most Israelis, Begin was happy to support the Israeli government's extension of its laws to East Jerusalem. The annexation he had wanted had finally happened.

Another moment that Begin had waited for since the inception of the state came ten years later, in the Likud election upset of 1977. For the first time in the country's history the Revisionists came in from the cold. Begin had the opportunity to put his long-held ideology into practice. His opening speech to the Knesset reflected ideas adopted at an early age and developed over a lifetime of application:

> We were granted our right to exist by the God of our fathers, at the glimmer of the dawn of human civilization, nearly four thousand years ago. For that right, which has been sanctified in Jewish blood from generation to generation, we have paid a price unexampled in the annals of the nations. Certainly, this fact does not diminish or enfeeble our right. On the contrary. Therefore, I re-emphasize that we do not expect anyone to request, on our behalf, that our right to exist in the land of our fathers, be recognized. It is a different recognition which is required between ourselves and our neighbours: recognition of sovereignty and of the mutual need for a life of peace and understanding. It is this mutual recognition that we look forward to: For it we shall make every possible effort.[99]

The right to biblical territory was an enduring theme, and Begin raised it continually. Asked once how he would like to be remembered, Begin replied, "As the man who set the borders of *Eretz Yisrael* for all eternity." Biographer Eric Silver notes: "That was not an ambition he discovered in his old age. From his adolescence in Poland, Begin had lived in the cultural and intellectual cloister of the Jabotinsky movement."[100]

In a surprising development, however, it was Begin's Likud administration that agreed to the return of the Sinai and peace with Sadat's Egypt. Whether this was an ideological volte-face or simply the wisdom of leadership in a heroic moment was difficult for observers to tell. Perhaps Begin was practicing his observant father's model of flexibility to the Sabbath rules. Perhaps, in his mind, the return of the Sinai was the payoff for continued retention of the West Bank. It is also possible that the Sinai did not represent the ancient border of Israel for Begin as much as some believed. There was debate, after all, about whether the biblical reference to the "river of Egypt" as the southern boundary meant the Nile or the Wadi al-Arish by the Gaza-Egypt border.

One area over which there could be no compromise, however, was Jerusalem. Begin was quick to point this out at the September 1978 Camp David talks that led to the 1979 peace treaty between Egypt and Israel.

According to Yoel Marcus,

> Begin turned to Article 6, in which Sadat was proposing that Israel withdraw
> from East Jerusalem which it had occupied in 1967, annexed and unified
> with West Jerusalem, and which it declared was its eternal capital. "So you
> propose to divide Jerusalem?" said Begin, adding, *"Never."*[101]

And so it was that when the agreement was finally signed, change in
the status of Jerusalem was noticeably absent. On July 30, 1980, the
Knesset reaffirmed what had been done in 1967 and passed the "Basic
Law: Jerusalem, Capital of Israel" in respect of the city. It declared,
"Jerusalem, complete and united, is the capital of Israel."[102] When the bill
was introduced by an ultranationalist Knesset member, Geula Cohen, it
was not initially supported by many either in government or in opposition. But it soon became politically inexpedient not to support it. Begin
was not going to be bested by the ultranationalists with respect to
Jerusalem. He had already made a public statement about the city earlier
in the month. He had suffered a coronary occlusion in June and had
issued the statement on Jerusalem from his hospital bed on July 6. It read,
"It is the national consensus and the policy of the Government of Israel
that Jerusalem, which has been reunited as a result of a successful legitimate self-defense, will remain forever united, forever indivisible, and forever the capital city of the State of Israel by virtue of right." On July 14,
on his release from hospital, he spoke again of the city's centrality to
Israel's identity.[103] Interestingly, Labor, too, decided to support the bill,
demonstrating once again that the Jerusalem issue cuts across party affiliation. The bill passed by 69 votes to 15. As a result, most of the remaining foreign diplomatic missions removed themselves from Jerusalem to
Tel Aviv. During the passage of the bill, Begin announced that he would
relocate his office to East Jerusalem. A building was prepared and furni-
ture moved in. The outcry within and outside Israel was such that he had
to abandon the idea, though four ministries and the national police headquarters did relocate.

In June 1981 Begin and the Likud were reelected. But the political aftermath of the disastrous 1982 IDF invasion of Lebanon to expel the PLO
proved devastating. Growing physical and mental fatigue following a fall in
late 1981, in which he broke his femur, compounded Begin's distress. The
death of his wife in November 1982 while he was on a visit to Washington,
D.C., caused him to descend into a clinical depression. He found it difficult
to shake his depressed state and became increasingly reclusive.[104] On his
resignation in September 1983, he told his cabinet, "I cannot go on." Rarely
seen thereafter in public, he died in 1992.

Summary: Menachem Begin

Menachem Begin was raised in the familiar pattern that established Zionist thought in so many of Israel's early leaders. His identity arose in part from his observant Jewish parents, who evinced a strong emphasis on Zionist goals. At the age of ten he was a member of the Jewish scouting organization Hashomer Hatza'ir, which educated the young about Jewish history and about life in the *Yishuv*, stressing immigration to Palestine as a way of self-fulfillment.

At the age of fifteen Begin became a member of Jabotinsky's Betar movement and was convinced that he would spend his life with the movement. As with other Zionist leaders, there came a defining moment when elements of his traditional background fused with the dynamism of the movement's teaching about settling the land, and the young follower became fixed ideologically. In Begin's case, the experience of meeting Jabotinsky gave him an idol, an extraordinary role model. Begin's identification with his leader was such that he virtually impersonated him, studying his dress, speech patterns, and mannerisms, and these aspects of Jabotinsky remained with him throughout life. Revisionism became his guiding philosophy, encouraging a militant and violent approach to establishing the state. Begin's determination and drive through seemingly impossible Second World War experiences is evidence of his unusually strong will. His twenty-eight years in the Knesset as opposition leader also confirm the strength of his ideological conviction. Never a gradualist, he insisted on the maximum immediate benefit for the state in any negotiation. Even in the peace negotiations with Egypt, he managed to avoid all concessions on the Palestinian Question and Jerusalem. In return for peace he gave only the Sinai, despite the fact that Sadat began the negotiations with specific demands that the Israelis recognize the Palestinians' right to self-rule and apply UN resolution 242 to the West Bank territories under Israeli control.

Begin's position on Jerusalem was also firmly embedded in his Jewish identity and Revisionist Zionist ideology. He was consistent in his beliefs about the city and its centrality to the Zionist cause. From the 1947–48 struggle for Jerusalem, through what he regarded as the abdication of the government's responsibility during the 1950s, to the push for the city in the 1967 war, he was always true to his identity and ideological core. As his biographer Eric Silver wrote, "the ideology was the man," "the trunk of the tree."[105]

Begin's maximalist persuasions dominated his approach to the Jerusalem Question. During the immediate period following the declaration of the State of Israel, he sought to defend Jerusalem with his Irgun fighters. Attempting to influence the situation on the ground once Ben-Gurion and the cabinet had agreed to the city's internationalization, he attempted to gain access to an inbound arms shipment. Ben-Gurion's opposition prevented any momentum on the Jerusalem Question through Begin's efforts at the time. However, just prior to the 1967 capture of Jordanian East Jerusalem, Begin played a significant role by pushing the prime minister, Levi Eshkol, to act decisively and capture the already surrounded city. The unintended consequences of the war put the Israelis in a position to act on Begin's own maximalist ideological imperative. His energies were fulfilled a few hours later as Israeli troops stood before the Western Wall. This time the interacting variables were in Israel's favor, and Begin seized the initiative, forcing the hand of the less decisive Eshkol. With his own rise to power in the 1977 elections, the stage was set for Begin's Likud party to attempt to gain more momentum on the Jerusalem Question. Though the 1980 "Basic Law: Jerusalem, Capital of Israel" was introduced into the Knesset by an ultranationalist, Begin was quick to seize the opportunity for parliamentary reaffirmation of Jerusalem as Israel's "undivided capital," announcing that he would relocate his office to East Jerusalem. It was only the interacting variable of public opposition to the move that caused him to reverse his plan. Menachem Begin's actions on the issue of East and West Jerusalem demonstrate his underlying drive, never forgotten over a lifetime, to create the momentum to make the whole city a sovereign Jewish/Israeli possession.

Yitzhak Rabin

Identity and Ideology

Yitzhak Rabin (1922–95) was born in Jerusalem to two recently arrived young Labor Zionists who had met in the Jewish Quarter of the Old City during the Arab riots of 1920. His mother, Rosa, came from Russia, emigrating to Palestine almost by chance in 1919. She had been influenced by the Jewish left-wing anti-Zionist party, the Bund, and was en route to Scandinavia or the United States when she met some young Zionists in Odessa on their way to Palestine. She impetuously joined them. After a year on a kibbutz in the Galilee she contracted malaria and went to stay with her uncle in Jerusalem, where she met and married Nehemiah Rubitzov (Rabin). He was from the Ukraine and had decided to leave after a pogrom in 1905, immigrating to Chicago. He became a tailor and a member of Po'ale Zion. After the Balfour Declaration and the British call for men to enlist in the Jewish Legion, he found himself in London with other legion members, including David Ben-Gurion, and then in Egypt with Vladimir Jabotinsky, from whom he learned Hebrew. The legion arrived in Palestine as the war came to an end.

Eventually the Rabins settled in Tel Aviv. Nehemiah was active in the Metal Workers' Union, holding meetings in their home. He was also a member of the Electric Corporation workers' committee. Rosa was involved with the Haifa Haganah and also volunteered time to community activities, including the education of working-class children. This left the couple little time for their own family during the week. As secular Zionists, they promoted a return to the land and insisted on duty to the Jewish cause.

After ten years of schooling (eight at the workers' school), Yitzhak Rabin was ready for agricultural school in the Galilee region. During his first year there his mother died from a persistent heart ailment, and he withdrew into his studies in grief, completing the year with high grades. The 1936 riots and several Arab attacks on the school resulted in Rabin's early military training under Yigal Allon, with whom he was later to spend many years. After one year at the school, the British closed the institution and Rabin went to work, first at a kibbutz on the Sea of Galilee, then in the Jezreel Valley, where the agriculture school resumed.

Completing his course during the early part of the Second World War, Rabin joined a group being readied to establish a new kibbutz. There he was recruited by the Haganah to join the Palmach (assault companies) as part of the Jewish Agency's plan to assist the Allies, who were under threat of Rommel's North African advance. Rabin chose to stay with the Palmach during the war years, rising through the ranks. Though imprisoned in 1946 by the British for his membership, he was in position to take on deputy command of the organization just before the informal war with the Arabs began in late 1947, following the UN resolution on partition.

Rabin and Jerusalem

In April 1948 Rabin, as commander of the Palmach's newly formed Harel Brigade, was given the task of completing Operation Nachshon. The isolated Jewish enclave in Jerusalem was connected to the coast by a narrow road corridor overlooked by Arab villages. The more than 90,000 Jewish inhabitants of Jerusalem were effectively besieged, and Rabin's units were to open up the Tel Aviv–Jerusalem supply route. But the impending evacuation of British troops from Palestine, and Jerusalem in particular, caused Ben-Gurion to order Rabin's brigade to Jerusalem itself. After a heavy firefight and many losses, they reached the city. Now Rabin was ordered to take the northern and southern parts of the city.

The proclamation of the State of Israel on May 14 brought immediate Arab military reaction. Rabin was called back to Jerusalem to help break through to the besieged Jewish Quarter. The commander of the Jewish forces in the city, David Shaltiel, proposed a plan of attack that appalled Rabin:

> I was furious with him and told him outright that his plan was idiotic and bound to fail. But Jerusalem was much too dear to me to refuse even an attempt; we would carry out the diversionary attack as he requested.[106]

As a Jerusalemite, Rabin viewed the city as "much too dear to me . . ."—a sentiment that appears repeatedly in his thinking. Shaltiel's plan was a failure, though Rabin's units were able to capture their objective. Soon Rabin was back at Shaltiel's headquarters, where, he writes, the commander proposed that the two Palmach companies occupying Mount Zion break into the Jewish Quarter by way of the Zion Gate.

> My rage was beyond restraint. "Where are all the troops?" I railed at Shaltiel. "Are the eighty exhausted Palmachniks I lent you the only force that the Jewish people can muster for the liberation of its capital?"

It seems that already in Rabin's mind the city was the new nation's capital—an early indication of his views on Jerusalem's role in Jewish life.

The Old City was defended by Jordan's Arab Legion to the point that the Jewish Quarter and its defenders had to surrender. Rabin watched from nearby and later recorded his impressions:

> On May 28 I went up to Mount Zion, where I witnessed a shattering scene. A delegation was emerging from the Jewish Quarter bearing white flags. I was horrified to learn that it consisted of rabbis and other residents on their way to hear the legion's terms for their capitulation. That same night the Jewish Quarter surrendered to the Arab Legion.

Clearly the failure to capture all of Jerusalem in 1948 was for Rabin almost a personal failure. He had been largely responsible for opening up the Jerusalem corridor to help in the relief of the city. Military strategy was one of his talents. Yet Shaltiel had not taken his advice about how to effectively attack the Old City. As a result, the Old City had been lost. Rabin's response to his next military experience with Jerusalem would reveal much about his feelings, described earlier in terms of being "horrified to learn" and witnessing "a shattering scene."

Following the 1948 war, the Palmach was disbanded and Rabin pursued a career in the IDF, rising through the ranks until in 1961 Ben-Gurion appointed him deputy chief-of-staff. In 1964, on Ben-Gurion's resignation, he became chief-of-staff under Levi Eshkol. It was in this role of chief military advisor to the prime minister that he entered the 1967 war.

With respect to the central front in the war, the Israeli cabinet did not want to engage Jordan and sent messages to Amman accordingly, even though the Jordanians had already started shelling the city. There was an Israeli plan in place for the capture of the West Bank and a separate one for Jerusalem, should it become necessary. On June 5 the cabinet decided against attempting to capture the Old City. On June 6 defense minister Moshe Dayan repeated the instruction not to take the Old City. The next day, however, he issued the order to capture the ancient citadel. According to Rabin,

> [w]ith the sense that time was pressing, at seven o'clock that morning Dayan entered the war room and finally issued the order for Jerusalem's Old City to be occupied as quickly as possible. The fact that our troops were moving in on the most coveted—and difficult—target in the war left us all with a sharp sense of anticipation.[107]

Here, in Rabin's retelling, the Old City moved from being an objective that the cabinet forbade to "the most coveted . . . target in the war." Clearly the Old City had a special meaning for the man who had fought there nineteen years earlier and failed. The opportunity to redeem oneself in relation to a national and religious icon is a powerful motivation. There were others who no doubt felt the same. One of Rabin's Palmach colleagues from 1948, Uzi Narkiss, was also involved. Rabin wrote of the final assault:

> I was asked to accompany the defense minister into the Old City, and we flew to the Jerusalem headquarters of Uzi Narkiss, GOC Central Command, where the air was charged with excitement. Uzi had been one of the officers of the Harel Brigade (which fought in Jerusalem during the War of Independence), so it was a great moment for both of us. In 1948 we had been forced to leave East Jerusalem in the enemy's hands, and ever since the outbreak of the present war we had been dogged by the feeling that we must not miss the historic opportunity again.

The language takes a surprising turn for the battle-hardened and usually emotionally reserved Rabin. Now the air is "charged with excitement," it is "a great moment," the opportunity is "historic." Early memories of the city flood back into consciousness. Secret hopes and latent emotions about the Western Wall come forth. According to Efraim Inbar, with regard to Jerusalem, Rabin, "like most other Jews, was unashamedly sentimental. The generations-long yearning for the Western Wall was central to his Jewish identity."[108] With respect to the emergence of latent feelings that day, Rabin said in a speech, "Rhetorical phrases and clichés are not common in our army, but this scene on the Temple Mount, powerful enough to break through their habits of reticence, revealed as though by a flash of lightning truths that were deeply hidden."[109] The following passage from Rabin's memoirs is one of the clearest expressions of the power and impact of personal and collective identity combined with ideological precepts:

> As we made our way through streets I remembered from childhood, pungent memories played on my emotions. The sheer excitement increased as we came closer to the Western Wall itself. It is still easy for me to conjure

up the feelings that assaulted me then, but it's very difficult to put them into words. The Wall was and is our national memento of the glories of Jewish independence in ancient times. Its stones have a power to speak to the hearts of Jews the world over, as if the historical memory of the Jewish people dwelled in the cracks between those ancient ashlars. For years I secretly harbored the dream that I might play a part not only in gaining Israel's independence but in restoring the Western Wall to the Jewish people, making it the focal point of our hard-won independence. Now that dream had come true, and suddenly I wondered why I, of all men, should be so privileged. I knew that never again in my life would I experience quite the same peak of elation.

When we reached the Western Wall, I was breathless. It seemed as though all the tears of centuries were striving to break out of the men crowded into that narrow alley, while all the hopes of generations proclaimed: "This is no time for weeping! It is a moment of redemption, of hope." Following the ancient custom, Dayan scrawled a wish on a slip of paper and pushed it in between two of the stones. I felt truly shaken and stood there murmuring a prayer for peace. Motta Gur's paratroopers were struggling to reach the Wall and touch it. We stood among a tangle of rugged, battle-weary men who were unable to believe their eyes or restrain their emotions. Their eyes were moist with tears, their speech incoherent. The overwhelming desire was to cling to the Wall, to hold on to that great moment as long as possible.[110]

Rabin's wife, Leah, wrote that her husband later described his visit to the Western Wall as "the peak of my life" and the "fulfillment of a dream."[111] As with Ben-Gurion at the wall in 1967 ("This is the greatest moment of my life since I came to Israel"), something emotionally profound happened to many Israelis when the Wall came into the State's possession. Inbar notes that, for Rabin, "the days of June 1967 closed a personal cycle and constituted historic justice."[112]

There were other successes for Rabin in the 1967 war, not least of which was the capture of the Golan Heights. But as his wife also wrote,

nothing matched the glory of unifying Jerusalem again. Israel had been a state for nearly twenty years but without a united Jerusalem, it was a state without its heart. There is a nostalgic Jewish prayer in the *Haggadah*, read at the conclusion of the Passover seder that expresses the hope "next year in Jerusalem." For nearly two thousand years a reclaimed Jerusalem was a holy mission. Suddenly Jerusalem united was a reality. This was a great triumph, but it was also a profound shock.[113]

From that time on, Yitzhak Rabin often alluded to a "redeemed" Jerusalem in his speeches. On June 28 he was awarded an honorary doctorate at the Hebrew University on the reopened Mount Scopus campus. In his speech he commented on the depth of emotion felt by the nation after the capture of the Old City and by many soldiers who had reached the Wall for the first time:

> The entire nation was exalted and many wept when they heard of the capture of the Old City. Our Sabra youth, and most certainly our soldiers, do not tend to be sentimental and they shrink from any public show of feeling. But the strain of battle, the anxiety which preceded it, and the sense of salvation and of direct confrontation with Jewish history itself cracked the shell of hardness and shyness and released wellsprings of emotion and stirrings of the spirit. The paratroopers who conquered the Wailing Wall leaned on its stones and wept—in its symbolism an act so rare as to be almost unparalleled in human history.[114]

In February 1968 Rabin became Israeli ambassador to the United States. In 1973 he was elected a Labor Party member of the Knesset, and in 1974 he was appointed minister of labor. In June he became prime minister, serving until 1976. Appointed minister of defense in 1984 in a government of National Unity, he oversaw the much-criticized punitive policy against the first Palestinian Intifada. In 1992 he became chairman of the Labor Party, which won the election that year.

At the introduction of his government to the Knesset on July 13, Rabin made the following comments about the Jerusalem Question in the context of ongoing peacemaking efforts:

> We see a need to stress that the government will continue to reinforce and strengthen Jewish settlement along the confrontation lines, because of its importance for security, and in metropolitan Jerusalem. This government, like all its predecessors, believes that there is no disagreement in this house concerning Jerusalem's being the eternal capital of Israel. Jerusalem, whole and unified, has been and forever will be the capital of the people of Israel under Israeli sovereignty, the focus of every Jew's dreams and longings. The government is firm in its resolve that Jerusalem is not a subject for bargaining. The coming years, also, will be marked by the extension of construction in greater Jerusalem. Every Jew, religious or secular, has vowed, "If I forget thee, O Jerusalem, may my right hand lose its cunning." This oath unites us all, and certainly applies to me as a native of Jerusalem.
>
> The government will safeguard freedom of worship for followers of all the other religions in Jerusalem. It will rigorously maintain freedom of access to the holy places of all religions and all communities, and will ensure that both those who visit the city and those who reside there are able to enjoy an orderly life, free of inconvenience.[115]

The language contains all of the usual references to the historic bond between the Jews and the city. Further it makes no concession to sharing sovereignty but rather speaks of reinforcing existing neighborhoods in metropolitan Jerusalem and the construction of new neighborhoods in greater Jerusalem. It rules out any bargaining over the city and relates the centrality of the city to Jews, whether religious or secular.

When he spoke on September 13, 1993, at the signing of the Israeli-Palestinian Declaration of Principles in Washington, D.C., Rabin said he had come "from Jerusalem, the ancient and eternal capital of the Jewish people. . . . to try and put an end to hostilities."[116] Notable even on this occasion, signaling as it did the formal beginning of the process of peace-making and the subject of Jerusalem's future, the prime minister closed down any discussion of altered sovereignty over the city.

He gave the same assurances on September 21, 1993, in a special session of the Knesset. Speaking about the interim agreements regarding Palestinian self-rule and the exchange of official letters with the PLO, he confirmed:

> In Washington, Foreign Minister Shimon Peres signed an agreement, a Declaration of Principles, for the interim period only. In this agreement, which will allow the Palestinians to manage their own lives, the following assurances are made to Israel:
>   Unified Jerusalem will remain under Israeli control, and the body that will be the administrative authority for Palestinians in the territories will have no authority there.[117]

Similarly, in December 1993 in a speech titled "On the Road to Peace," Rabin discussed his feelings on shaking Yasser Arafat's hand in public earlier that year. Then at the close of the speech he appeared to break abruptly with the prepared script and announced:

> There will be no change, no change whatsoever, in another matter, one that is the very heart of the Jewish people, and its very soul: Jerusalem. In whatever negotiation, we will be firm in our stand that Jerusalem is and will continue to be united and our eternal capital. From our perspective, Jerusalem of Gold, of Copper, and of Light—is ours.[118]

Visiting Casablanca for an economic summit on October 30, 1994, Rabin delivered some remarks before King Hassan II of Morocco, who at the time was head of the Arab League's committee on Jerusalem. Rabin said:

> As we sat in Jerusalem almost three thousand years ago, no doubt nowadays, Jerusalem will remain united under Israel's sovereignty, the capital of Israel and the heart of the Jewish people. We learned from you, Your Majesty, to tolerate and to respect other religions, and we will allow free access, free practice, administration of the shrines holy to the Moslems and Christians, but it is still early to raise this.[119]

The perspective on Jerusalem's future propounded here is one that does not allow for any change in sovereignty as perceived by Israel since 1967. Religious freedom of access is all that is allowed by this scenario. Even so, having put forward the argument, Rabin withdraws it, since it is "still early to raise this." The trial balloon having been floated, it is promptly removed from sight again. The signal has been given, however, that there will be no compromise.

The constant need to reaffirm the centrality of Jerusalem to the state and its unaltered sovereignty appears rooted in more than a normal desire to reassure on matters of publicly doubted policy. On receiving the Nobel Peace Prize in December 1994, Rabin said:

> I am here as the emissary of Jerusalem, at whose gates I fought in days of siege; Jerusalem, which has always been and is today the eternal capital of the State of Israel and the heart of the Jewish people who pray toward Jerusalem three times a day.[120]

In his Jerusalem Day speech to the Knesset in May 1995, Rabin reminisced about the failure to capture the Old City in 1948 and spoke of separation from the Western Wall in terms of trauma and of its possession by alien peoples:

> We did not then succeed in liberating the Old City, and over the years, we lived with the painful feeling that the city was divided and that the remnant of the Temple was in the hands of foreigners. For 19 years, the paths to the Western Wall were desolate: "The market square is empty, and no one visits the Temple Mount in the Old City," in the words of poet Naomi Shemer.[121]

It is not surprising that he saw the Palestinians as foreigners, considering his upbringing and training. According to Uri Avnery he had been schooled to see Arabs as people who rioted and were murderers.[122] In the same Jerusalem Day speech, Rabin noted the unity of all parts of the Israeli political spectrum with respect to Jerusalem and went on to make the case for a continuing uncompromising stand on the city's future and its sovereignty:

> We are divided in our opinions, on the Left and the Right. We argue over courses of action and over purpose. I believe that there is no argument on one matter[:] the wholeness of Jerusalem, and its continued existence as the capital of the State of Israel. I said yesterday, and repeat today, that there are not two Jerusalems; there is only one Jerusalem. From our perspective, Jerusalem is not a subject for compromise. Jerusalem was ours, will be ours, is ours and will remain as such forever.[123]

On June 27, 1995, Rabin addressed a group of school children in Tel Aviv. Addressing his familiar theme in new terms, he said, "If they told us that peace is the price of giving up on a united Jerusalem under Israeli sovereignty, my reply would be 'let's do without peace.' "[124]

Yitzhak Rabin was assassinated in November 1995 by a Jewish religious extremist at a rally in support of the Oslo peace initiatives. Leah Rabin spoke to an American audience after his death and confirmed her husband's commitment to Jerusalem's inviolability, despite the impending final-status talks on the city, to which he had agreed:

> I know Yitzhak was absolutely resolute and had decided and was convinced that Jerusalem, the symbol of Jewish life, of Jewish eternity . . . [sic] For 2,000 years Jews have been wandering and dispersed all over the world. Jerusalem was a symbol and was a center in their Jewish identity and their Jewish tradition and their Jewish faith and their Jewish heritage. . . . This is our symbol of our unity, and for 19 years, from 1948 to 1967, Jerusalem was divided. Yitzhak regarded it as an open wound. He was unhappy with it and regarded himself as a very, very privileged and happy man to have been the commander of the IDF to unite Jerusalem, and I think that is someone who had a very great sensitivity to Jewish life, to Jewish tradition and faith, to Jewish nationality, to the survival of the Jewish people, and to the raison d'être of a Jewish homeland. For him Jerusalem was out of the question and undiscussable.[125]

Summary: Yitzhak Rabin

Yitzhak Rabin was Israel's first native-born prime minister. And he was born in Jerusalem, which gave him an additional reason for identification with the city, beyond that expected of the Jewish community. He was the son of passionate Labor Zionists, brought up from an early age to serve and to practice duty to the nation. His secular upbringing did not deter him from identifying with the traditional symbols of Jewish identity. This became clear when the opportunity to fight for Jerusalem came his way in both 1948 and 1967. It was evident in his statements about the city as it was captured by the Arab Legion and in his emotional remarks about the Western Wall when he reached it in 1967. Perhaps more than any other Jewish or Israeli leader, Rabin's expressiveness about the Old City and the significance of its capture stand out. What is equally striking is his continued rejection of any compromise on the city's sovereignty, even after the Oslo Agreements and the awarding of the Nobel Peace Prize. Though the Oslo Agreements were not designed to address the Jerusalem Question specifically (the issue was left for subsequent final-status talks), the rhetoric from Rabin, confirmed by his widow, signaled that there would be no compromise on the sovereignty of the Jewish identity markers, the core elements of Jewish Jerusalem: the Western Wall and the Temple Mount.

Momentum with respect to the Jerusalem Question is seen in most of Rabin's interaction with the city, even his disappointing 1948 war experiences. The road to Jerusalem for relief columns was secured. The constraints of that war imposed by his superior Shaltiel's actions and the failure of the Haganah to dislodge the Arab Legion from the eastern part of the city did not prevent Israel coming into possession of West Jerusalem. The 1967 capture of the Old City was the single most positive experience of momentum on Jerusalem for Rabin, as he led troops into the city in his role as commander of the IDF. Thereafter, as defense minister and prime minister, he continued to uphold the new status quo/stasis, insisting on Israel's right to the entire city, until the groundbreaking Oslo Agreements. Even then his demand was to delay the subject for final-status talks. It seems clear from his remarks and actions in the two years before his death that any compromise on his part vis-à-vis the city's status was constrained by his view of Israeli security considerations, and the Jerusalem component of his own identity-ideology nexus.

Shimon Peres

Identity and Ideology

Shimon Peres (1923–) was born Shimon Persky in Volozin, Byelorus, a town whose one thousand families all spoke Hebrew as their first language. In 1934, at the age of eleven, he emigrated to Palestine with his family. Soon after, he became a member of the Labor Zionist youth movement, Hanoar Haoved. He attended high school in Tel Aviv and spent two years at a Youth Aliya children's village, Ben Shemen. In 1943 he became secretary of Hanoar Haoved and was part of a training group that founded Kibbutz Alumot, where he stayed until 1947.

At this early stage Peres became a protégé of Ben-Gurion and progressed rapidly. On Ben-Gurion's direction he began work at Haganah headquarters in 1947. He became intimately involved with defense matters as head of the Defense Ministry Mission to the United States (1949–52). From 1953 to 1959 he worked for Ben-Gurion directly as director-general of the Defense Ministry. During this period he was involved in planning the 1956 Sinai campaign, initiating defense agreements with France and Germany, and initiating Israel's electronics, aviation, and nuclear developments.

As part of the second generation of Mapai-Labor leaders, Peres became a Knesset member in 1959. He served as deputy defense minister until 1965, when he joined Ben-Gurion as secretary-general in a new party, Rafi. In 1968 he brought the party back to its roots, and the Israel Labor Party officially came into being. A member of the cabinet until 1977, Peres was minister for economic development of the administered areas, minister for immigrant absorption, minister of transport and communications (1970–74), minister of information (1974) and defense minister in the Rabin government (1974–77). He was chairman of the Labor party through the initial Likud period and beyond (1977–92).

Peres came to an agreement with Yitzhak Shamir to form a National Unity government from 1984 to 1988, serving as prime minister for the first two years, then as deputy prime minister and minister of foreign affairs (1986–88). In the second such government, 1988–90, he was deputy prime minister and minister of finance.

In 1992 he joined archrival Yitzhak Rabin's Labor government in the role of foreign minister. With the prime minister, Peres shared in the development of the Oslo Agreements with the PLO, for which he was awarded the 1994 Nobel Peace Prize along with Rabin and Yasser Arafat.

One of his early teachers was Labor Zionist Berl Katznelson. Katznelson was also from Byelorus and founded the Tel Aviv newspaper *Davar*, of which he was editor in chief until his death in 1944. He educated Peres on a weekly basis for four years. Peres later paid tribute to him for the role he played in his intellectual development. "I see him as a mentor, as a teacher in the Indian tradition. . . . He had the most inquiring mind I have ever encountered, non-conformist, widely-read, erudite."[126]

Under Ben-Gurion, Peres functioned in various sectors of the defense establishment. Accordingly his career evidences a strong Zionist commitment to state security issues that in the early 1960s coincided with the "iron wall" perspective. At that time Peres viewed Israel's position in the Middle East as an anomaly. He believed that by nature Israel was more European than Middle Eastern. The task therefore was to "de–Middle Easternize" Israel. He expressed this viewpoint in a 1960 interview, in which, according to Brecher, he added that "Israel has virtually no contact with the Arabs and should ignore them, concentrating rather on internal development and security."[127] In this period Peres was the most committed Ben-Gurionist, regarding the Arab states as a permanent enemy besieging Israel, an enemy that understood only force, and to whom concessions would be self-defeating.[128] But by 1964 he had come to believe that Israel was in a position of military strength and could bargain for peace with the Arabs accordingly.

From then on, Peres traveled a substantial distance in his approach to the Palestinian community. In the context of the shift in Israeli-Palestinian relations in the early 1990s, he remarked, "Morally, I think that many Israelis, deep in their hearts, are happy with the idea that we shall no longer dominate the lives of another people."[129] Perhaps it was in recognition of his debt to Ben-Gurion that he came to the conclusions he did. Peres said at the same time,

My own mentor was David Ben-Gurion. What I learned from him as the most important lesson is that the highest degree of wisdom is the moral call. All told, nothing is wiser than to be decent, fair and honest.[130]

Peres and Jerusalem

Following the 1967 war, Peres said that with the Palestinians the issue was "not so much a matter of territory, but of human relations. . . . We do not want to make them Israelis and we respect their national aspirations." With regard to making peace, he commented further:

> We are ready to pay the highest price for peace. I can't tell you today what that price will be. . . . But it is certain that we will make sacrifices. . . .
> We are ready to hand over some of the territories. . . . It goes without saying that Jerusalem is not negotiable, that the Golan Heights are *essential to Israel's security*."[131]

At this point Jerusalem was not even an item for discussion. Yet by the late 1980s Peres was willing to negotiate with the Palestinians in a way that was not anticipated by his earlier stance. Brecher noted what could be a salient point in this radical change in Peres's approach. He wrote, "By temperament and behaviour he is a technocrat, who has long since abandoned ideology as a guide to policy."[132] As early as 1966 Peres said that he belonged to "a generation of dialogue rather than rigid ideology."[133] Certainly by the 1990s Peres preferred to express faith in science and technology as a key to Israel and Palestine's joint future in the Middle East. In the second half of the 1990s, he was an architect of several joint business ventures and business parks.

As a result of his apparent about-face, Peres has been described as a hawk turned dove. Asked in 1999 whether his perspective had changed over the years, he replied:

> I have changed because the situation has changed. When I thought that Israel was in danger, I was a terrible hawk. I thought it my duty to do whatever I could to defend Israel to make it stronger. But that wasn't a purpose; this was a must. Once I felt that we could go for peace, I changed, because that *is* a purpose. War is a must, peace is a goal, and I don't hesitate to admit it—full-heartedly.[134]

But does a claim to support dialogue over rigid ideology and a commitment to peace necessarily lead to a new position on Jerusalem, a position that is at odds with one's past? After all, a former defense minister does not easily forget the battles fought over the city, nor the euphoria over its capture. In April 1993 Peres announced that for the first time the government would have formal contact with a Palestinian representative in East Jerusalem, Faysal Husayni. Yet concurrently he announced "that Jerusalem will remain united as the capital of Israel and under Israeli sovereignty."[135]

That same year Peres wrote a book outlining his vision for the Middle East. With respect to Jerusalem, he repeated the concept of religious openness but remained immovable on the issue of Palestinian sovereignty in the Old City:

> While insisting on preserving Jerusalem's status as a united city under Israeli control, Israel fully understands the Holy City's significance to Christians and Muslims as well as to Jews. The general consensus in Israel is that Jerusalem should be under Israeli political control, but the city will be open to all believers, of all faiths and nationalities. Perhaps this is the modern context for Zechariah's ancient prophecy "Jerusalem shall be inhabited without walls" (Zechariah 2:4). The wall Sultan Süleiman constructed on the foundations of King Herod's wall continues to adorn Old Jerusalem, but it will not bar anyone from reaching any place in the Holy City. And the joyful prayer of the Jewish cantor, the Muslim muezzin, and the Christian choir will always rise from Jerusalem. This will be true for the other places throughout the country, too. Nowhere in the world is there a country quite like the land of Israel, where so many weapons and so many holy places occupy such a small area.[136]

During a Foreign Ministry seminar on September 11, 1994, a year after the Oslo Agreements, Peres answered questions about the role of the PLO in East Jerusalem. He was insistent on the nonnegotiability of Jerusalem's sovereignty:

> While we have recognized the PLO, we didn't designate any role to the PLO in Jerusalem. . . . The status of Jerusalem is clear. It is part and parcel of Israel, of its sovereignty and of its authority. We didn't share it. We permit normal life, like any community. But we didn't change the status of Jerusalem.[137]

In 1995, following the assassination of Yitzhak Rabin and now once again prime minister, Peres confirmed that Jerusalem would remain Israel's united capital in perpetuity.[138] In response to a question posed four years later about any change he might want to make to this 1995 statement, he said:

> I think there is no need to change it. I can think of so many other alternatives—why touch this one? You know, Jerusalem may be the only issue on the Israeli position which escapes strategy and politics. This is the only place that has the aura of holiness. And the difference between politics and holiness is that when holiness begins, compromise stops. Even reason stops. If somebody says it is holy, that's the end of reason.[139]

Here Peres gives his reason for refusing to compromise on Israeli sovereignty over the whole city and in particular the Temple Mount and the Western Wall. Remarkably, the technocrat-scientist-pragmatist advances *holiness* as a defense of the Israeli position on Jerusalem. The man of reason defends what happens when "reason stops." Again we are on ideological ground, dealing with issues and symbols of identity.

In June 1999 Peres denied any validity to the Palestinian historical and political claim, asserting in effect that only a religious claim could stand. In the context of a question about the centrality of Jerusalem to Jewish identity and Zionist ideology, he said:

> It's not just ideology. It's also history. Historically, Jerusalem was never an Arab capital. Even when the Jordanians occupied East Jerusalem, they never made it the capital. On the other hand, as far as Jewish history is concerned, we didn't have any other capital but Jerusalem. So it's almost normal that we should look upon Jerusalem as our center of prayers, of hopes, and of administration at the same time.
>
> Things are a little bit more complicated when it comes to the religious (not the political) side. There are at least three major religions—Jewish, Christian, Muslim—and maybe it is here that we have to look for some new approaches. It looks to me like Jerusalem is closed politically but open religiously, and the claims of the Arabs and the Palestinians are more religious than political.
>
> You know, one day Arafat told me he would like to have a sort of Muslim Vatican in Jerusalem. I asked him who would be the "pope" in that case. I'm not sure we got the ready-made answer, but anyway, he chose a certain direction.[140]

Visiting India in January 2001, Peres continued this theme when he said,

> While the modern city of Jerusalem can be divided demographically between Israel and the Palestinians, the holy city of Jerusalem will have to be shared religiously. . . . The holy city spread over an area of 800 meters is full of complications. There can be a compromise on politics, but not on religion.[141]

The concept of religious sharing underlay Peres's call in 2003 for international supervision of the holy sites in the Old City. His suggestion was to put the sites under UN stewardship, with the secretary-general serving as mayor.[142]

The increase in terrorism post-2001, once the Sharon government was in office, produced numerous changes, not least of which were the construction of the separation barrier and the disengagement from Gaza and the northern West Bank. In January 2005, Peres and the Labor Party formed a coalition with the Sharon government, which gave Likud the necessary majority to effect the disengagement. But Peres and Sharon did not necessarily share the same view on resolving the Jerusalem Question. Peres, ever the pragmatist, had shifted from his own earlier position. On June 6, Peres spoke of the Israeli "mistake" in occupying all of East Jerusalem.

"Whoever thinks that 240,000 Arabs from East Jerusalem could be annexed while Jerusalem stays a Jewish capital is as mistaken as those who say the city can be divided with fences and walls. . . . If there isn't peace in Jerusalem, there won't be peace in the country."[143] One month later, he said that "there is no chance of reaching a conclusive agreement with the Palestinian Authority without giving back Hebron and dividing Jerusalem" [into two sovereign capitals].[144]

Thus, although Peres often spoke of the nonnegotiability of Jerusalem and related to it as an identity marker for Zionism, pragmatics dictated an evolving position on the city's final disposition as two political state capitals and a religious "world capital" at the same time.

Summary: Shimon Peres

Shimon Peres experienced many of the same identity-forming aspects of Jewish life in Eastern Europe as other Zionist leaders. He was raised in a small Jewish community in the Zionist tradition by parents who made the journey to Palestine from Byelorus in 1923. Hebrew was the first language of his surroundings. At age eleven he was taken to live in Tel Aviv, where he joined the Labor Zionist youth movement, becoming a leader in his late teens. Personally selected by the leader of the Jewish people in Palestine, Ben-Gurion, Peres reflected many of his mentor's political perspectives and interests as a young man. Ben-Gurion's passion was for settlement, immigration, and building up the defensive capabilities of the incipient state. Peres interfaced for most of his career with the technological and scientific side of the defense industries. His view of the Arabs was undoubtedly skewed during this period by his defense role and by Ben-Gurion's prevailing vision and values. Accordingly Peres was uninterested in rapprochement with the Palestinians. He was by his own admission "a terrible hawk." The change in identity that he undertook in the 1980s was occasioned by the growing realization that further progress for the state could not be achieved by utilizing the ideological positions of earlier years with respect to the Palestinians. This is perhaps due to a combination of the influence of his mentors, Katznelson and Ben-Gurion. Peres admired Katznelson for his independent mind, his erudition, and his nonconformist approach, while Ben-Gurion apparently inspired him to higher moral vision.

Once the State had achieved a degree of security through defense buildup, Peres was willing to consider other options for its advancement. There was a level of pragmatism and realism in his thinking about the conflict and the prospects for Israel's economic progress in the Middle East that allowed him to take ideological risks. However, there were lengths to which the dove would not go, and this fact speaks to the issue of Jewish identity.

He spoke of his preference for building a hotel rather than a weapon, of soft borders with the coming Palestinian State, of joint Israeli-Palestinian trade and technology projects, yet at the same time he denied any negotiation on the political issue of sovereignty over Jerusalem. In a clash of existential need and defense of identity, Peres could say at one and the same time that

> for the sake of Israel being democratic and Jewish, we need a Palestinian state. Not just a Palestinian state, but a democratic Palestinian state. Not just a democratic Palestinian state, but an affluent Palestinian state. . . .
>
> From our point of view, the better the Palestinians shall have it, the better a neighbor we shall have. . . .

and

> You know, Jerusalem may be the only issue on the Israeli position which escapes strategy and politics. This is the only place that has the aura of holiness. And the difference between politics and holiness is that when holiness begins, compromise stops.[145]

With respect to stasis and movement on the Jerusalem Question, Peres's example demonstrates that even with openness to change in some aspects of the identity-ideology nexus vis-à-vis relationships with the Palestinians, a Zionist can remain resolute with respect to Jerusalem. It is a curious anomaly of the man that he can admit that he has moved from the position of hawk to dove over the decades and at the same time make little change on the sovereignty aspect of the Jerusalem issue. His experience with Jerusalem tracks those of his mentor, Ben-Gurion, and his rival-turned-peace-partner, Yitzhak Rabin. The day after the capture of the Old City in 1967, Peres shared in Ben-Gurion's moment of greatest satisfaction, accompanying him to the Western Wall. Since then his record generally shows support of Israeli stasis on the matter of sovereignty, and some movement toward accommodation of Palestinian demands to have their capital in East Jerusalem.

Concluding Thoughts

The Zionist identity-ideology nexus is a constant in the seven Jewish/Israeli personalities examined here. With respect to identity, there are certain significant commonalities in each individual's development. It goes without saying, though perhaps it should not, that all had Jewish parents who recognized their roots to a greater or lesser extent. None denied them. Most of those parents sympathized with or supported the Zionist cause. The seven were born in Eastern Europe (1), or in the Russian Pale of Settlement (5), or in the Jewish community in Palestine (1). Even those most assimilated—Herzl and

Jabotinsky—show the effect of early Jewish influences on identity. Herzl attended Jewish primary school and, despite his subsequent irreligious outlook, was outraged at the age of twenty-two by an anti-Semitic work. This led to his resignation from a student society in 1883 over its anti-Semitic attitudes. The die was cast. The anti-Semitism unleashed by the Dreyfus affair ten years later catapulted Herzl, the assimilated writer, into a lifelong search for a Jewish homeland. As for the urbane, secular, and brilliant Russian-language author Jabotinsky, it was in the aftermath of the anti-Semitic Kishinev pogrom of 1903, when he heard Herzl speak at the Zionist Congress, that he committed himself wholeheartedly to Zionism. His mother's positive response to his question at the age of six as to whether the Jews would one day have their own land now assumed greater meaning.

Several of the personalities expressed themselves at an early age in terms of identity in relation to Zionism and its precepts. Weizmann announced his interest in Zionism and return to the land and Jerusalem at ages eleven and fifteen. Ben-Gurion said that he dreamed of the return to Zion from the age of three. The death of his deeply observant mother when he was eleven plunged him into a depression, from which he emerged at fourteen a fully convinced Zionist. Begin became a convert to the cause at age fifteen when he joined Jabotinsky's youth movement, Betar. Once he heard the leader speak, he identified with him, idolized him, and took on his Zionist mission.

The next generation of leaders included Rabin and Peres, both of whom were committed to Zionism at an early age and both of whom demonstrate that identity and ideology can shift somewhat through experience. Rabin was raised by secular Labor Zionist parents and at the age of fourteen was involved in military training during the 1936 Arab Revolt. His dedication to the military was to dominate his career. Rabin's role in the 1948 battle for Jerusalem was an extraordinarily formative experience that melded with his Zionist beliefs and prepared him for his decisive role in the 1967 war. However, he was the one to agree to a new direction in Arab-Israeli relations, eventually signing the 1993 Oslo Agreements with his sworn enemy, Yasser Arafat.

Peres followed a similar path. Raised in a Zionist home in Byelorus and Palestine, he became a member of a labor youth organization at the age of ten, and in his teens proved such a talented leader in the movement that he was selected by Ben-Gurion as a protégé. His commitment to Israeli defense provided him with the career path that brought him to senior leadership in the Zionist hierarchy. Like Rabin, he saw the need for an ideological shift in respect of the Palestinians, sharing in the Oslo process. However, also like Rabin, he never lost sight of his ideological commitment to Israel's continued right to exist as a Zionist entity, nor to Israeli sovereignty over Jerusalem.

Applying Daniel Katz's four types of latent forces in the individual, which can be aroused in the service of a nationalist identity, it is evident from the early life stories of all seven personalities that emotional and behavioral conditioning to elements of what would become Jewish/Israeli nationalism occurred. There are differences of degree in each case, Herzl being at the less intense end of the spectrum and the others clustered at the more intense end. As a result, in line with Katz's second latent force, all display personal identity as nationals or incipient nationals with a common history, fate, and culture. In all cases there is evidence of the third element: compensatory identification with some aspect of "the nation" to resolve personal insecurities. Witness, for example, Herzl's life-changing reaction to reporting firsthand on the Dreyfus affair; Weizmann's plunging into the Hebrew University project at a time of career disappointment; Ben-Gurion's emergence as a Zionist following his mother's death; and Jabotinsky's response to the 1903 pogrom in Kishinev in terms of promoting the idea of a Jewish self-defense force. In line with Katz's formulation, there is also extended instrumental involvement in the national structure to the degree that it comes into existence over time. Involvement in the Zionist project gave each of the seven personalities reason for the highest level of instrumental involvement in the national or incipient national structure.

Turning now to the propositions regarding the identity-ideology nexus set out in chapter 1, do we find support for them with reference to the Jerusalem Question in the thinking and practice of the seven Jewish/Israeli leaders? Taking the three founders first, in the cases of Herzl, Weizmann, and Jabotinsky there is certainly evidence of significant personal identification with Jerusalem during their childhood, adolescent, and adult stages, and it is expressed in their writings and public statements as the opportunity arises to confirm that identification.

Second, there is evidence in all three cases of latency of identity and ideology in the face of the effect of stronger interacting variables, leading to stasis over the city's future. Understandably, for each of them there were more important priorities at the time of their contribution to the development of the Zionist project. In Herzl's case, his attention was focused on establishing the very concept of a homeland, the search for suitable territory, and immigration to the new land. Similarly, Weizmann was dedicated to achieving the minimum conditions for a homeland and pursuing Herzl's priorities. With the issuing of the Balfour Declaration, the work of creating a homeland had only just begun. He spent most of the subsequent thirty years as president of the World Zionist Organization, and until the declaration of the State of Israel, he was fully occupied with the vicissitudes of the Zionist endeavor as Britain pulled back from its initial commitment in 1917. Weizmann's energies went into attempts to garner international support for a Jewish state and the development of the Hebrew University.

The time was not yet right for concentration on the Jerusalem Question and its resolution. Jabotinsky's maximalist views of the territory required for the Jewish state were equaled only by his passion for the development of Jewish military capacity. While the Jerusalem Question did not occupy much of his attention, even the scant biographical references to his interest in the city demonstrate his ideological passion for it. Indeed, when all three personalities make statements about the city's future, it is in terms of Jewish/Israeli ownership of part or all of it as a natural consequence of the return to the land.

Of the three founders, proposition three finds support only in the experience of Weizmann. Momentum on Jerusalem came for him since he lived long enough to see the de facto division of Jerusalem between Israel and Jordan in 1948. It seemed to encourage him that the entire city would one day be in Israel's hands.

The four prime ministers, Ben-Gurion, Begin, Rabin, and Peres, manifest evidence of all three propositions. The first proposition is fulfilled simply by the circumstances of their Jewish background and upbringing. Like their Zionist forebears, they differ in degree of affiliation with Jerusalem, but in each case the evidence of identification with the city is sufficient to meet the conditions of the first proposition. David Ben-Gurion's shadow falls across the history of the *Yishuv* and the State of Israel like no other. His single-minded dedication to the building of the State—from his early introduction to Zionist aims as a child, to his announcement of the establishment of the new nation, to his celebration of the outcome of the 1967 war—speaks eloquently enough of his continuity with Zionism's philosophical foundations. The resolution of Menachem Begin, despite impossible physical odds, to follow through on his convictions, drawn at an early age from the teaching and example of Vladimir Jabotinsky, is a testimony to the strength of his ideological roots. Yitzhak Rabin's unwavering commitment to the ideals of Labor Zionism, modeled on the example of his Zionist parents and augmented by his own extensive military training in the service of the State, attest to the sureness of his ideological foundations. Finally, Shimon Peres's long journey from hawk to dove, while fully supportive still of the Zionist ideal and Zionism's essential identity, rests in personal convictions drawn from his free-thinking Zionist mentors.

Periods of both stasis and movement are evident in each leader's experiences with the Jerusalem Question, according to the strength or weakness of interacting variables. Critical situations arose in the wars of 1948 and/or 1967, when each man's latent or suppressed identification with Jerusalem was freed as he experienced war's effect on the city and its Jewish inhabitants. It was the interactive variables of the identity-ideology nexus, together with the unexpected outcomes of these wars (in particular the

1967 war) with respect to Jerusalem, that appeared to propel each man into activities that demonstrate evidence of maintaining, defending, and enhancing Jewish and Israeli rights to the city. Further, once the whole city was in Israeli hands, the inability of each man to compromise on possession of Jewish/Israeli Jerusalem was clearly couched in terms of their individual ideology-identity nexus.

Analysis of periods of stasis and movement on the Jerusalem issue during the lifetimes of the seven personalities suggests that either condition is characterized by the presence of an object of latent associations and the attendant ability to exert overwhelming force in support of such preexisting identity and ideological factors. In the case of stasis, it appears to be the result of a preponderance of conditions favoring the dominant party, including its ability to exert sufficient force in fulfillment of its identity and ideological imperatives, territorial possession, and ineffectual outside (international) intervention. When there is movement, it appears to result from a sudden dislocation of current conditions that in turn provide significant opportunity for expression of the same kind of imperatives, held latent until the breakpoint. Once again a preponderance of force is crucial to gaining new ground and shifting possession of territory. Along with lack of effective international intervention, these appear to be the triggers that bring momentum and change in the Jerusalem equation. Rather like the cumulative effect of a series of small earthquakes triggering a major temblor, interactive activation of the variables can give new momentum in the service of the identity-ideology nexus.

The focus of the study now shifts to the Palestinian case and examines the Jerusalem Question through the biographies of seven influential Palestinian figures. Do their life stories parallel the patterns of their Jewish/Israeli counterparts with respect to the three propositions developed in chapter 1?

CHAPTER 5
ARAB AND PALESTINIAN PERSONALITIES

In parallel with the preceding chapter, the life histories of seven Palestinian leaders and their relation to the development of Palestinian nationalism and the Jerusalem Question are now examined. The leaders are al-Hajj Amin al-Husayni, Ahmad al-Shuqayri, Yasser Arafat, Ahmad Quray', Hanan Ashrawi, Faysal al-Husayni and Ahmad Yassin. Do their biographies provide support for the three propositions concerning the identity-ideology nexus put forward in chapter 1? And how well does Mullins's five-part typology apply to Palestinian nationalism?

With respect to the first aspect of the typology—historical consciousness—there is ample evidence in Middle Eastern history that a distinct Arab identity has existed for hundreds of years within Palestine's generally recognized geographic boundaries, and that a Palestinian national consciousness has been extant for about a century. Some Palestinian scholars have tried to trace such identity much earlier, claiming that the origins of the Palestinian people reach back before the emergence of the tribes of Israel to the times of the Phoenicians and Canaanites. Benvenisti mentions this alternative history as sourced in an unnamed Palestinian history book, but he believes that the question of who is right is superfluous. "[E]ach side has mined stones for the construction of its myths—and for throwing at each other."[1] On the other hand, Rashid Khalidi speaks of "extreme advocates" of the view that "Palestinian nationalism has deep historical roots." They read back into Palestinian history "a nationalist consciousness and identity that are in fact relatively modern." He notes the predilection of such extremists "for seeing in peoples such as the Canaanites, Jebusites, Amorites, and Philistines the lineal ancestors of the modern Palestinians."[2] The Bible names a tribe within the Canaanites, the Jebusites, as the inhabitants of Jerusalem at the time Israel's King David captured the city around 1000 B.C.E.[3] However, the Phoenicians and the Canaanites were not Arab peoples. The Arabs' primary distinguishing characteristic is their common Arabic language. The degree to which the modern Palestinian is Canaanite and/or Phoenician in origin is moot due to the absence of historical evidence. However, a strong claim can be made for tracing the ancestral line of the Arabs from the patriarch Abraham, an immigrant to Canaan from Chaldea.[4]

From the later Muslim perspective, awareness of Arab Palestine's general geographic boundaries can be established in print around 1000 C.E. in the "merits of Jerusalem" literature *(Fada'il al-Quds)*, which celebrated the city's holiness within Islam.[5] This literary genre continued to have its impact for several centuries after the Crusades.[6] The emergence of the constituents of a specific Palestinian national identity within the Ottoman Empire can be established around the time of the first wave of Jewish immigration into Palestine (1882–1903).[7] The concept of *Filastin*, denoting either the whole of Palestine or the Jerusalem *sanjaq* alone, was widespread among the educated Arab public at the end of the Ottoman period.[8] Separate Palestinian consciousness can alternatively be dated to the 1918–20 period, when Amir Faysal established an Arab government in Damascus and supporters from Palestine joined him.[9]

Historical consciousness in terms of the past is thus well established for Arab and then Palestinian national consciousness. And as with its Zionist counterpart, Palestinian nationalism meets Mullins's requirement that an ideology's historical consciousness also include present and future perspectives. Historical consciousness in all three aspects differentiates ideology from myth and utopia, which exist disconnected from exact time and place (in both "sometime" and "nowhere"). Palestinian nationalism has a present orientation and the vision of a future. As noted earlier, ideological futures are based on "concrete programs and strategies having immediate social relevance."[10] Examples of this are the social programs for Palestine put into effect in the 1970s and 1980s by the secular nationalist PLO in exile in Lebanon and Tunisia. Similarly, the Palestinian politico-religious organization Hamas, which subsumes Palestinian nationalism within its Islamic identity, has since the late 1980s created social programs to assist Palestinians, mostly in Gaza, with the long-term political goal of an Islamic state on the whole territory of Palestine. As an extension of such social programs, Palestinian nationalism, subsumed or otherwise, "informs political action" and "tends to explicate the significance of events, situations and possible courses of action."

Does Palestinian nationalism have cognitive power—the second element in Mullins's typology? To qualify in this category it must provide its adherents with the ability to filter meaning from everyday events. There is surely no doubt that for those Palestinians living in the midst of the daily conflict, Palestinian nationalism provides a prism through which to understand both who they are and what their future ought to be. The goals of an independent

Palestinian state and the return of refugees and land indicate the cognitive power available within Palestinian nationalism.

Mullins's third component is an ideology's capacity for the evaluation of policies and programs. For example, Palestinian nationalism allows its adherents to make judgments about what should and should not be done in its name, what support it can and cannot give. More precisely, the beliefs of some Palestinian nationalists (PLO) allow them to evaluate the arguments of other Palestinian nationalists (Hamas or Islamic Jihad) and vice versa, as well as the ideas of Israelis and Zionists, regarding the long-term consequences of certain activities for the establishment of the Palestinian state.

The fourth criterion—action orientation (cause for doing)—is the mobilizing aspect of ideology and results from a combination of its elements—"cognitions, evaluations, ideals, and purposes." Palestinian nationalism has a history of mobilizing the Palestinian people to demand return of their ancestral lands in a number of ways. The right of return of refugees has also been a constant element in the Palestinian nationalists' appeal for international justice.

The fifth and final component in Mullins's typology is logical coherence. An ideology must not be chaotic and it cannot be illogical. It must be internally consistent and separable from propaganda and popular ideas without substance. In this regard, for almost 100 years Palestinian nationalism has expressed the necessary "conceptions, reasons and justifications" to account for its existence.

Like Zionism, as shown in chapter 3, Palestinian nationalism also has a powerful religious aspect, whether it is Muslim or Christian. This is much more the case at the beginning of the twenty-first century than in the 1950s and 1960s, and especially in respect of the Old City and its religious sites. Commitment to Islam or Christianity affects the adherent's view of Jerusalem's significance, though not necessarily one's opinion of where its sovereignty should rest. Like their Israeli counterparts, the Palestinians experience the magnet of identification with the city and its associated ideological components. This is demonstrated in the biographies of the seven Palestinian personalities to whom the inquiry now turns. Once again each biographical study concludes with a summary of the individual's identity-ideology nexus.

Al-Hajj Amin al-Husayni

Identity and Ideology

Al-Hajj Amin al-Husayni (1895?–1974) was born into the notable Husayni family in the waning days of the Ottoman Empire. A native of Jerusalem, he spent his childhood in the Shaykh Jarrah area of the city. His great grandfather could trace his roots to Husayn, son of the fourth caliph, 'Ali ibn Abi Talib, and his wife, Fatima, daughter of the Prophet Muhammad. His family roots in Jerusalem went back to 782, and before that for two hundred years in Wadi al-Nusur, a small village near the city. His predecessors had held the positions of mufti of Jerusalem, naqib al-ashraf in Jerusalem, and shaykh al-haram al-qudsi. After removal from the role of mufti as a result of their opposition to Ibrahim Pasha's domination of Palestine (1831–40), the family regained the office and held on to it into the twentieth century. Hajj Amin's grandfather, Mustafa, and his father, Tahir, held the title mufti of Jerusalem.

As a child Amin, together with his two brothers, went to the mufti's office at the Haram and, with their father's encouragement, heard the political, legal, and religious discussions of the day, including his concerns about increasing Jewish immigration.[11] Tahir was appointed by the Ottomans to keep a watching brief on the sale of property to the Zionists. In 1908, when Amin was thirteen, his father died and Kamil, his brother, became mufti. Amin attended Muslim elementary school in Jerusalem, and in 1912 Kamil sent him to Cairo's al-Azhar University, famed for its reputation in Islamic and Arabic studies. There he became well acquainted with a friend of the family, Arab reformer Muhammad Rashid Rida. Influential in the formation of Amin's political ideas, Rida emphasized Islamic revival. Amin was "a devout Muslim who believed that the role of Islam was inseparable from politics and that religious symbols should be used to unite the Arabs."[12] His involvement in a fledgling Muslim and Christian Arab student society opposed to Zionist immigration was an early demonstration of his sentiments.

In 1913 Amin earned the right to the title "al-Hajj" by making the pilgrimage to Mecca with his mother. Returning to Jerusalem, he taught Islamic studies and wrote political articles about the threat of Zionism. In 1914 he was admitted to the Military Academy in Istanbul, only to have his studies curtailed by the First World War. Although his postings in the Ottoman army did not provide much combat experience, the life of a soldier strengthened him. His ranking as an officer in 1916 gave him the necessary training to command men.

Though at first loyal to the Ottomans, Amin al-Husayni was disillusioned by their treatment of Arab nationalists, several of whom they executed in 1916 for fear of losing control of their Arab lands. He returned to Jerusalem in 1917, having decided to join the Arab Revolt in support of Amir Faysal Husayn, whose father, the sharif of Mecca, had formed an alliance with the British against the Germans and their Ottoman allies. The sharif had agreed to initiate an Arab uprising against the Ottomans and had begun the revolt in 1916. Al-Husayni recruited Palestinians for an Arab army that would fight for the independent state in the Middle East that the British had promised the sharif.

In 1918 al-Husayni became president of the Arab Club, a literary and political society organized to further the Palestinian cause against Zionism. He was driven by antipathy to Zionism, made only more profound by the recent Balfour Declaration. He began to view Faysal's proposed Syrian-Palestinian state as an answer to Jewish encroachment on Palestinian lands. At Faysal's invitation, he attended the General Syrian Congress in July 1919, sharing in the passage of resolutions against Zionism and Jewish immigration.

When Faysal was crowned king of Syria in March 1920, al-Husayni and several notables in Jerusalem organized a march in support of the new Arab monarch and used the occasion to protest against Zionism. Al-Husayni announced to the crowd that Faysal was their king. Within a short time, fighting broke out in the Jewish Quarter of the Old City, and Arabs killed three Jews and injured many others. A group of Jabotinsky's Jewish fighters retaliated and killed and injured some of the protesters and other Arabs who were onlookers. British police stepped in to bring the fighting to an end. As a result, al-Husayni was sought for questioning but he evaded capture, arriving in Damascus some time later. In his absence, he was sentenced to ten years imprisonment, while Jabotinsky received fifteen years (a sentence that was quashed a few months later). With the imposition of French rule in Syria in July 1920, Faysal's hopes for a state collapsed, and al-Husayni traveled to Transjordan and went into hiding among the bedouin.

Soon pardoned by the British high commissioner, Herbert Samuel, al-Husayni returned to Jerusalem to be with his ailing brother, Kamil. The grand mufti died, and after a difficult and complicated election process, Samuel named al-Husayni as mufti in May 1921. His power was consolidated in 1922 when Samuel granted him the title of president of the newly formed Supreme Muslim Council. Al-Husayni now had control over the religious and financial affairs of the Haram and the associated charitable endowments.

Al-Hajj Amin al-Husayni and Jerusalem

From an early age Amin al-Husayni identified strongly with Jerusalem and the Haram. Born into a family tracing its descent from the Prophet, he was imbued by his conservative religious father and his pious mother with a love for his country and his city. According to his unpublished diary, as a soldier he carried a poem that read, "This [Palestine] is my country and the country of my ancestors—I will sacrifice myself for the sake of its sons."[13] He also spoke of Jerusalem's people, who he said were "honest, self-sacrificing, sharing, courteous, inseparable, and loyal." In another piece of wartime poetry in his diary he wrote, "Whenever I mention Jerusalem my tears flow."

The depth of al-Husayni's devotion to Jerusalem and its Islamic sites was revealed more fully once he became mufti. For the next few years he set about renovating the two holy sites on the Haram, the al-Aqsa Mosque and the Dome of the Rock. Through fund-raising for the venture, the mufti gained credibility across the Muslim world and at the same time gained recognition as a Palestinian nationalist.[14]

Until 1928–29, when riots at the Western Wall spread throughout Palestine, al-Husayni kept a low profile with the British and remained faithful to his promise to stay out of politics. The riots were precipitated by a minor incident on Yom Kippur 1928, when a female Jewish worshiper struck a British official after he removed a screen separating men and women at the prayer site. The Muslim authorities were informed of the incident and of the attempts of the Jews to introduce additional furnishings into their worship in the narrow space in front of the Wall. Over the months that followed, both Jews and Arabs exploited what should have remained a petty quarrel.

Philip Mattar exposes the significant background to the events, as well as the errors in the conventional historiography.[15] The mufti was blamed for inciting his people over the incident. Yet al-Husayni was not involved at the time and did not become engaged until six days later. On the other hand, the Jewish reaction was swift and transformed a religious spat into a political issue. The Jews complained to the British government and the League of Nations; they held a protest march against the British, went on strike, and published inflammatory newspaper articles. The mufti was aware of various recent attempts by Jews to purchase property in front of the Wall and even to acquire the Wall itself. His suspicions were aroused by the Jewish rhetoric that flowed after the confrontation at the Wall and by the passions that the site brought forth. He was naturally protective of the Western Wall of the Haram, a significant site for the Muslim community since Muhammad's horse, Buraq, was believed to have been tethered by the inside wall at the southwest corner of the enclosure. Al-Husayni may well have feared that, unchecked, the Jews would eventually seek to take over the Haram and attempt to rebuild the temple on its original site.[16]

In 1922, British cabinet minister and financial supporter of Jewish projects Sir Alfred Mond (later to become Lord Melchett) had "declared in public . . . that the day of the reconstruction of the Temple was very near."[17] There was also evidence that the Jews had requested the British to force the sale of adjacent Muslim charitable or *waqf* property, or even to expropriate the Wall. As a result, the mufti became actively involved in defending Muslim rights to the site. He warned the British administration of the Zionists' designs. He claimed that they were being carried out with a view to influencing the British and other governments, as well as the League of Nations, so that the

Jews could "take possession of the Western Wall of the Aqsa Mosque known as the Buraq, or raise claims over the place."[18] Interestingly, the phrase "take possession" matches the language of the demand for "handing over the Wailing Wall to the Jews" made by Weizmann to Balfour in 1918.[19]

In November 1928 al-Husayni initiated the Buraq campaign to promote the defense of Muslim rights to the Wall. He wanted to educate the Arab and Muslim world about the issue and encourage compliance with the 1852 status quo arrangements for the holy sites. The mufti was eager to promote the neglected holiness of the Wall to the Muslims. The same month, representatives from Palestine, Syria, Lebanon, and Transjordan attended his General Muslim Conference and agreed to resolutions backing his campaign. Al-Husayni was still willing to cooperate with the British authorities, as they assured him that the status quo regulations upheld by them provided the security he demanded for the Haram.

The continued tensions of the next several months led to an outbreak of violence in Jerusalem in August 1929, which over a few days spread throughout Palestine and resulted in the deaths of 133 Jews and 116 Arabs. Al-Husayni was not an inciter of the violence. He had politicized the issue of the Wall, but he had not called for violence. Further, he tried to prevent the outbreak when, on the basis of a letter bearing his forged signature, Palestinians gathered at the Haram to defend the area against the Jews. The Shaw Commission, authorized by the British to investigate the disturbances, concluded that Jewish demonstrators had initiated the violence to which Arab militants had responded; that the situation had spiraled out of control; and that al-Husayni was not to be blamed. It was noted, however, that he had played a role in the escalation of politicized feelings.[20]

The commission's findings encouraged the mufti to continue on a co-operative course with the British. He sent delegations to London to discuss the creation of a parliamentary system for Palestine that would include the Jews. He was even able to set aside some of his feelings over the British government's reversal of the 1930 White Paper's recommendation that Jewish land sales and immigration should be curtailed. The British government issued the 1930 Passfield White Paper in the wake of the 1929 riots and two government studies (the Shaw Commission Report and the Hope-Simpson Report). The White Paper was considered very favorable to the Palestinians. The tone of the paper was anti-Zionist, and Jewish immigration was to be limited. (In 1929 Sydney Webb, the new British colonial secretary—soon to become Lord Passfield—had told Weizmann that he was opposed to larger numbers of Jews immigrating to Palestine. According to Yoram Hazony, it was "a none-too-subtle way of saying that he intended to work to suspend the very concept of a British-Jewish mandate in Palestine."[21]) The Passfield White Paper provoked a strong reaction from

Jewish organizations around the world. British prime minister Ramsey MacDonald subsequently wrote to Weizmann "clarifying" the government's position and raising immigration to higher levels. Taking a moderate approach to this retreat on the part of the British, in December 1931 al-Husayni successfully brought together in Jerusalem 130 participants from the Arab and Muslim world in the General Islamic Conference. His aim was to create an Arab-Muslim version of the World Zionist Organization. Significantly, two of the items on the six-point agenda were the defense of Muslim holy places and the founding of a Muslim university in Jerusalem. The opening of the conference coincided with the annual celebration of the Prophet's night flight from Mecca to Jerusalem. Rashid Rida, al-Husayni's friend and mentor, was in attendance. From the mufti's point of view, the timing and details of the congress reinforced several issues of personal identity.

Growing Palestinian disillusionment with British rule and their continued support of Jewish immigration and land acquisition gradually overtook any long-term impact of the conference. The mufti's moderation came under criticism from the younger, more radical Palestinian elements. His election in April 1936 as president of the Arab Higher Committee made little difference to his standing, and by the summer al-Husayni found himself being required to support the Arab Revolt without ever having agreed to its instigation.

The mufti was ready to discuss the possibilities of partition raised by the report of the 1937 Royal Commission on the revolt, though his supporters were not. Continuing disappointment with the British, however, led to his decision to oppose them violently. As a result he became a prime candidate for arrest and forced exile. In October 1937 he escaped to Beirut by sliding down a rope from the Haram's walls under cover of darkness. After some time, he was caught and put under house arrest.

In 1939 the British government issued a White Paper that was again very favorable to the Palestinians. Al-Husayni rejected it out of bitterness toward the British, against whom he was now willing to fight militarily. Thus, at the onset of the Second World War, the mufti refused to support the Allied cause. He fled Beirut for Baghdad, where he was welcomed by Arab nationalists as a key figure in their own struggle against the British. His involvement in Iraqi politics and the collapse of a nationalist attempt to liberate Iraq from British rule in April-May 1941 placed him once more on their wanted list. At the end of May he was forced to flee to Iran. Refuge there proved impossible, and by November he was in Berlin discussing a secret agreement with Adolf Hitler. He remained there for the rest of the war, directing propaganda, sabotage, and Muslim recruiting efforts in support of the Axis powers. Despite various Zionist attempts to prove that al-Husayni was a war criminal because of his stated approval of the Nazis' Final Solution, sufficient evidence was never provided to indict him. In his memoirs, the mufti did admit that he had opposed the transfer of European Jews to Palestine in 1944, suggesting to the German foreign minister Ribbentrop that they be sent to Poland.[22]

In June 1946 al-Husayni made his way back to the Middle East, finding refuge in Cairo. There he attempted to influence Palestinian affairs by lending his support to the Arab League, which had been formed in 1944. The League's proposal for an independent Palestinian state by 1949 met with the mufti's approval, since he viewed himself as the obvious choice for leader.[23]

King Abdullah of Jordan, however, opposed al-Husayni in his presumed leadership of a future Palestinian state. Abdullah was coming to his own arrangements with the Jewish community in Palestine in a series of meetings that began in August 1946.[24] In one of those meetings he told his Jewish interlocutor, Elias Sasson, that the mufti should be killed.[25] Abdullah even referred to al-Husayni as that "devil straight from hell."[26] The idea of assassinating the mufti was not a new idea. Abdullah had proposed the same to the Jewish Agency's Pinhas Rutenberg in 1939.[27] He may have repeated the idea to Golda (Meyerson) Meir in secret talks on November 17, 1947.[28] Perhaps the mufti heard about Meir's visit to Abdullah, since ten days later he asked for his own secret meeting with the Jewish Agency to discuss a compromise on the Palestine issue. The mufti was in Lebanon and sent the following message to his representative in Haifa:

> The Mufti requests you to contact Dr. Mordechai Eliash [a leader of the Zionist religious Misrachi Party] and ask him to propose secret talks between the Jewish Agency and the Mufti prior to the final decision of the United Nations General Assembly. These talks are to be conducted without the mediation of any of the Arab countries.[29]

The proposed meetings were to take place at the mufti's residence in Lebanon. Ben-Gurion called a special meeting of the agency, and after much discussion a message was returned to the mufti saying that the Jews would negotiate with any Arab leader except Amin al-Husayni.[30]

In 1946 the Arab League had installed the mufti as chairman of a newly formed Arab Higher Committee to look after Palestinian affairs. Relations were cordial until the league proposed that Arab armies enter Palestine. The mufti was convinced that he and his own fighters could oust the Zionists. He also knew that King Abdullah had his own designs on Palestine. Once the UN passed the resolution for the partition of Palestine in November 1947, Amin al-Husayni organized Jaysh al-Jihad al-Muqaddas (the Holy War Army) under the leadership of Abd al-Qadir al-Husayni. Unfortunately for the Palestinian cause, however, Abd al-Qadir was killed at Qastel, near

Jerusalem, on April 8, 1948—the day before the Deir Yassin atrocity that set in motion the flight of many Palestinians from their homes and villages.

In a desperate attempt to hold on to any possibility for a Palestinian state under his control, al-Husayni finally persuaded the Arab League to establish an All-Palestine Government (APG) in Gaza in September 1948. The league had rejected his previous attempts because of internal rivalries and the opposition of King Abdullah and the Iraqis. At the end of September the mufti went to Gaza from Cairo, where the Palestine National Council met and elected him president. An independent democratic state was proclaimed in all of Palestine. The capital of the state would be Jerusalem, and the flag would be the sharif's standard from the 1916 Arab Revolt: black, white, and green stripes with a red triangle. However, the newly proclaimed state was soon a forlorn hope. On October 1, 1948, the same day that the APG issued its declaration of independence, King Abdullah held a meeting of his own First Palestinian Congress in Amman. Five thousand Arab Palestinian notables attended. The delegates denounced the APG, swore loyalty to Abdullah, and resolved that Transjordan and Palestine were indivisible.[31]

A few days later the Egyptian prime minister, al-Nuqrashi, sent military police to accompany the mufti back to Cairo. When he refused, he was taken by force and put under police surveillance. Although the APG had been recognized by the Arab states—Egypt, Saudi Arabia, Iraq, Syria, and Lebanon—it was quickly shunned and became largely irrelevant as the division of Palestine between the Zionists and the Hashemites became a reality.

The mufti was now marginalized and spent most of his final years in Cairo. With the rise of Jamal Abd al-Nasir, he took refuge in Beirut, where he died in 1974. The Supreme Muslim Council in East Jerusalem requested that, according to his wishes, his body be buried in a Jerusalem cemetery overlooking the Haram. The Israeli government refused to allow their old enemy his last wish, and he was buried instead in the cemetery of "The Fallen of the Palestinian Revolution" in Beirut.

Summary: Al-Hajj Amin Al-Husayni

Amin al-Husayni was born in Jerusalem into a family whose history and influence were difficult to avoid. From the perspective of early identity, he was integrated into the religious ethos of Muslim Arab society at the highest levels. He claimed lineage to the Prophet. His immediate forebears were holders of chief leadership positions in Jerusalem, including the offices of mufti and warden of the Haram. Amin was experienced from an early age in the workings of the Haram and its *waqf* institutions. His education was conventionally Islamic both in Jerusalem and in Cairo, where he attended the 1,000-year-old center of Islamic scholarship, al-Azhar University. Amin's devotion to Islam was evidenced by his pilgrimage to Mecca at age eighteen with his widowed mother. His association with the Muslim reformer Rashid Rida broadened his political views and expanded his horizons on the interplay between Islamic revival and politics.

The Haram became the center of his life, and he believed that religion and politics should be fused in the search for Palestinian self-determination. Politics was therefore a constant element in his understanding of the Haram's importance. He was able to use the 1928–29 Western Wall disturbances to further Palestinian national consciousness. In 1931 he called for the defense of the Muslim holy places and the establishment of a Muslim university in Jerusalem.

Inevitably his role, his beliefs, his essential identity, and his nationalist ideology would bring him into conflict with Zionism and its leadership. Jerusalem and the Haram were not only the religious center of his life, they also became the political center. In 1948, consistent with the aims of Palestinian nationalism, the Palestine National Council, of which the mufti was president, declared Jerusalem as the capital of the All-Palestine Government. Al-Husayni's last request to be buried within sight of the Haram brought his identity and ideology back full circle and at the same time demonstrated the reason for the frustration and bitterness of his life vis-à-vis the Zionists, who refused to honor his dying wish.

In terms of stasis and momentum on the Jerusalem issue, the 1920s provide the most relevant material in the case of the mufti's involvement. There can be no question of his strong identification with the city and in particular its Muslim holy places. His campaign to make Jerusalem more significant to the Muslim world, by fund-raising for the renovation of the Haram properties and by drawing attention to Zionist attempts to possess the Western Wall, created momentum within the Palestinian community for retention of the Muslim sites. In this case the interacting variables of Zionist pressure on Muslims to sell the Wall and property adjacent to it, pronouncements by leading Zionists about rebuilding the temple, and general support for the mufti by Mandate officials, coalesced to bring the Jerusalem Question to a condition of momentum for the Palestinians and stasis for the Zionists until the Royal Commission Report of 1937.

Ahmad al-Shuqayri

Identity and Ideology

Ahmad al-Shuqayri (1908–80) was born in Tebnin in southern Lebanon. The al-Shuqayri family traced their origins to the Arabian Peninsula territory of the Hijaz and had emigrated to Egypt. However, Ahmad's father, Shaykh

As'ad al-Shuqayri, was born in Acre in Palestine, and his mother was Turkish. At the time of the boy's birth, the shaykh was in exile in Lebanon for his opposition to the policies of the Ottoman sultan Abd al-Hamid. In 1908, following the Young Turks Revolution, Shaykh As'ad was elected a member of the Ottoman parliament for Acre. He returned to Acre and became "the highest ranking Palestinian of the new regime."[32] He was a Muslim cleric, a graduate in religious law from al-Azhar University in Cairo, and appointed mufti to the fourth corps of the Ottoman army in Syria-Palestine during the First World War.

In 1915, while Ahmad was living in Tulkarm in Palestine with his mother, she fell ill and died. He was seven years old. The following year Ahmad went to live with his father in Acre. There he completed his early schooling, moving to Jerusalem for secondary school. In 1926 he began studies at the American University of Beirut but was expelled after a year for participation in an Arab student demonstration on Martyrs' Day, May 6. He returned to Jerusalem, taking up legal studies at the Institute of Law. At the same time he became a writer of considerable rhetorical style for the nationalist newspaper, *Mir'at al-Sharq (Mirror of the East)*. He subsequently worked with a leading Palestinian lawyer, Awni Abd al-Hadi, cofounder of the first political party in Palestine, al-Istiqlal (the Independence Party).

By the early 1930s Shuqayri was one of the young leaders in the party. Along with other members, he advocated energetic opposition to the Zionists and to the British Mandate. Their aim was Palestinian parliamentary rule. Perceived as far less moderate than the mufti, these young activists became popular with a restive public. As a result, by late 1933 the mufti had all but crippled al-Istiqlal.[33] During the 1936–39 Arab Revolt, Shuqayri represented Palestinians who had been indicted within the British court system.

In the early part of the Second World War, Shuqayri opened a law office in Acre, where "power was mainly concentrated in the hands of [his] family."[34] He subsequently took up the post of director of the Arab Media Office in Washington, D.C., and in 1946 became head of the Central Arab Media Office in Jerusalem. Like many Palestinians during the 1948 war, he was forced to flee and went to Lebanon. When the APG was proclaimed, foreign minister Jamal al-Husayni announced that Shuqayri would be a representative to the UN. The failure of the APG led to his appointment by the Syrian government to their UN delegation (1949–50). He also served as assistant secretary general of the Arab League in Cairo until 1957. The Saudi Arabian government then asked him to serve as minister of state for UN affairs (1957–63).

In his various capacities at the UN, he made many speeches on behalf of Palestinian causes. In a 1958 address, he called for the repatriation of those

Jews who had immigrated to Palestine after 1947. He said:

> The solution lies in the de-Zionization of Israel. . . .
> . . . Palestine is an integral part of the Arab homeland, and such it has
> been since time immemorial. The Arab nation now on its march towards
> final liberation will not give up one single inch of their sacred territory.[35]

He believed that the UN should reconsider its 1947 resolution calling
for the partition of Palestine into a Jewish and an Arab state. He called for
"restoration of the geographic unity of Palestine as part and parcel of the
Arab homeland" and "demilitarization of the whole country." He envisaged
"a democratic state where all the inhabitants have equal rights and duties,
Moslems, Christians and Jews alike."

In August 1963 the Saudis dismissed Shuqayri from his UN appointment.
Since Ahmad Hilmi, the first Palestinian representative at the Arab League,
had died in June, the Egyptians proposed that Shuqayri should succeed
him. Despite Jordan's opposition, the league's Political Committee
confirmed his new role in September.[36] But the Egyptians had more in
mind. It seems that Nasir was anxious to find a new unifying cause for
Egyptian leadership of the Arab world following the 1961 collapse of his
union with Syria in the United Arab Republic. The Palestine issue offered
that possibility.[37] Apparently as early as September Nasir gave Shuqayri the
task of planning a Palestinian entity.[38]

In January 1964, at Nasir's instigation, the Arab League held the First
Arab Summit in Cairo, ostensibly to discuss Israel's imminent diversion of
the headwaters of the River Jordan. But Nasir took the opportunity to bring
forward the idea of the new Palestinian organization. As a result, the thirteen
Arab League leaders attending the summit agreed to a study into the feasi-
bility of establishing an organization to promote "the nationalist energies of
the Palestinian people."[39] They entrusted Shuqayri "with putting some flesh
on the summit's bare bones of an idea."[40]

His draft constitution called for a Palestinian General Assembly to
meet for the first time on May 14 in Jordanian East Jerusalem.[41] The
assembly was to convene every two years, rotating between Jerusalem and
Gaza. Shuqayri's preparations included many journeys around the
Palestinian Diaspora, seeking support from individuals and governments.
In February he met with King Husayn and, in order to gain the monarch's
favor, promised that

> [t]he emanation of the Palestinian entity from Jerusalem does not seek to cut
> off the West Bank from the Hashemite Kingdom of Jordan; we seek the
> liberation of our violated homeland to the West of Jerusalem.[42]

Four hundred twenty-two Palestinian representatives from the Arab world and Europe attended the founding conference of the PLO in East Jerusalem in May-June. Shuqayri was elected president of the conference and chairman of the Executive Committee of the PLO. He was even able to keep his promise to King Husayn by inserting into the 1964 National Covenant an article that specified:

> This Organization does not exercise any territorial sovereignty over the West Bank in the Hashemite Kingdom of Jordan, on the Gaza Strip or in the Himmah Area. Its activities will be on the national popular level in the liberational, organizational, political and financial fields.[43]

In his draft constitution Shuqayri had proposed that the Arab countries train young Palestinians in their armed forces with a view to creating a viable Palestine Liberation Army (PLA). He wrote, "The Arab states shall avail the sons of Palestine the opportunity of enlisting in their regular armies on the widest scale possible."[44] In addition, he proposed that "[p]rivate Palestinian contingents shall be formed in accordance with the military needs and plans decided by the Unified Arab Military Command in agreement and coopera-tion with the concerned Arab states."[45] This was not the same as the concept of armed struggle through commando operations incorporated into the char-ter following the 1967 war. Exactly what Shuqayri intended with respect to armed struggle in his draft constitution is perhaps moot. The fact is that King Husayn opposed him, fearing that Nasir was attempting to enter Jordan by the back door with the Palestinians as his proxies. The king was insistent that Palestinian commandos not launch operations from within his territory. In April 1966 Husayn closed the offices of the PLO in Jordan, and Shuqayri "launched a campaign of vilification against the 'reactionary' governments of Jordan, Saudi Arabia, and Tunisia."[46] In February 1967 he was wounded in a never-solved assassination attempt.

In December, following the 1967 war, seven members of the PLO Executive Committee demanded that Shuqayri resign over criticisms of the PLO's role in the lead-up to the conflict. Shuqayri was accused of elitism and of having lost touch with the Palestinians in the streets and refugee camps. The deputy chairman of the Arab Bank, Abd al-Majid Shuman, had tried to get Shuqayri and Yasser Arafat, leader of the underground Palestinian guerilla organization, al-Fateh, together, but they "never really got on, they were quite different people."[47] When Shuqayri refused to resign, Shuman, who was chair-man of the Palestine National Fund, suspended his access to finances. Shuqayri appealed to Nasir, but no help came and he resigned on Christmas Eve, 1967.

With his influence in Palestinian affairs now nonexistent, Shuqayri took up residence in Cairo. In the late 1970s he became disgusted with Anwar Sadat's attempts to find a peace formula with Israel. He considered the Egyptian president's signature on the 1978 Camp David Accords and the subsequent peace treaty to be acts of treason against the Arab cause. Thereafter he preferred not to live in Cairo and in 1979 moved to Tunisia, where, after a few months, he became chronically ill. He died in Amman in 1980 while undergoing medical treatment. In accordance with his last request, he was buried in a cemetery in the Jordan Valley overlooking Palestine, adjacent to the tomb of Abu 'Ubayda, a Companion of the Prophet.

Shuqayri and Jerusalem

Shuqayri was the son of a devout Muslim cleric. He was schooled partly in Jerusalem, practiced law, and lived through two crucial periods there—the 1928–29 Wailing Wall disturbances and the 1936–39 Arab Revolt. With his background, it is reasonable to surmise the centrality of Jerusalem in his thinking, and his speeches and writings appear to confirm that interest. His well-known positions on the essential Arab character of Palestine and a return to its configuration under the original mandate indicates that with respect to any sharing of Jerusalem's sovereignty he was very conservative, even closed-minded. He addressed the crucial issue of Jerusalem's holy sites on October 1, 1958, and proposed the appointment of a UN representative "on matters pertaining to the status quo of religious shrines and the free access to the holy places."[48]

Three years later he again spoke to the General Assembly on the Palestine question, this time in the context of the division of Berlin. Of Jerusalem he said:

> For the last thirteen years, the holiest city, held in veneration by the three religions of the world, Jerusalem, has been breathing day and night in an atmosphere of hardship a thousand times more monstrous than those created in divided Berlin. Yet, to the Western powers, divided Berlin is everything, and divided Jerusalem is nothing.[49]

In the same speech he pointed out the effect that the division of the city was having on its Palestinian inhabitants. Quoting Adlai Stevenson, who had visited Palestine in 1953, he noted that barbed wire divided children from their schools, one half of a village from the other, farmers' lands from their homes, "and Jerusalem itself divided." He warned:

> The problem of Palestine is relatively dormant now, but it may explode at any moment. As long as Israel is there, divided Jerusalem may prove to be more dangerous to world peace and security than divided Berlin.
>
> For our part, we shall do everything in our power to help Palestine regain its unity, Jerusalem redeem its integrity and the people rebuild their national entity.

Later the same month he took the opportunity to rebut Golda Meir's recent speech, in which she had said that all of the issues between Israelis and Arabs could be solved by negotiation. Shuqayri took the issues one by one, *beginning with Jerusalem*. He noted that the UN had decided that Jerusalem should be internationalized and that Israel had rejected the resolution, moving its parliament to the city and declaring Jerusalem its capital in 1949. He quoted Ben-Gurion's unequivocal response—that Jerusalem was "Israel's crown and capital, irrevocably and for all men to see."[50] Shuqayri's conclusion: "On the basis of defiance and negation there can be no negotiation." He also addressed the Israeli arms buildup in the context of Meir's comments on disarmament:

> Even Jerusalem, the holy, was made a military arsenal by Israel. Time and again, Israel has refused the demilitarization of Jerusalem, time and again decided by the United Nations. In the fall of this year, the Security Council called upon Israel not to hold a military parade in Jerusalem, being outlawed under the armistice agreement. Israel held the parade and defied the Security Council, and the lady is bold enough to propose regional disarmament. Instead of quoting the prophet Isaiah to beat swords into plowshares, let Israel beat her guns out of Jerusalem—let the holy become again holy. Instead of being militarized and Israelized, let it be demilitarized and freed from Israel. So far, year in and year out, Israel has been shipping enormous arms from the United States and the United Kingdom and France, with the lady from Israel, year in and year out, pleading for disarmament.

Shuqayri was a brilliant orator, but his words about Jerusalem appear to spring from more than speech-making ability. During the eighteenth session of the UN on November 5, 1963, he spoke about the liberation of Palestine as the only way to address the Israeli occupation. By this time he was no longer Saudi Arabia's delegate but chairman of the Palestine Arab Delegation, and he had just been assigned the task of planning a new Palestinian entity aimed at uniting Palestinian energies against the Zionists. In introducing his delegation to the Special Political Committee of the UN General Assembly, he framed their backgrounds in a telling way:

> As to their domicile, my colleagues come from different parts of Palestine. Some come from Jerusalem, wherein lies the church of the Holy Sepulchre and the Mosque of Omar, in living testimony to the national fraternity of the Moslems and Christians of Palestine, a fraternity reflected in the composition of our delegation. Some others come from Galilee and you know what is Galilee—those of you who had been taught the New Testament in their childhood in school; you know what is Galilee and the holiness of Galilee, which has witnessed the miracles of the Great Master, Jesus Christ. Others have come from the South with its ancient pilgrimage routes to the Holy Places in Mecca. Others come from the Coast—the historic crossroads to the

three continents of the world. We all come from Palestine—we are all Palestinians . . . now and for all time to come.[51]

Although he went on to describe each delegate's profession and the diversity of their occupations, it seems that the sacred, the holy, the religious, was important to him in expressing origins. He continued with the thought that the unity of the Holy Land was an essential part of its character:

> [S]cattered as we may be, we come to you in one delegation, representing one people for one Palestine, free and undivided, independent and unpartitioned; and herein lies the solution of the Palestine refugee problem, a solution based on the unity of the Holy Land—and I emphasize the unity of the Holy Land because it cannot be a Holy Land if it is partitioned; holiness is indivisible.

Summary: Ahmad al-Shuqayri

Ahmad al-Shuqayri was raised by his well-educated and well-traveled father, and schooled in Islamic law at one of the premier universities in the Middle East. His father was a free thinker who opposed the policies of the Ottoman sultan and was prepared to pay the price for opposition. Ahmad was raised in Palestine, subjected to the loss of his mother at an early age, and set on the path of higher education under his father's wing. The pursuit of law took him to Jerusalem and introduced him to the circle of free thinkers who were impatient with the mufti's gradualist approach to Palestinian rights. A leading Palestinian lawyer and political leader, Awni Abd al-Hadi, became his mentor. Shuqayri was active in the 1936–39 Arab Revolt in Jerusalem, defending Palestinians who had been accused within the British court system. His commitment to the Palestinian cause was evidenced by his many fiery speeches at the UN during his successive tenures as Syrian, Saudi Arabian, and Palestinian representative. His acceptance of the role of Arab League representative of the Palestinian people and then chairman of the PLO governing body again demonstrates his essential identification with the cause. Even in decline his vociferous opposition to Anwar Sadat's peace treaty with Israel emphasized his conviction about the uselessness of negotiations to achieve Palestinian rights.

The impassioned orator had less to say about Jerusalem itself than about the overall problem of Zionism's intrusive effect on Palestine as a whole. No doubt this was a function of his place in time. His UN speeches on the Palestine Problem were more detailed when it concerned the 1948 refugees, the dispossession of home and homeland, continued Israeli expansionism, and Israeli military actions as in the Suez crisis. When he did address the issue of Jerusalem, however, his comments were no less passionate than his lengthier speeches on the Palestine Problem. He spoke in terms of legitimate ownership and custodianship of the holy sites.

Stasis on the Jerusalem Question marked the period, when under other conditions Shuqayri's voice might have made a difference. During his tenure as UN spokesman for various Arab nations and bodies, the environmental constraints on any resolution to the impasse over the divided city were so great that his actions had little effect. Of the fact that he had a strong identification with the city there can be little doubt. He simply lived at a time when the latency of his identification found no outlet beyond impassioned oratory.

Yasser Arafat (Muhammad Abd al-Rahman Abd al-Ra'uf Arafat al-Qudwa al-Husayni)

Identity and Ideology

Yasser Arafat (1929–2004) was born in Cairo, the sixth of seven children. His father, Abd al-Ra'uf Arafat al-Qudwa al-Husayni, was part Egyptian and part Palestinian from Gaza; his mother, Zahwa, was from the Palestinian Abu Sa'ud family in Jerusalem. The couple had moved from Jerusalem to Egypt in about 1927. Though various biographies have suggested Jerusalem or Gaza as the place of Arafat's birth, the discovery of his Egyptian birth certificate ended that speculation.[52]

Descent is traced through the father in the Arab world, making Arafat a Gazan; his attempt to claim origins in Jerusalem is therefore significant. Perhaps he promoted the myth of a Jerusalem birthplace to create the public image of a "son of Jerusalem." Specifically he claimed that he was born in a Muslim *waqf* in Jerusalem.[53] This is probably a reference to the Abu Sa'ud family home, a compound of several residences and buildings abutting the Western Wall, all of which the Israelis would later demolish as they prepared the plaza in front of the Wall in 1967.

After the death of his mother in 1933, the four-year-old Arafat and his younger brother lived at this family compound until 1936. There, at age seven, he participated in the Arab Revolt against the British and Zionist presence in Palestine, slashing car tires and throwing rocks.[54] Arafat was eventually taken back to Cairo, where he grew up and gained most of his education. His father married twice more, and Arafat's eldest sister spent a considerable amount of her time raising him.

He viewed his time in Cairo as a form of exile. Unlike his Palestinian contemporaries who were driven from the land, however, Arafat's exile was imposed by his father's search for business opportunities. Danny Rubinstein suggests that this lack of the true exile's experience of suffering may account for Arafat's desire to connect with Jerusalem or at least to create mystery about his origins. It may also be that he sought to make a connection with the city as the traditional home of Arab Palestine's leadership elite.

His early identity also seems to have been shaped in part by the loss of his mother and the resulting stay in Jerusalem at the family home next to the Haram and the al-Aqsa Mosque. However, when asked about his birth, he answered, "I was not born until I became Abu Ammar," in reference to his adopted revolutionary name.[55] It was a way of signifying that his identity was wholly that of the Palestinian struggle. Again Rubinstein notes that Arafat did not have a history of dispossession in his earlier life, as have so many of his fellow Palestinians. He writes, "The only one of the eminent people in the Palestinian leadership who has never written memoirs or descriptions" of loss of family, home, village, and land is Yasser Arafat. The statement that he did not exist until he became Abu Ammar is an important comment on how he viewed his identity. For someone who did not suffer the same sense of direct loss of homeland as his fellow Palestinians, yet aspired to lead them, this is a significant remark. The symbolism behind his adopted name is equally noteworthy. It is an inversion of the name of the Prophet Muhammad's friend and companion in arms, Ammar Ibn Yasser.[56]

When Arafat was about sixteen, the mufti of Jerusalem returned to Cairo from exile in Nazi Germany. He gathered his supporters and attempted to reengage in the struggle for Palestine. Arafat was sometimes at the home of the mufti in the Heliopolis suburb of Cairo. There he heard about "Arab nationalism, Islamic movements and secret military plans."[57]

Around this time, two visitors from Jerusalem attracted Arafat's attention. One was his relative, prominent religious leader Shaykh Hassan Abu Sa'ud, a close colleague of the mufti; the other was a more distant relative, Abd al-Qadir al-Husayni, a Palestinian military leader who organized young men for help in the struggle. Abd al-Qadir's son Faysal, who was seven at the time, recalled Arafat's learning to make bombs and cleaning guns at their home in Cairo.[58] Arafat soon began helping deliver arms for use in Palestine.

Overcome by the death of Abd al-Qadir in the battle for Jerusalem, Arafat and other students joined the war in Palestine in May 1948. In Gaza he helped the Ikhwan al-Muslimun (Muslim Brethren)[59] in an attack on a settlement, but professional Arab soldiers soon deprived them of their weapons. In Jerusalem he met up with soldiers in the Arab Legion, who also prevented him from fighting. According to Alan Hart, it was the beginning of Arafat's disillusionment with outside Arab forces.[60] The shock of the Arab defeat in the 1948 war was such that eventually Arafat was motivated to join others in forming a fighting force of their own.

But first, at twenty-one years of age, he returned to Cairo University and his engineering studies. He became involved in student politics and did some basic military training in explosives and landmines. At this time the mufti encouraged him in his pursuit of student leadership. In 1949 he became a member of the Egyptian Union of Students, then chairman of the Federation of Palestinian Students. In 1951 he was involved in training students to engage in anti-British guerilla actions in the Suez Canal Zone. The following year he became chairman of the Palestinian Students Union, a position he held for the next four years. As a result of the Suez Crisis, the Palestinian students formed a commando unit to serve beside Egyptian volunteers. As a reservist second lieutenant and engineer, Arafat was sent to the Canal Zone to help with minesweeping operations. Qualifying in civil engineering that year, he went to work for the Kuwaiti Public Works Department in early 1957. The political atmosphere was more open than in Egypt, and in October 1959 Arafat and four friends were able to found an underground organization, al-Fateh. The concept of armed struggle became part of their vocabulary, and they aimed to fight against Israel for their Palestinian homeland without the help of Arab outsiders.[61] Arafat's style was marked by gradualism, however, and for several years al-Fateh remained under cover, working through their underground publication *Filastinuna: Nida al-Hayat (Our Palestine: The Call to Life)* and the General Union of Palestine Students (GUPS).[62]

Arafat and his colleagues did not welcome the 1964 formation of the PLO under Ahmad al-Shuqayri. They regarded it as another feeble attempt to involve Arab powers in the Palestinian issue, without any real promise of success.[63] As a result they took independent action and started very basic terrorist operations. Their first attack under the pseudonym *al-Asifa* (the Tempest) was against the Israel Water Carrier in January 1965, but the explosives were discovered. The operations continued through that year. As a result of the first raids, Shuqayri and some of the other Palestinian nationalists were furious with al-Fateh. Some in the Arab mass media in Egypt, Lebanon, Saudi Arabia, and Jordan denounced the actions as the work of either Muslims in the pay of the CIA, pan-Arab revolutionaries, or international communists.[64]

The disastrous defeat of the Arab forces in the 1967 war and Shuqayri's loss of the PLO leadership put al-Fateh in a strong position to dominate the movement. The turning point came in March 1968, when an Israeli force moved on al-Fateh's Jordanian headquarters in the village of al-Karameh. The Israelis were forced to retreat, and word of the great Palestinian victory spread. As spokesman, Arafat made the most of the fact that the Israelis had to withdraw under Palestinian fire.[65] In the months that followed, funds and recruits poured in to al-Fateh's offices. In the wake of the 1967 Arab defeat, such armed opposition to the Israelis, even with limited success, was encouraging to most of the Arab world.

In July 1968 the Palestinian National Covenant became the Palestinian National Charter and was modified to stress an independent national identity as well as the exercise of armed struggle. As part of the integration of the commando groups, al-Fateh came within the PLO fold with 38 percent of the seats in the Palestine National Council (PNC). Arafat's popularity led to his election as chairman of the Executive Committee of the PLO in 1969. The changes that had been made to the Palestine National Covenant with respect to the promotion of armed struggle and commando operations could now become reality from within the PLO hierarchy.

By 1970 King Husayn could no longer tolerate the presence of al-Fateh and the Popular Front for the Liberation of Palestine (PFLP) within Jordan's borders. The two organizations posed a threat to his sovereignty: he could neither control their attacks on Israel from Jordanian territory nor sustain the effect of Israeli reprisals. That summer the PFLP hijacked passenger planes and forced them to land in Jordan. The ensuing civil war (Black September) saw King Husayn expel the Palestinians first from Amman, and then from the northern part of the country by July 1971. Arafat took refuge in Beirut and gradually regrouped.

In the 1970s a shift began to take place in the PLO's approach to achieving its goal of liberating Palestine. No longer would armed struggle be the only tool. In June 1974, following the 1973 Arab-Israeli war, the PNC indicated for the first time that political negotiation could be added to the PLO's means of achieving statehood. The Palestinian Authority could now be established "on any liberated part of Palestine."[66] At the Arab Summit in October, the PLO gained recognition in the Arab world as the "sole legitimate representative of the Palestinian people."[67] In November the United Nations invited Arafat to speak before the General Assembly. Later that month, the PLO was granted observer status at the UN.

A major shift also occurred on the Israeli political front in the late 1970s. The Likud Party, under the leadership of Menachem Begin, came to power in 1977. It was the first time the Revisionist stream of Israeli politics had assumed the leadership, and it was to have a devastating impact on the PLO and Yasser Arafat. In 1982 the Israel Defense Forces invaded Lebanon and besieged Beirut, forcing Arafat and his administration to leave. They were allowed to set up headquarters in Tunis, the farthest they had been from Palestine in their years in exile. One disadvantage of the distance was that it prevented the administration from exercising early leadership of the First Intifada, the grassroots uprising in Palestine that began spontaneously in Gaza in late 1987.

The Intifada had at least two far-reaching effects on the Palestinians and the Israelis. Inside Gaza and the West Bank, the lot of Palestinian residents became even more difficult as IDF operations caused the quality of everyday life to deteriorate further. In reaction, moderate elements began to demand that the PLO leaders in Tunis recognize the State of Israel, accept a two-state solution, and announce a Palestinian state, albeit with its government in exile. On the Israeli side, public support grew for an autonomous Palestinian entity, while at the same time demands came from some segments for a greater crackdown on the Intifada. Since both perspectives were represented in the national unity government, it was unable to move beyond inaction, paralyzed by the impasse.[68]

A further development in the PLO's pursuit of political means in its struggle against the Israelis came in November 1988. At a meeting of the PNC in Algiers, Arafat gained support for recognition of the State of Israel, acceptance of all relevant UN resolutions as far back as November 29, 1947, and adoption of the principle of a two-state solution. The PNC also issued a declaration of Palestinian independence. In the weeks that followed, under American pressure, Arafat clarified the practical effect of these declarations. The PLO renounced all forms of terrorism, accepted UN Security Council resolutions 242 and 338 as the basis for peace negotiations with Israel, and recognized Israel's right to exist.[69]

The demise of the Cold War and the end of the Gulf War created new opportunities, and the United States and Russia convened the two-track October 1991 Madrid Peace Conference to address the Arab-Israeli and Israeli-Palestinian conflicts. The conference was the first time that Palestinian representatives attended with their Israeli counterparts, though they were required by prime minister Yitzhak Shamir to be part of a joint Palestinian-Jordanian delegation. The fiction that the Israelis were not negotiating with the PLO had to be maintained.[70] It led ultimately to ten rounds of inconclusive bilateral meetings between the same Palestinian representatives and the Israelis in Washington, D.C. In June 1992, as the lengthy process was under way, a new Israeli government led by Yitzhak Rabin came to power. But even the change from the stonewalling Likud to the more conciliatory Labor leadership seemed to make little difference in terms of breakthrough progress.

Then, with the bilateral talks logjammed in Washington, Israeli foreign minister Shimon Peres agreed to the opening of a secret channel in Oslo in January 1993 between Israelis and representatives of the PLO. At last Arafat in Tunis and the State of Israel in Jerusalem were discussing their mutual futures as directly as they could without the top leaders meeting face-to-face. The resulting Declaration of Principles (Oslo Agreements) was signed in Washington, D.C., on September 13, 1993, confirming mutual recognition between the PLO and Israel and the creation of an independent Palestinian Authority in Gaza and Jericho. Arafat entered Gaza in the summer of 1994 to set up his government in

Palestine. In 1994 he shared the Nobel Peace Prize with Yitzhak Rabin and Shimon Peres.

Arafat and Jerusalem

Arafat had an early identification with Jerusalem. As a young boy living with his mother's relatives in the mid-1930s, he heard stories retold of "Haj Amin's inspiring work to organize the Arabs and of Sheik Hassan's heroic efforts to stop the Jews from expanding their place at the wall."[71] The activist shaykh, who was a leading mufti in charge of the courts of Islamic law in Jerusalem, "preached Arab nationalism to those who came to pray at al-Aqsa Mosque."[72] He intervened at the Wall on Yom Kippur 1928, under the watchful eye of the mufti from a window above, and went through the crowd of Jewish worshipers to extinguish their illegal lights and close their books.[73] This was the catalyst for the 1928–29 Wailing Wall disturbances across Palestine.[74] This early home environment was formative for Arafat: "It was Sheik Hassan Abu Saud and Haj Amin al-Husseini who played major roles in directing Arafat's life."[75]

Arafat had little opportunity to visit Jerusalem after his early childhood, apart from several clandestine trips in the summer of 1967 when he crossed into the West Bank and, in disguise, traveled to Nablus and Ramallah. Years later, when asked if he would accept an invitation to go to Jerusalem as Anwar Sadat had done, Arafat replied that he did not need to be invited; he could get there on his own as he had four times before.[76]

One of the effects of the 1948 war was to heighten Palestinian expressiveness about Jerusalem. The vast majority of Palestinians have never returned after dispossession of their land in the western part of the city. Between 1948 and 1967, they were simply unable to do so. It was cold comfort that the Jordanians occupied East Jerusalem and the Old City, but at least the Haram was in Muslim hands. Israel's capture of the Old City and its destruction of sections of the Arab Quarter in 1967 meant that Jerusalem's sovereignty was more compromised than ever in Palestinian eyes. Despite retaining functional control over the Haram, the Palestinian *waqf* authorities were always subject to the imposition of Israeli rule. As a result, declarations about Jerusalem as the center of Palestinian identity became more frequent and more forceful. The increasing influence of the PLO after 1967 also meant that "the Palestinians, more than ever before, now reaffirmed their national identity . . . 'Arab Jerusalem' became its shining symbol."[77]

The most concrete expression of Jerusalem's centrality to the Palestinians came on November 15, 1988, when the Palestine National Council, meeting in Algiers under Arafat's chairmanship, announced "the establishment of the State of Palestine in the land of Palestine with its capital at Jerusalem."[78]

The advent of the Oslo peace process introduced a new complication in the Jerusalem Question, as certain Palestinian-Israeli issues were now negotiable while others were postponed for final-status agreements. Jerusalem would be one of the last items to be negotiated. This extended timeline and the return of the Likud party to power under Benjamin Netanyahu allowed for the creation of more Israeli "facts on the ground" in Jerusalem. Reacting to Netanyahu's mid-1998 announcement of the expansion of greater Jerusalem's boundaries, Arafat held a special meeting of the Palestinian Legislative Council (PLC). He said:

> The battle for Jerusalem is a battle of life and death for the Palestinian people. . . . The patience of the Palestinian leadership and the Palestinian people has run out. Let Netanyahu and his government know that Jerusalem is a red line, and that there is not one person among us who would make concessions on any grain of soil of Jerusalem.[79]

Two years later, in August 2000, in the wake of the impasse at the Camp David II talks, Arafat addressed religious and political leaders from sixteen Muslim countries attending the meeting of the Organization of the Islamic Conference in Agadir, Morocco. Signaling that there was a point beyond which he could not compromise, he spoke of Jerusalem as "the essence of the Palestinian issue and the most dangerous and sensitive of all issues. This is a red line which can't be crossed."[80]

In early September, Arafat addressed the summit of the Millennium Assembly of the UN. On the subject of Jerusalem, he said:

> As for Holy Jerusalem, the cradle of Christianity, and the site of Prophet Mohammed's ascension to Heaven, we have agreed to share the city, in contrast to the attempts at monopolizing it, as a response to exclusivity and rejection of our rights. At the same time we remain committed to our national rights over East Jerusalem, capital of our state and shelter of our sacred sites, as well as our rights on the Christian and Islamic holy sites, maintaining that the city should be accessible to all, and open onto its western side.[81]

In February 2002, during his Israeli-imposed isolation at the Muqata (his compound in Ramallah), Arafat released an op-ed piece to the *New York Times*. He wrote about the PLO's vision for peace. Specifically about Jerusalem, he said:

> The Palestinians have a vision of peace: it is a peace based on the complete end of the occupation and a return to Israel's 1967 borders, the sharing of all Jerusalem as one open city and as the capital of two states, Palestine and Israel.[82]

A few days later a BBC reporter interviewed him in Ramallah. At the end of a difficult session she asked him, "But what about Jerusalem?" "You will visit me there," he cried, "in my capital."[83] Three days later, reacting to his continued confinement in Ramallah by the Israelis, he called up the image of Jerusalem for his followers in a public address: "This people is mighty and steadfast and together we will reach Jerusalem, Jerusalem, Jerusalem."[84] It was reminiscent of a line in Palestinian poet Mahmud Darwish's eulogy of Nasir: "And you will see us marching forward, forward, forward."[85]

According to the official PLO Web site, the Palestinian position on Jerusalem is "straightforward": East Jerusalem is part of the territory over which the Palestinian state will exercise authority once the state is established. It will be the capital. The Declaration of Principles on Interim Self-Government specifies that all of Jerusalem, East and West, is open for permanent status negotiations. Jerusalem should be an open city, with no physical partition. Since most of the holy sites are in East Jerusalem, including those in the Old City, the State of Palestine will guarantee freedom of worship and access.[86]

This was the position Arafat upheld until his death. In late 2004 his health suddenly deteriorated, and after suffering a stroke, he died in a Paris hospital on November 11.[87] The following day he was given a private state funeral in Cairo before being taken to Ramallah for burial at the Muqata. Israel had refused to allow his last wish to be buried near the al-Aqsa Mosque. But his colleagues, with an eye on the future, prepared an easily moveable coffin to be relocated once the Jerusalem Question is resolved. Thus, even in death, Yasser Arafat continues to hold out the broader fulfillment of his promise to the British journalist: "You will visit me there, in my capital." Perhaps the veteran Palestinian revolutionary will be proved right after all and many will visit him alongside the military hero Abd al-Qadir al-Husayni at the Haram.

For Arafat, securing sovereignty over East Jerusalem became not only a viable and necessary goal for the Palestinian state; it was also a symbol of the struggle, to be called up whenever needed. It was such an evocative identity element, rich with historical and religious overtones and with the collective memory of dispossession, that it was a powerful rallying cry.

Summary: Yasser Arafat

In terms of the elements of his identity, Arafat displayed similar fundamentals to other Palestinian leaders: he was born into a Palestinian family with roots in Gaza and Jerusalem. After the premature death of his mother, his influential Jerusalemite relatives——the Abu Sa'ud family——afforded him protection and solace in their home adjacent to the primary site of Islamic identity in the city, the Haram. At this time his adoptive family told and retold stories of their bravery and political fervor in the face of the Zionist threat to the city and particularly the Western Wall. Not surprisingly, Arafat participated as a child in the 1936 Arab Revolt in the city. Lectured in his teens by the exiled mufti and his distant relative, Abd al-Qadir al-Husayni, Arafat became a gunrunner for the Palestinian cause in Gaza.

These were all formative experiences for his adult identity as the enduring Palestinian guerilla and political leader par excellence. He ultimately claimed that he did not exist (had no identity) until he adopted his nom-de-guerre, Abu Ammar, from the Companion of the Prophet, Ammar Ibn Yasser. His ideology was formed out of this crucible, beginning with the teaching he received from his relatives about Arab and Palestinian nationalism and his early commitment to armed struggle. His role as a Cairo University student leader in support of the Palestinian cause moved him toward the joint founding of al-Fateh, which came to dominate the PLO. While Jerusalem had not featured very strongly in his political expression prior to the 1967 defeat, understandably it was soon spoken of as the lost center of Palestinian life and related to his personal aspirations for the incipient State of Palestine.

The loss of Jerusalem's integrity in 1948 signaled a period of stasis in its Palestinian history. Inevitably at that point in the conflict, what was momentum for the Israelis regarding the city was stasis—or rather retrogression—for the Palestinians. While Arafat could claim identity with the city, momentum toward resolution of the Jerusalem Question could only begin for him once the peace process was under way. The prior constraints of Jordanian rule and the Hashemite hold on the holy sites in the Old City, together with Israeli possession post-1967, made it difficult for Arafat or his PLO colleagues to address the issue. The Oslo process did lead to agreement on negotiations over the future of the city as a final-status element. It was the combined effect of the interaction of variables such as the 1988 recognition of the State of Israel and the renunciation of violence, the 1991 Madrid talks, and the secret Oslo negotiations that made movement on the Jerusalem Question a final-status issue for both parties. In terms of stasis and momentum, 1993 saw the Jerusalem Question break out of the limbo that had bedeviled it since 1948. Once the possibility of change on the issue was mentioned in the framework of resolution of the larger issue of the two-state solution, there was a qualitative difference between these and any previous discussions.[88] The reality that the Jerusalem Question could be resolved now existed. It was a case of willingness of both parties to adjust identity and ideology in the face of historic possibilities that brought momentum. The constraints that appeared afterward—Camp David II failure, Likud intransigence, intensified Palestinian terror operations, Arafat's isolation, and massive Israeli military intervention—do not mean that the issue of Jerusalem will not be resolved. What Arafat and his Israeli interlocutors saw as a significant opportunity in 1993 may yet produce negotiated resolution of the Jerusalem Question.

Ahmad Quray' (Abu Ala')

Identity and Ideology

Ahmad Quray' (1937–), also known as Abu Ala', was born in Abu Dis, a Palestinian village to the east of Jerusalem. His father was born in Jerusalem itself. Ahmad trained as an economist and first worked as a mathematics teacher. Though he was a member of the Ikhwan al-Muslimun, he was impressed by the Fateh publication *Filastinuna* and became an early member, joining the organization in 1968. That same year he left Palestine and worked in Jordan, Saudi Arabia, and Lebanon. Expanding his experience, he matured as a businessman and banker and in the 1970s began to manage the very successful SAMED (Palestine Martyrs' Works Society) Institute in Beirut. The organization was the PLO's economic arm, with thirty-six individual companies manufacturing household goods, foodstuffs, and other commodities. At the time it was also the largest holding company in Lebanon.

In 1983 Quray' became head of the Economic Department of the PLO Executive Committee. Under his management, the investment fund supporting the PLO economy had diverse projects in Africa, Eastern Europe, and Central America by 1989. In 1992 he prepared a far-reaching analysis of the PLO's financial future and showed that it was dire. The study proposed economic cooperation with Israel in a new Middle East and set the stage for the role Quray' would play in the Oslo talks. Following the Madrid talks, he became advisor to the "non-PLO" Palestinian delegates in the multilateral talks in Washington.

When the Oslo channel was opened in 1993, Quray' was the chief negotiator for the PLO. Despite his extensive background with the PLO, when the Israeli intelligence community responded to Yitzhak Rabin's request for an assessment of Quray', they could deliver only a four-and-a-half-page document. This made Rabin wonder whether the negotiator had much influence with Yasser Arafat.[89] At the same time Quray' became managing director of the Palestinian Economic Council for Development and Reconstruction (PECDAR). He also prepared the "Program for Development of the Palestinian National Economy (1994–2000)." Between 1994 and 1996, he was minister of trade and minister of industry in the Palestinian National Authority (PNA). Elected in January 1996 in the Jerusalem constituency to the Palestinian Legislative Council (PLC), Quray' was chosen as Speaker. He is also a member of the International Board of the Peres Center for Peace. From November 2003 until Arafat's death, he served as prime minister, a position he retained in Mahmoud Abbas's government from February 2005 until January 2006.

Quray' and Jerusalem

At the first meeting in the Oslo talks with Uri Savir, his Israeli counterpart, Quray' asked about Savir's origins. As Savir recounts:

> He said: "Where do you live?"
> I said: "In Jerusalem. . . . Where do you come from?"
> He said: "From Jerusalem. . . . Where does your father come from?"
> I said: "From Germany."
> He says: "Aha! . . . My father comes from Jerusalem."
> So I said: "Maybe let's go back to King David."
> And then he said something which was very smart. He said: "Look, let's make the first agreement. Let's never negotiate over the past. Let's try to create a different future, 'cause if you try to resolve the past—that was the meaning—you're always going to end up in a discussion over right or wrong. In the future, it's about two rights."[90]

The interesting aspect of this exchange was that an attempt was made by Quray' to distance himself from the historical arguments about primary possession. While he no doubt has the same attachment to the city as those born there, he was willing to step back from the endless argument about who was there first. Under the circumstances, it was a wise negotiating stance. But in January 1997 he stated that East Jerusalem as a whole and the Haram in particular must be under Palestinian sovereignty: "Jerusalem is the most important cause for the Palestinian leadership and there can be no peace without Jerusalem, whose return was explicitly mentioned in the international resolutions."[91]

Later that year he emphasized, "[T]he Palestinian state . . . is Jerusalem. The state means Jerusalem, and a state of which Jerusalem is not the capital will not be a state."[92]

In a speech to the Washington Institute in 1998, he addressed the final status of Jerusalem as part of the framework for peace. He said in part:

> I believe we will recognize the special importance of the city [of Jerusalem] for the three monotheistic religions—Islam, Judaism and Christianity. International law and a large number of resolutions and conventions issued since the occupation of east Jerusalem all affirm its status as an integral part

of the Arab territories occupied in 1967. And it is on this consensus that any future solution must be based, clearly acknowledging the Palestinian rights in Jerusalem and refusing Israeli claim to exclusive rule of governance.[93]

Quray' also knows that the Palestinians and the Israelis cannot solve the issue of Jerusalem in a vacuum. The Palestinians are aware that the Muslim and Christian worlds, with long historical perspectives of their own, are looking over their shoulder as the Palestinians negotiate Jerusalem. In 1999, putting the argument in religious and historical terms, he said:

> [W]e cannot make the decision alone without consulting the Arabs and the Muslims in the world. Jerusalem is not only for the Palestinians. Muslims everywhere look to Jerusalem like they look to Mecca. It's the holy place of all Muslims and Arabs; therefore, it is a Palestinian decision, but with Arab and Muslim support—and Christian. The Christians, the Muslims and the Arabs must support the solution; otherwise it will not survive. We cannot avoid it.[94]

Quray' was also clear about the centrality of the city to the Palestinian identity. And, like his colleagues in the PLO hierarchy, he knows that sovereignty of the Old City is crucial to any agreement. The PLO will not be able to sell any agreement on Jerusalem to its supporters if it fails to confirm full sovereignty over the Haram and the majority of Arab East Jerusalem for the Palestinian state:

> Jerusalem is the capital of the Palestinian state. It is the head, the heart of the Palestinian state—the heart of the Palestinian identity. Without Jerusalem, I don't think peace will be achieved. Therefore, this is the most important element of the peace process.
> . . . The nonnegotiable issue in the conflict over Jerusalem is sovereignty. Sovereignty is not negotiable. Modalities can be negotiated: what kind of security, how to reach the religious places, transportation, taxes—even municipal wards can be negotiated. But the matter of sovereignty is nonnegotiable. . . .
> . . . I'm speaking about sovereignty in East Jerusalem for the Palestinians and in West Jerusalem for the Israelis. Sovereignty in East Jerusalem is not negotiable for the Palestinians.

Ahmad Quray' is an economist, a banker, and a manager of successful manufacturing companies. He is a man who can cut through the emotion of a situation and get to the practicalities. But on the issue of Jerusalem he has to acknowledge his own identity-ideology nexus. His birthplace is Abu Dis, a suburb of East Jerusalem, which was proposed as the compromise capital of the Palestinian state.[95] The idea was that an extension of Jerusalem's boundaries could easily incorporate the village, thus solving the problem of definition. But even though Quray' owns a significant amount of residential and business property in Abu Dis, and though the PLC building is there, he denies that the village can ever replace Jerusalem itself as capital of the Palestinian state: "Abu Dis is a village two kilometers from Jerusalem. It's part of East Jerusalem, not an alternative to Jerusalem. Abu Dis without Jerusalem is zero; it is nothing."[96] The truth is that no Palestinian with East Jerusalem as an identity component would accept anything but the Haram, the Arab Quarter, and the eastern Palestinian suburbs as identifiably East Jerusalem.

In August 2005 Quray' made a statement on behalf of the Palestinian Council of Ministers, immediately prior to Israel's Gaza and northern West Bank disengagement. He reaffirmed

> that the legitimate rights of the Palestinian people . . . comprise [among others] . . . the establishment of a viable and sovereign Palestinian state on the territories occupied by Israel in the June 1967 War, with Jerusalem as its eternal capital.[97]

Summary: Ahmad Quray'

With a birthplace in sight of the Old City and a paternal link to Jerusalem itself, Ahmad Quray' can claim authentic physical identification with the city. Once he was persuaded to leave the Muslim Brethren by the Fateh publication *Filastinuna*, his ideological stance became more narrowly focused on indigenous Palestinian concerns than provided for by the agenda of the Ikhwan. Trained in mathematics, economics, and banking, he became a natural choice for work in the administration of the PLO's financial operations. His rise through the PLO hierarchy demonstrated Yasser Arafat's considerable confidence in his loyalty and ideological agreement, to the extent of naming him successor in the event of his own incapacity. The position held by Quray' on the Jerusalem Question is uncompromising: East Jerusalem's sovereignty is nonnegotiable.

The Oslo talks, in which he was a prime player, provided him with the opportunity to delay discussion of the Jerusalem Question until final-status talks—but this alone was progress for the Palestinians; at least the subject was acknowledged. The subsequent Camp David II and Taba talks went much further. As with Arafat, the Jerusalem Question gained momentum for Quray' in the environment created by the interaction of unforeseen variables—the PLO's new stance, the end of the Cold War, the Madrid talks, the landslide election victory of Labor, and the unusual willingness of moderate Israelis to negotiate as never before.

Hanan Mikha'il-Ashrawi

Identity and Ideology

Hanan Mikha'il-Ashrawi (1946–) was born into a wealthy Christian Arab family in Nablus, the youngest of five girls. Her mother was a devout, conservative Episcopalian Christian from Beirut, while her Palestinian father, Da'ud Mikha'il, came from a long-established Ramallah family of Greek Orthodox affiliation. At the time of her birth he was stationed in Tiberias as a physician in the Palestinian army under the British. When he heard of an intended attack on the Palestinian community there, he took the family to Amman, and a short time later the 1948 war broke out. In 1950 they returned to Ramallah, the Mikha'ils' ancestral town, which became part of the annexed Jordanian West Bank one year later. There Hanan grew up and still maintains the family home.

In the years that followed, King Husayn legalized political parties, permitting Ashrawi's father to express his political views by joining the National Socialist Party led by Sulayman al-Nabulsi. But by 1957 relations between King Husayn and al-Nabulsi, who was now Jordanian prime minister, became so strained that the king dismissed the cabinet. The leftist National Socialist Party paid the price: all political parties were suppressed; some leaders fled into exile; others, including West Bank organizer Da'ud Mikha'il, were imprisoned. Ashrawi's father was sentenced to six years for what King Husayn was persuaded were anti-Jordanian views. It seems that the king himself, who was a family friend, did not know of the imprisonment at the time it occurred. Da'ud's daughter Huda remarked, "I don't think he [the king] knew till after the fact."[98] The family appealed, and after four years the king commuted the sentence.

In 1964 Ashrawi went to study at the American University of Beirut. At the same time her father was working with Ahmad al-Shuqayri on his new project, the PLO, recruiting and making field surveys for him in Palestine. According to Huda, Da'ud believed that a new political organization was necessary and that Palestine could be "liberate[d] by logic."

In Beirut, Ashrawi joined GUPS. There she was introduced to al-Fateh and the concept of military struggle for Palestine. Al-Fateh expected members of GUPS to work with the Palestinian refugees in two large camps in Beirut. Ashrawi "taught classes in 'what we called consciousness raising and political awareness' " and took journalists through the camps. In the fall of 1969 she attended a GUPS convention in Amman as the only elected female delegate and met Yasser Arafat for the first time.[99] Eventually she would leave Fateh, but only after many years.

In 1970, unable to return to the West Bank because of Israeli permit restrictions, Ashrawi went to the United States to pursue a doctorate in medieval English literature. She went back to Ramallah in 1973 and the following year took up the post of head of the English Department at Birzeit University (1973–78, 1981–84). By the mid-1970s Ashrawi was already thinking independently of a two-state solution to the Palestine Problem. As a result she and other Palestinians became involved with Israeli activists seeking the end of their government's occupation. Together they formed what she refers to as "the first Palestinian-Israeli underground political organization"—the League of Communist Workers.[100] In 1986 she was appointed Dean of the Faculty of Arts at Birzeit (1986–90) and remained a faculty member until 1995.

Arafat chose Ashrawi as official spokesperson for the Palestinians at the 1991 Madrid Peace Conference, at which the Israelis had refused to meet directly with members of the PLO or Palestinian residents of Jerusalem. Ashrawi played her role so skillfully that she quickly became the most eloquent and recognizable public representative of the Palestinian position in Madrid and at the ensuing bilateral talks with Israel in Washington, D.C. During the period leading up to the signing of the 1993 Oslo Agreements, she was also a member of the Leadership/Guidance Committee and the Executive Committee of the Palestinian team. Having become critical of the PLO's approach in the Washington talks, however, she and several colleagues tried to resign their positions in 1993. Arafat refused to accept their resignations.

The following year she founded the Palestinian Independent Commission for Citizens' Rights. In 1996 she was elected to the Palestinian Legislative Council, Jerusalem District, and at the same time became Palestinian Authority minister for higher education and research (1996–98). When she was demoted to minister of tourism in a cabinet reshuffle in 1998, she chose to resign, citing Arafat's handling of the peace process and his failure to dismiss certain ministers named in a report on corruption.[101] She went on to found the Palestinian Initiative for the Promotion of Global Dialogue and Democracy (MIFTAH) in August 1998.

Appointed spokesperson for the Arab League in 2001, she resigned after less than a year, saying that the varying agendas of the member nations' information ministers made it difficult for the Arab League to express a unified message.

Ashrawi and Jerusalem

Prior to an onerous trip to the United States to discuss matters with secretary of state Warren Christopher in 1993, Ashrawi described her feelings about the city and the way it had changed. One of the issues on the agenda with Christopher was Jerusalem. She wrote:

> Jerusalem was being altered before our very eyes, its people evicted and dispossessed, its ancient walls studded with soldiers, its rolling hills violated

with settlement fortresses, its open roads blocked with military checkpoints, and its spirit soiled by possession as the conqueror's spoils. It lay stifling under siege, slowly strangulating, bereft of the lifeblood of its own children, groaning under the boot of military occupation. And we mourned Jerusalem instead of reveling in its magnificence. We watched the city that had been our core and cornerstone become a city without a soul.[102]

She speaks of the city as having been the core and cornerstone of Palestinian life. Her partner in the discussions with the secretary of state was Faysal al-Husayni. He was from a notable generations-old Jerusalem family and the son of the Palestinian military hero Abd al-Qadir al-Husayni. One year earlier Faysal had established his family's East Jerusalem property, Orient House, as a center for Palestinian diplomatic exchanges with foreign representatives.

Being a resident of the Jerusalem area, Ashrawi carried a significant burden as a negotiator who might not be appreciated by her own people in the end. Speaking of the historic core of identity that Jerusalem holds for its inhabitants, and the weight of her responsibilities, she wrote:

As a Ramallah-Jerusalemite, I inherited the legacy and deprivation of both, and as a Palestinian I felt the eye and weight of history as a personal intrusion. The Palestinian people as a whole habitually exacted a heavy toll from those who dared intrude on the course of their fate, particularly from those who presumed to lead or speak on their behalf.[103]

Excluded from the Oslo negotiations as part of the elaborate smoke-screen to keep them secret, Ashrawi was not pleased with the results of the process. Ironically Ashrawi was the one who brought together Ahmad Quray' and Ya'ir Hirschfeld, the Israeli academic who played a key role in establishing the Oslo talks.[104] It was not the countless hours she spent as part of the parallel and fruitless Washington talks that concerned her. Ashrawi was worried that the compromise of postponing discussion of the rights of refugees, Israeli settlements, human rights, and Jerusalem would give the Israelis opportunity to create more "facts on the ground." In the days leading up to the signing of the Declaration of Principles in Washington, Arafat had explained his strategy to her, without giving away the secret talks. He said that he accepted Jericho as the first step in Israeli withdrawal and Palestinian sovereignty, because that way he could get to Jerusalem and from there to Gaza, thus linking them together with the West Bank.[105]

When Arafat asked Ashrawi to explain the Oslo negotiations to King Husayn, she did so personally in an off-the-record visit. The suggestion had been made that sovereignty of the Haram/Temple Mount should be left to rest with God. The king had obviously warmed to this idea. Writing about the meeting, Ashrawi commented:

> King Hussein expressed real concern about the fate of Jerusalem. "Jerusalem is not just the holy places," I said. "It's a living, throbbing city with national, political, and historical Palestinian rights, with institutions, human beings, homes, and land that have to be protected."
>
> I was worried that the perceptual spiritual shift to celestial Jerusalem might undermine our terrestrial city. By granting God sovereignty over the sacred aspects of Jerusalem, we might be sanctioning Israel's actual and illegal exercise of sovereignty in the secular domain.[106]

She based her fears about this possibility on much bitter experience. As she explained three years later in respect of the proposed settlement on the northern edge of Bethlehem at Jabal Abu Ghunaym (Har Homa),

> [f]or 30 years Israel has been confiscating our land in Jerusalem, has willfully and systematically prevented any building in Jerusalem, Palestinian building, while it systematically brought in Israeli Jewish settlers, and . . . has isolated Jerusalem from the rest of Palestine. It has besieged Jerusalem within a sea of settlements, and this latest settlement will close the ring around Jerusalem and totally cut it off from the rest of the Palestinian territory.[107]

Giving a briefing to the American Committee on Jerusalem in Washington, D.C., in March 2000, she commented again on the Jerusalem issue. The idea had been suggested by the Israelis that an Arab suburb or village adjacent to East Jerusalem would suffice for the Palestinian capital. It was a not-so-subtle attempt to give the Palestinians something and yet avoid the sovereignty issue within Jerusalem. Ashrawi went to the heart of the matter when she said:

> We have never had a problem defining Jerusalem. We know what it is, we know where it is, we know its character, we know its institutions, we know its significance not just in history, to the past, not just to the present, but also to the future of the whole region.
>
> Jerusalem holds the key to peace for Palestinians and the rest of the Arab and Islamic world and with the region as a whole. It defies exclusive possession. It does not belong to Israel. According to [UN Resolution] 181, Jerusalem is not even subject to Israeli sovereignty, whether it is East or West Jerusalem. This is a corpus separatum. But again, according to international law, Jerusalem is occupied territory. And the boundaries of East Jerusalem are the same as those of 1967.
>
> Nobody recognizes the illegal annexation or expansion of Israel's municipal boundaries. Even the US doesn't do that, which should tell you how taboo that is.
>
> We are not in the process of accepting substitutes for Jerusalem, of accepting the parceling out of Jerusalem, of accepting Israeli sovereignty over Jerusalem,

of accepting functional tasks in Jerusalem as a substitute for actual sovereignty. We think that the negotiations on Jerusalem, as well on all other permanent status issues, should be firmly based on international law.[108]

Summary: Hanan Mikha'il-Ashrawi

When identity and ideology are considered, Hanan Ashrawi's biography demonstrates a rather different profile than those examined thus far. The basis for her role rests in part on the influence of her parents, particularly her physician father, whose politically independent frame of mind brought him into conflict with the king of Jordan over his role in that country's National Socialist Party. His imprisonment lasted four years during a formative period of Hanan's life. Her father's later involvement with the PLO under Shuqayri was in support of what he characterized as liberation by logic.

Some of these strands of independence and defiance are apparent in Ashrawi's own political career. She joined and resigned from the PLO; she resigned in protest from her role as spokesperson of the Palestinian Delegation of the Washington talks; she refused to accept a new cabinet post from Yasser Arafat; and she resigned from the job of spokesperson of the Arab League. She has identified corruption within the PLO and formed her own Palestinian organization for global dialogue on democracy. Clearly a free thinker, her willingness to participate in an early underground Palestinian-Israeli dialogue indicates her openness and independence. Her views on Jerusalem rest in identification with the city as a Ramallah-Jerusalemite. She is protective of Palestinian rights to the city and fearful for its physical future as the core of Palestinian life.

Reflecting on how her involvement in the whole peace process had come to fruition in the hours before the 1993 White House ceremony, Ashrawi describes a chain of events that may have started the process for her. It is a list of possible interacting variables that may have produced the momentum that brought her and the PLO to Washington that day. She wonders whether it was James Baker's initiation of contacts with her and her colleague, Faysal al-Husayni, in Jerusalem prior to the Madrid talks, or her involvement in the First Intifada. Was it her encouragement of the initial meeting between Hirschfeld and Ahmad Quray' a year earlier, or her formative student years in Beirut?[109] As she mused, the Jerusalem Question was still unresolved, but Ashrawi had witnessed the beginning of momentum on the issue through the interaction of some of these events. Her future negotiating position, if she would have a role to play, was sure to reflect her views on the legality of the Palestinian claim and her own identification with the city.

Faysal al-Husayni

Identity and Ideology

Faysal al-Husayni (1940–2001) was born in Baghdad, Iraq. His father was the famous Palestinian guerilla fighter Abd al-Qadir al-Husayni. His grandfather, Musa Qasem Pasha al-Husayni, was mayor of Jerusalem until the British removed him from office in April 1920 for opposing their pro-Zionist policy. Faysal was a descendant of the Prophet Muhammad, the nephew of al-Hajj Amin al-Husayni, and a distant cousin of Yasser Arafat. It was said of him, "his roots lie deep in the legend, lore, and religion of Palestine, stretching back to the beginning of the seventeenth century, when the post of *mufti* (the highest Muslim authority on religious law) of Jerusalem was held by Abdel Kader ibn Karim al-Din Husseini."[110]

Faysal al-Husayni was educated in Cairo, Baghdad, and Damascus as a result of his father's itinerant life as a freedom fighter and his own desire to further the Palestinian cause. When the mufti was forced to flee Jerusalem in 1937, he was accompanied by several of his supporters, including Abd al-Qadir. By 1939 the mufti had traveled through Lebanon and Syria and had arrived in Iraq, where Faysal was born in 1940. The mufti was soon on the run again, and Abd al-Qadir attempted to follow him into refuge in Iran. However, the Iranians would not allow the mufti's fellow fighters to enter with him, so Abd al-Qadir returned to Iraq and was imprisoned by the British until 1944.

At the age of four, Faysal, his parents, his brothers, and his sister went to live in Saudi Arabia. While there Abd al-Qadir was forced to teach his four boys at home, as the school system would not allow them to attend. Faysal later said that this was the only time he saw much of his father. In 1946 the family was allowed to settle in Cairo. The mufti arrived there at the same time, following his exile in Europe. From Egypt he and Abd al-Qadir launched operations against the Jewish community in Palestine. A regular visitor to the al-Husayni home at this time was sixteen-year-old Yasser Arafat, who soon became involved in the 1948 war.

In the battle for Jerusalem, when Faysal was eight years old, his well-known father was killed by a Jewish soldier at Qastel and became "the first martyr of Palestine." Faysal recalled that his mother showed no grief in front of her children and that it was a few days before he himself felt the loss of his father. In the months that followed, the mufti (often accompanied by Arafat) would visit the bereaved family. Arafat coached the nine-year-old Faysal on how to address those who would ask about his father in years to come. Faysal could recite one of his father's songs, he said. It was about a mother and child in conversation. The child says, "Talk to me about the land; is it right that the Zionists got our land? Give me my sword, Mother, and I will go and fight for our land." For the next several years Faysal sang this song before Egyptian audiences remembering his father's death.

In his teen years Faysal was supportive of Nasir's approach to the Palestinian cause, believing that pan-Arabism was the best vehicle for realizing Palestinian aspirations. But this perspective was to change. In 1957 he joined the Arab Nationalist Movement, which clashed with Nasir only a few years later. In 1958 he completed high school and went to the University of Baghdad to study geology. Although the mufti had had a profound influence on his nephew, Faysal was beginning to see that the religious leader represented the old way of looking at the Palestine Problem. The founding of al-Fateh in 1959 by his childhood friend Yasser Arafat and his colleagues further changed his mind. By 1961, with the collapse of the United Arab Republic, he concluded that the pan-Arab approach was failing.

With Shuqayri's appointment as chairman of the PLO, Faysal al-Husayni took on the role of deputy manager of the Public Organization Department (1964–65) in Jerusalem. After two years he became disillusioned with Shuqayri's lack of results and decided to complete his military training in Syria, where he graduated from the Damascus Military College in 1967. Sent by the Syrians to Lebanon, he recruited and trained more than 1,200 members for the Palestine Liberation Army. Their base was the Shuqayri estate near Beirut. The outcome of the 1967 war changed al-Husayni's plans, however, and he decided to return to Jerusalem.

By chance that summer in the West Bank he met Arafat, who was recruiting for Fateh. He asked why Faysal was there, assuming someone must have sent him. Al-Husayni replied in words that became a trademark statement: "I'm here because I want to be here. This is my land, my property is here, and my family is here."[111] Arafat suggested that he use his recent military training to help Fateh, but al-Husayni now said that he preferred to pursue political approaches against the Israeli occupation. However, he was willing to conceal a couple of weapons in his Jerusalem home for Arafat. This led to the first of many experiences with police questioning and detention.

While in prison in March 1968, he gave an interview to *Ha'aretz*, in which he recognized the rights of Jews to have a homeland in Palestine. It was the day after the battle of al-Karameh in Jordan, where Fateh inflicted heavy losses on the IDF. The PLO was four months away from renaming and rewriting parts of the Palestinian National Covenant to reflect Palestinian commando-led armed struggle. Arafat was less than a year away from becoming PLO chairman. In that climate, al-Husayni's moderate views seemed out of place. It would be twenty years before they would come to center stage.

The 1970s were a lean time for al-Husayni. Without an Israeli identity card—part of the continued harassment he suffered—employment and travel were very difficult. He worked as an X-ray technician at a family-owned clinic (1973–77) and in 1979 founded the highly reputed Arab Studies Society in Jerusalem. Al-Husayni was placed under house arrest and city arrest and was imprisoned without trial more than once by the Israelis between 1982 and 1987.

In a Likud-sponsored attempt to counterbalance Shimon Peres's peace efforts with King Husayn in 1987, al-Husayni was invited into discussions about limited autonomy with a member of the Likud central committee, Moshe Amirav. For his efforts, he was suddenly detained by the Israeli *Shin Bet* and prevented from attending a conference in Geneva to discuss a memorandum about autonomy. It seems that Yitzhak Shamir had not objected to the arrest. Al-Husayni spent the next ten months in prison, while the First Intifada was in progress.

When he was released in June 1988, he wrote a proposal for a Palestinian declaration of independence and the establishment of a provisional government, with Arafat as head but with a broad-based elected legislature of Palestinians living under occupation. The "Husayni document" was an attempt to redirect the uprising away from violent confrontation. As a result, he was rearrested. In all he spent forty-two months in prison and a further five years under house arrest.

Al-Husayni was a member of the PLO Executive Committee and the Higher Islamic Council in Jerusalem (1982–2001), as well as coordinator of the Palestinian advisory council at the Middle East Peace Conference in Madrid in 1991 and a participant in the continuing bilateral talks with Israel in Washington through 1993. A constant proponent of dialogue with the Israelis, he became the Palestinian National Authority's representative in Jerusalem as minister without portfolio. His office at his family's Orient House in East Jerusalem was the nerve center for Palestinian contacts with international representatives following the opening of the 1990s peace process.

In May 2001, while in Kuwait for a conference, he died suddenly of a heart attack. He was buried next to his father on al-Haram al-Sharif, in a funeral service attended by his family and Yasser Arafat.

Faysal al-Husayni and Jerusalem

In his 1968 prison interview with *Ha'aretz*, al-Husayni was asked how he felt about Jerusalem after the Israelis captured it. He said:

> I was outraged when I saw my city, al-Quds under foreign rule, Israeli rule. A considerable part of it was taken in the past. Now everything was taken, and it's being named differently: "Urshalim." They are also changing the Arabic

names of streets. They are forcing a foreign rule upon us. They are forcing a foreign lifestyle upon us.[112]

Yet this perspective did not lead al-Husayni to bitterness. He preferred to coexist with the Israelis, recognizing that they had to live together for the benefit of each people. He said that in the twenty years since 1948, things had changed. He was prepared to allow the Jews to live in their homeland in peace as long as the Palestinians were allowed to do the same.

The development of this approach was observable through the 1980s. In a 1990 interview, al-Husayni was asked about the idea of the transfer of the indigenous Palestinians to Jordan. He replied, "You can't tell the Palestinians that they are Jordanians, or where they are, where is their land. Only I can tell you who I am and where is my land."[113] Asked about his preferred solution to the Jerusalem Question, he responded:

You know I'm from Jerusalem. I hate to see Jerusalem divided. Unfortunately, Jerusalem now is divided. Obviously you can go now and you can see that there are two cities—a city under occupation and a free city. . . . I can see Jerusalem can be one city with two capitals: a Palestinian capital in the east part, an Israeli capital in the west part. And I believe that we and the Israelis insist that Jerusalem must be part of us. So we can reach this deal.

In 1991, in the run-up to the Madrid Peace Conference, al-Husayni and his colleagues Hanan Ashrawi and Zakariyya al-Agha had several meetings with U.S. secretary of state James Baker and his team. Each of the Palestinians had an issue he or she felt more strongly about than the others. Ashrawi writes:

Each one of us had his or her obsession. Faisal's was Jerusalem. It is undoubt-edly inscribed in his heart. It was more than a political issue for him, it was a personal, emotional commitment. He came from a long line of Jerusalemites who have held positions of authority—both secular and religious—for cen-turies. I once heard him declare: "I'm a Palestinian and I love Palestine. I'm a family man and I love my wife and children. But first and foremost I'm a Jerusalemite. For that I'm willing to die."[114]

Israeli prime minister Yitzhak Shamir prevented East Jerusalemites from joining the Madrid talks, saying it would compromise Israel's annexation of the city by recognizing Palestinian existence there, and for fear that it might indicate that Jerusalem could be discussed. Yitzhak Rabin, on the other hand, agreed to allow al-Husayni to join the 1993 peace talks if he would buy a house on the West Bank, outside of East Jerusalem, his family home.

In May 1995 al-Husayni spoke during a demonstration against Israeli expropriation of Palestinian land. Standing next to the walls of the Old City, he said, "I dream of the day when a Palestinian will say 'Our Jerusalem' and will mean Palestinians and Israelis, and an Israeli will say 'Our Jerusalem' and will mean Israelis and Palestinians."[115]

In the period following the Oslo Agreements, al-Husayni became more and more disappointed with the lack of progress in the peace process. In December 1999 he spoke at an Arab League Conference in London, during which he laid out a Palestinian view of Jerusalem's future prospects. Commenting on the city's centrality in the peace process and to Palestinian identity, he said:

> Jerusalem is the most important issue to be resolved in order to achieve a lasting peace between Arabs and Israelis. Without an acceptable solution to the Jerusalem issue there will be no peace in the region. . . .
>
> . . . Israel desperately wants to annex Jerusalem and its holy sites but not its Palestinian inhabitants. Palestinian Jerusalemites are not part of the Israeli vision for Jerusalem and the Israelis have created conditions on the ground that force us to leave Jerusalem and change our identity as Palestinians.
>
> But we have resisted these measures. By fighting to preserve our identity as a people and our right to live in the City, we have preserved the [sic] Jerusalem as our capital and our cultural and economic center. This fight has not been restricted to the inhabitants of Jerusalem but was joined by all the Palestinians.[116]

By the time of Ariel Sharon's infamous visit to the Haram in September 2000, al-Husayni could only comment that "the Israelis are trying to take our holy place."[117] It was as if the wheel had come full circle and he was repeating the words of his relative the mufti in 1928 when the Wailing Wall riots broke out.

At the time of his death, al-Husayni was in Kuwait for a conference to discuss a freeze in the cooperative trade relations of several Gulf States with Israel. Despite his disappointment with lack of progress toward a Palestinian state, the Palestinian Academic Society for the Study of International Affairs could say in an obituary that he "pursued tirelessly his dream to see Jerusalem as the capital of a free Palestine."[118]

Summary: Faysal al-Husayni

The salient elements of identity in Faysal al-Husayni's biography include the enduring image of his famous warrior father, his own intimate connection with Jerusalem's history (his grandfather was mayor, his uncle the mufti Amin al-Husayni), his descent from the Prophet Muhammad, and his passion for the city as the heart of Palestinian life.

The death of his father when he was eight years old emphasized his family's struggle for justice for the Palestinian people. For several years he explained to audiences his father's philosophy by way of a patriotic song about the land of Palestine. As time went on, his ideology shifted from support for pan-Arabism, to enthusiasm for the first incarnation of the PLO under Shuqayri, to acceptance of his distant cousin Yasser Arafat's leadership.

Al-Husayni's willingness to suffer imprisonment without bitterness for his pro-Palestinian positions made him a formidable foe. Perhaps it was this lack of bitterness against his enemies that led him to a two-state solution ahead of his time. His participation as head of the Palestinian Delegation to the Washington talks confirmed his central role in indigenous Palestinian life. With respect to Jerusalem, he was abundantly clear: East Jerusalem would be the capital of the Palestinian state in a negotiated settlement with the Israelis, sooner or later.

With his colleague Hanan Ashrawi, Faysal al-Husayni experienced the early stages of the 1990s peace process at close quarters. A man devoted to patient and persistent negotiation, he was confident in the overall justice of his cause and anticipated that the momentum gained in the Oslo process would eventually triumph despite the setbacks. About a year before his death, he wrote an op-ed piece for the *Los Angeles Times*, in which he argued for fair rule of "The Holy City." He said in part:

> Palestinians want a Jerusalem that is shared, not divided. Ours is the only realistic alternative for a city that is so important to so many people. There is no reason why Jerusalem cannot become the symbol of reconciliation in the Middle East instead of continuing to be an obstacle to peace.[119]

Al-Husayni had endured many experiences that would have convinced most that bitterness was justified and that stasis was all that could be expected on the Jerusalem Question. The interaction of the variables of the early-1990s peace process seemed to justify his optimism that eventually the problem would see resolution.

Shaykh Ahmad Isma'il Yassin

Identity and Ideology

Ahmad Isma'il Yassin (1936?–2004) was born in al-Jura (al-Majdal district), a fishing village near Asqalan (Ashkelon), to Sa'dah Abdallah al-Habeel. The family was moderately prosperous and owned land in the northern part of the British Mandate's Gaza District. When Ahmad was around three years old, his father died. During the 1948 war, at about the age of twelve, the boy fled with his family to the Gaza Strip, where they were housed in the Shati refugee camp near Gaza City. As a teenager he was seriously injured in an accident that left him quadriplegic.

Influenced by Muslim Brethren teachers in his youth, he joined the society in 1955. At the time the organization was outlawed in Egypt and Gaza in response to its 1954 attempt on Nasir's life. During this period, Yassin and Yasser Arafat became acquainted as student members of the same organization.

Ill health would trouble Yassin throughout his life. Confined to a wheelchair following the accident, he eventually began to suffer from muscular atrophy, chronic respiratory problems, deafness, and near blindness. Yet, despite his paralysis and other health problems, after studying in Cairo Yassin qualified as a teacher and worked in that capacity in Gaza from 1957 to 1964.

He returned to Egypt as a graduate student in English at Cairo's Ayn Shams University (1964–65). In 1965 the Egyptian authorities imprisoned him for a month on suspicion of subversive activities in connection with the Muslim Brethren. The influential leader of the Brethren in Egypt, Sayyid Qutb, was imprisoned at the time and executed the following year for his alleged role in an attempted coup to overthrow Nasir. Subsequently Qutb's writings would become instrumental in persuading many Islamic groups, including Yassin's, to take up violence against non-Islamic regimes.

On his release Yassin was sent back to Gaza, where once more he emphasized *da'wa*—religious preaching and education as the communal means to establishing an Islamic society. Together with other Muslim leaders, he benefited from the Israeli administration's determination to undermine the secular nationalist PLO agenda by promoting cultural and religious societies such as Hamas. Though he had not received formal religious training, Yassin traveled "from the Galilee to the Negev to preach and lead Friday prayers"[120] following the 1967 war. Eventually he became known by the honorific religious title "shaykh," in recognition of his spiritual role.

Yassin now worked for almost a decade to revive the Muslim Brethren in Gaza and to develop its institutional and social infrastructure. In 1973 he helped found the welfare organization al-Mujamma' al-Islami (the Islamic Center). It was based in the Zaytun section of Gaza in the Jurat al-Shams Mosque, and Yassin was its spiritual leader. It soon became the public face of the Muslim Brethren and controlled all of the Muslim religious institutions in Gaza. The Islamic Center was legalized in 1978, with the encouragement of the Israeli administration. The Israeli military governor of Gaza, Yitzhak Sager, admitted that al-Mujamma' was indirectly funded by Israel to create an option to the PLO. Yitzhak Rabin and Hamas official Mahmud Zahar met for discussions on frequent occasions, as did others from both sides.[121] One year later Yassin founded the Gaza Islamic Society in sympathy with the aims of the Ayatollah Khomeini's Iranian Islamic revolution.

Yassin's passion for Islamic militancy led in 1984 to his being sentenced by the Israelis to twelve years in prison on the grounds of possession of weapons and explosives. The imprisonment followed immediately on his retirement from teaching because of increasing physical disabilities. Within a year, however, Yassin was released in a prisoner exchange between Israel and Ahmad Jibril's Popular Front for the Liberation of Palestine–General Command.

Free once more, Yassin devoted himself to religious, educational and social endeavors, working again from the Islamic Center. On December 12 and 14, 1987, a few days after the beginning of the First Intifada, the shaykh announced the establishing of Harakat al-Muqawama al-Islamiyya (Islamic Resistance Movement), also known by the acronym "Hamas," which is the Arabic word for "ardor" or "zeal."[122] This was the beginning of a presence for the Muslim Brethren in Gaza and the West Bank as representatives of political Islam. The following year, Hamas published the Islamic Covenant, detailing its ideology and practice.

The shaykh espoused belief in "the establishment of an Islamic state in Palestine by means of *jihad* [in the sense of armed struggle] against Israel as a long-term goal that required preparatory educational groundwork."[123] This entailed directing the education of the young for resistance against the Israeli occupation. A key step was his encouragement of militants to take control of the Islamic University in Gaza, an extension of al-Azhar in Cairo. Established in 1978, the university was funded by Saudi Arabia and Jordan. But its allotment was cut off by a penurious PLO in 1985, and the Islamic Center was able to step in and provide the necessary funds. Within just a few short years, five thousand students at the university were overwhelmingly loyal to the Islamist position.

The First Intifada, which began in Gaza on December 9, 1987, provided an opportune moment for the public inauguration of Hamas. The Mujamma' leaders had previously abstained from armed struggle, but now it was in their interests to promote the uprising as a means of mobilizing the masses and publicizing the ideological difference between itself and the PLO. Almost from the beginning, Yassin's religious perspective and commitment to Islamic fundamentalism caused him to clash with the secular nationalism of the PLO. He differed ideologically, especially as the goal of the PLO shifted from eradication of the Zionist presence through armed struggle to its accommodation and acceptance of the two-state solution. From time to time since 1988, Hamas officials have softened their positions on the possibility of a truce, the end of suicide bombings, participation in PNC elections, Israel's right to exist, the demand that all of Palestine become an Islamic state, cessation of violence, even allowing for "discussion of all matters."[124] Despite Hamas's rhetoric following its 2006 election victory, it is important not to lose sight of their occasional tendency to moderate their positions.

Yassin was arrested again in May 1989 and given a life sentence in October 1991 for his role in the execution of four Palestinians accused of collaboration with the Israelis. He was also sentenced to fifteen years for his implied role in the kidnapping and death of two Israeli soldiers. Nevertheless, despite his restricted leadership (he was able to communicate only by letter from prison), his colleagues continued to develop the infrastructure of Hamas. In line with Yassin's principles, they continued to take care of welfare, health care, vocational training, and educational and political needs in Gaza and the West Bank. The military wing, comprising Izz al-Din al-Qassam Battalions, was also set up in the early 1990s and committed itself to punishment of collaborators and to violent resistance to the State of Israel and its citizens by various means, including suicide bombings. Khaled Hroub also mentions that as early as 1983 Yassin had established a security apparatus, which stored arms, assassinated collaborators, and manufactured bombs.[125]

Hamas declared its opposition to the Oslo Agreements, describing them as illegitimate and inconsistent with UN Resolution 242, and vowed to continue its campaign of violence. But the signing of the Oslo II Agreement in 1995 produced a drop in ratings for Hamas among Palestinians. Yassin's personal support declined from 20 percent to 14 percent, whereas Arafat's increased from 44 percent to 58 percent.

Yassin was released from jail in October 1997 in another prisoner swap between Israel and Jordan, his ill health having provided additional impetus to the negotiation. A few days later, on October 6, he returned to Gaza as a hero and was welcomed as the "king of the intifada."[126] The next day he announced: "If Israel withdraws completely from the West Bank and the Gaza Strip and it removes all of its settlements, I will make a truce with it."[127] This comment caused a rift in the organization between the military and political wings.

Though he was still recognized as the spiritual leader, Yassin's influence had waned somewhat in day-to-day affairs and practical decision making while he served his life sentence. Once he was back in person in Gaza, however, the shaykh was ready to reassert his leadership. In 1998, now contradicting some of his lieutenants, he admitted that he saw no difference between the political and military branches of Hamas: "We cannot separate the wing from the body. If we do so, the body will not be able to fly. Hamas is one body."[128]

Yassin and Jerusalem

During Yassin's period of leadership, the claim was made that Hamas did not depend on any one person, that decisions were made on a joint basis through the Unified Consultative Council *(majlis al-shura al-muwahhad).* At the same time it was readily admitted that Yassin "is the only individual in the movement who has the power to impose his personal views on others."[129] In the Hamas Charter, Yassin's ideological views are clearly expressed. Islam is where the organization "reaches for its ideology."[130] The movement

> has a comprehensive understanding and precise conceptualization of the Islamic precepts in all domains of life: concept and belief, politics and economics, education and society, jurisprudence and rule, indoctrination and training, communications and the arts, the hidden and the evident, and the rest of life.[131]

The charter makes reference to Jerusalem in the context of the Muslim history of Palestine. It draws attention to the "ideological invasion" of Muslim lands once the Crusaders had defeated Salah al-Din. "The Orientalists and missionaries" brought about the invasion. Further, they

> paved the way for the imperialist attack in which [General Edmund] Allenby claimed when he entered Jerusalem: "Now the Crusades are over;" and General Guroud [sic] stood by the tomb of Saladin and said: "We have returned, O Saladin." Imperialism helped the ideological invasion establish its roots firmly and it still does. And all that was preparation for the loss of Palestine.
>
> We must instill in the minds of Muslim generations that the Palestinian cause is a religious cause. It must be solved on this basis because Palestine contains the Islamic holy sanctuaries of the al-Aqsa Mosque and the Haram Mosque, which are inexorably linked, as long as the heavens and earth exist, to the night journey (isra) of the Prophet of God (may peace be upon him), who ascended to the heavens (miraj) from there.[132]

In an interview at his Gaza home in February 1998, Yassin indicated the impossibility of compromise over Jerusalem. He said that peace could be achieved only once all the land is returned to the Palestinian people and an independent state called Palestine is established, with Jerusalem as its capital.[133] Further, in April that year, after a period of infighting between internal elements of Hamas in which bomb maker Muhi Sharif was killed, Yassin issued a call to the Arab world that was thought to be an attempt to shore up his conflicted organization. He expressed himself in familiar terms: "We are calling upon you to pray that God will help Jerusalem be rescued from the Israeli occupying enemy."[134] At the time Yassin was on a four-month tour of eight or more Muslim countries, by the end of which he was reputed to have collected $50–300 million in Saudi Arabia and Iran for his causes.

During his stop in Syria, he said that Hamas would keep fighting Israel "until the liberation of all Palestine."[135] He added, "[T]he first quarter of the next century will witness the elimination of the Zionist entity and the establishment of the Palestinian state over the whole of Palestine."[136] The comment was consistent with the Hamas Charter's reminder to Arab countries and Islamic governments that "when the Jews occupied immaculate Jerusalem in 1967, they stood on the stairs of the blessed al-Aqsa Mosque and loudly chanted: *'Muhammad has died and left girls behind.'* "[137]

Jerusalem, then, features in the charter in the way one might expect in an ideological document based on Islamic perceptions of the city. However, one article dealing with "the people of other faiths" is couched in the language of conciliation about the future of Jewish and Christian access to the holy sites:

> In the shade of Islam it is possible for the followers of the three religions, Islam, Christianity, and Judaism, to live in peace and harmony. This peace and harmony only is possible under Islam, and the history of the past and present is the best written witness of that.
> Followers of other religions should stop fighting Islam over ruling this area, because when they rule there only is murder, punishment, and banishment. They make life hard for their own people, not to mention the followers of other religions. The past and present are full of examples to prove this.[138]

In April 2002, a spokesman for Yassin made some intriguing remarks in light of a Saudi peace plan for resolving the Arab-Israeli conflict. Isma'il Abu Shanab, a member of the five-person Executive Committee of Hamas, confirmed that he was speaking for the entire organization when he said that "the Hamas covenant calling for 'every inch of Palestine' from the Jordan River to the Mediterranean Sea is 'theoretical,' and that Hamas must now be 'practical.' "[139] He continued:

> There has been generation after generation (of war). Now there is a generation who needs to live in peace, and not worry about their safety. . . . So it is a generation that wants to practice living in peace and postpone historical issues. We speak of historical Palestine, and practical reality.

This led to consideration of the Jerusalem Question. Abu Shanab commented that a return to pre-1967 borders would mean that the Palestinians would immediately take over East Jerusalem, including the Jewish holy sites and the Western Wall. Interestingly, he did not require Palestinian control over the whole of Jerusalem. Hamas, he said, would agree to international law guaranteeing freedom of access and worship for all:

> Such a law could enforce access to worship for all the world. We would accept this. The Jews do not need to worry about this. They will have free access and be welcomed to all religious sites. We have nothing against the Jews, nothing against the Christians.

While there was speculation that the purpose of such an interview, filled as it was with concessions, was to avert a potential massive Israeli intervention in Gaza in the wake of several catastrophic suicide bombings, it nevertheless continued the retreat from inflexibility already noted. In the same way that the PLO had moved away from earlier irredentist positions, so Hamas now seemed to be willing to consider political options and practicalities. Even at the Haram, worshipers might eventually coexist with those at the Western Wall below.

Abu Shanab was assassinated by Israeli forces in August 2003 in Gaza City. Less than a month later, a similar attempt to assassinate Ahmad Yassin failed. But in March 2004 he, too, was killed in a targeted Israeli rocket attack as he exited a mosque in Gaza City.

Summary: Shaykh Ahmad Isma'il Yassin

Ahmad Yassin's identity became fused with the tenets of Islam in a particular fundamentalist form. There were other important elements that provided shape to his identity, including the death of his father when he was three, dispossession in 1948 from the family's land, exile in a Gaza refugee camp, and a critical life-changing injury at age fourteen. The capacity to sustain himself amidst terrible suffering remains a testimony to his enormous willpower and conviction.

Influenced strongly by the Muslim Brethren in his teens, he adopted the movement's religious credo to such an extent that he became a religious teacher and preacher. The new Palestinian state would be created on the foundation of Islamic fundamentalist teaching. Intertwined with his religious convictions was his acceptance of the radical teachings of the Egyptian Muslim Brethren's ideologue Sayyid Qutb, who advocated the violent overthrow of non-Islamic powers. Yassin's sympathies were made plain by his founding of the Gaza Islamic Society in support of Ayatollah Khomeini's Iranian revolution. With respect to the secular PLO and its acceptance of the two-state solution for Palestine, Yassin formed Hamas in 1987 in direct opposition, insisting that Palestine be freed from Israeli control in its entirety and be created anew as an Islamic state. Understandably Hamas's underlying religious convictions mean that Jerusalem is more than simply a potential capital city; it is at its heart a religious shrine, the place from which Muhammad ascended to heaven. Though Hamas would provide access to the city's holy sites to adherents of Judaism and Christianity, there could be no compromise in terms of the Muslim sovereignty of the city.

Stasis characterized Shaykh Yassin's relationship to the Jerusalem Question largely because of the uncompromising nature of his ideological stance (lifelong antipathy to the Zionist presence), and the unremitting opposition of the Israelis to his organization once it was identified with suicide bombings. Whatever glimmer of momentum there has been in Hamas's experience has come as a result of mollifying statements released by its leadership at strategic moments in the organization's relentless struggle with the Israelis. The possibility of compromise on the goal of an Islamic state encompassing all of mandatory Palestine will be an important element in momentum on the Jerusalem Question as far as Hamas is concerned.

Concluding Thoughts

When Katz's four types of latent forces are considered in respect of the seven Palestinian personalities reviewed in this study, it is clear that they have been mobilized in the service of the Palestinian nationalist identity as much as their Jewish/Israeli counterparts have with regard to the Zionist identity. It is evident from the details of their early life stories that emotional and behavioral conditioning to the elements of Palestinian nationalism occurred. Individual differences resulting from different emphases within families and experiences, including among other things religion, wealth, parental loss, and dispossession, account for variations in the channeling of individual energies for the Palestinian cause. But there is sufficient commonality in their conditioning to the essentials of Palestinian nationalism that the seven personalities can be placed on a continuum of Palestinian identity. In other words, all display personal identity as nationals or incipient nationals with a common history, fate, and culture (Katz's second latent force).

In all cases there is evidence of the third element: compensatory identification to resolve personal insecurities. For example, Amin al-Husayni's father died when the boy was thirteen, and by the age of seventeen, the young man had come under the compensatory influence of family friend Rashid Rida, the Muslim reformer. Amin's convictions about the interrelation of Islam and politics were formed at this critical stage. In Shuqayri's case, the death of his mother thrust him into his influential father's political, legal, and Muslim clerical circle in Acre. The strands of his future career in Palestinian political and diplomatic life were beginning to be woven together. Arafat's loss of his mother at age four resulted in a formative three-year stay with his mother's family, who lived adjacent to the Western Wall in several houses connected with the Haram and the al-Aqsa Mosque. There he became familiar with the religious and political convictions of his influential extended family members, including Amin al-Husayni. At age seven he was a participant in the 1936 Arab Revolt. When Faysal Husayni was eight, he was schooled in the Palestinian cause by Amin al-Husayni and Yasser Arafat in memory of his famous father, Abd al-Qadir al-Husayni. Ahmad Yassin's journey was filled with personal crises and compensatory ideological activities. His reaction to parental loss, dispossession, refugee life, and a crippling accident was to become, under his teachers' influence, a member of the Muslim Brethren while in his teens. Ahmad Quray', disillusioned with pan-Arabism and the outcome of the 1967 war, became an early member of al-Fateh as a way of resolving his personal dilemmas. And Hanan Ashrawi, whose free-thinking father was lost to her for four years while he was in a Jordanian prison for his political views, doubtless followed his lead in establishing her own political and socially active identity within Palestinian life.

In line with Katz's formulation, there is also instrumental involvement in Palestinian national structure to the degree that it exists. Active support for the Palestinian cause gave each of the seven personalities reason for the highest level of instrumental involvement in the national or incipient national structure.

Finally, in respect of the three original propositions, despite their diverse backgrounds these seven Arab and/or Palestinian personalities demonstrate convincing evidence. The amount and strength of evidence varies with where they are located on the time line of the past hundred years, and with their individual opportunities for expression on the Jerusalem Question. All show commitment to East Jerusalem and the relevant holy sites within the Old City and adjacent areas. All demonstrate understanding of the link between the city's symbolic and political importance in nationalist terms. All express themselves on the issue, seeking public support for their stand.

Amin al-Husyani was personally devoted to the religious and political destiny of Jerusalem within the overall framework of Palestinian nationalism. Once it became clear that Amir Faysal's monarchial pretensions in a joint Syria-Palestine would come to naught, Amin discontinued his support and launched his own campaign to renovate the Haram and its mosques as symbols to which Palestinian nationalism could gravitate. This led to public pronouncements, especially during the Wailing Wall crisis of the late 1920s, in defense of Muslim rights to the area and against Zionist encroachment. The mufti was never willing to compromise on the city's physical Muslim core.

Ahmad al-Shuqayri's upbringing under his father's devoted Muslim-clerical, Palestinian-political, and secular-legal tutelage provided him with a wealth of experience and example to draw on in his successful international diplomatic career. His rhetorical abilities from the days as a leader in the first Palestinian political party al-Istiqlal to his years in various capacities at the UN were marshaled in support of the Palestinian cause, including the resolution of the Jerusalem Question.

Yasser Arafat's commitment to the successful end to the Jerusalem impasse is surely one of the most obvious of the case studies undertaken here. From early identification with the city through his mother's Jerusalemite family of religious and political leaders, including the mufti and Abd al-Qadir al-Husayni, to his insistent, vociferous, and uncompromising public demands that East Jerusalem be the capital of the State of Palestine, Arafat never failed to make his ideological position known.

Ahmad Quray' may be a pragmatic economist and banker with a broad grasp of the realities of the Palestinian economy, but he is also personally linked with East Jerusalem and understands its emotive significance to his people and the Arab world. He has made one of the most straightforward comments on Jerusalem's centrality to Palestinian identity and nationalist aspirations: "It is the head, the heart of the Palestinian state—the heart of the Palestinian identity." He readily concedes that without resolution on East Jerusalem as the Palestinian capital, there can be no answer to the Jerusalem Question.

The evidence for Faysal al-Husayni's Jerusalem-based identity and ideological conviction about the city could hardly be stronger. With some of the deepest historical roots in Muslim Palestine and the nationalist movement, al-Husayni nonetheless represented the moderate end of the spectrum on the Jerusalem Question. Taken on balance, his adult life demonstrated that ideological conviction did not have to mean the use of violence to bring a resolution. He was willing to accept a two-state–two-capital solution before most of the other members in the PLO. His passion for the city was paramount; as he said, he would die for it—perhaps the strongest statement of any of the seven personalities regarding their identity and ideological commitment to Jerusalem.

Like Faysal al-Husayni, Hanan Ashrawi stands apart from most of the personalities reviewed here because of her capacity for independent thought and action. Her concerns are expressed on a broader canvas than most. As an academic, Christian, feminist Palestinian, she is capable of decisive, principled action. With respect to the propositions at hand, her biography provides sufficient evidence for an identity-based and ideological position on the city. She readily acknowledges East Jerusalem as the core and cornerstone of Palestinian identity and life and is eloquent in its defense.

The seventh personality occupied a position on the spectrum that was far to the right and represented extreme violence and radicalism in pursuit of a solution to the Jerusalem Question in the larger context of the Arab-Israeli conflict. Ahmad Yassin chose the path of Islamic revival as the base for his activism. While his approach created a broad net of social, educational, and welfare services, it did so with the goal of creating a fundamentalist Islamic state across the whole of pre-1948 Palestine. Accordingly Yassin's perspective on the Jerusalem Question confirms all three propositions. His identity as a fundamentalist Muslim cleric, ideologically committed to the violent teachings of the executed Egyptian Muslim Brethren leader Sayyid Qutb, meant that in a Palestinian context, East and West Jerusalem must be the capital of the state. Thus neither the centrality of the Haram nor the sovereignty of the city could ever be compromised.

The findings on all fourteen personalities in this study lead overwhelmingly to the conclusion that the identity-ideology nexus, in combination with the various interacting variables of their times, is a powerful tool in clarifying why there have been periods of both momentum and stasis on the Jerusalem Question. The implications for future momentum and resolution are taken up in the concluding chapter.

CONCLUSIONS

In his work on the role of alternative ideas in the collapse of communism in the late-twentieth-century Soviet bloc, Robert English quotes James Joll, who said of the causes of the First World War, "It is only by studying the minds of men that we shall understand the causes of anything."[1] The importance of ideas (and, by extension, of identity and ideology) in the minds of men and women underlies the present study. It has examined the formation and continued development of the identity-ideology nexus with respect to the Jerusalem Question in the life histories of fourteen Middle East personalities—all significant actors at various stages of the more-than-one-hundred-year-old Arab-Zionist conflict.

With respect to the three propositions put forward in chapter 1, the study has found (a) evidence of significant personal identification with Jerusalem during the childhood and subsequent life stages of these individuals, expressed in adulthood as the opportunity arises to confirm that identification; (b) that for both Jews/Israelis and Arabs/Palestinians, a preponderance of unfavorable interacting variables in the form of external events and conditions causes latent forces in the identity-ideology nexus regarding Jerusalem to remain quiescent, resulting in stasis over the Jerusalem Question; and (c) that for both Arabs/Palestinians and Jews/Israelis, the triggering effect of favorable interacting variables causes hitherto latent forces in the identity-ideology nexus regarding Jerusalem to become active, resulting in movement on the Jerusalem Question. Moreover, the identity-ideology framework is shown to provide a more fundamental explanation for intransigence on the Jerusalem Question than economic, security, or legal arguments can furnish. Paradoxically the framework also offers more hope for momentum and change.

In early childhood—stage three of Erikson's eight stages of identity development—"ideal prototypes" are experienced in the nuclear family. At stage five the young adolescent discovers "ideological perspectives."[2] Difficult disruptions and positive transitions at these two critical life stages have been noted in all of the biographical studies undertaken. In other words, both identity and ideology matter in a fundamental way at the personal and collective levels. In all fourteen cases the degree and depth of identification with Jerusalem is certainly impressive and has led to some new interpretations of existing materials.

First, it is generally held that the founding fathers of Zionism were agnostic or atheistic—certainly secular—and that therefore Jerusalem held no spiritual interest or connection for them. It turns out that a more careful reading of Herzl's diaries, for example, shows a man who, while an assimilated European Jew, still expressed himself with a sense of perhaps unconscious religious attachment to Judaism. The same may be said for Jabotinsky and Ben-Gurion. Correspondence with Ben-Gurion's official biographer, Shabtai Teveth, yielded a surprising corroboration of what Ben-Gurion's identity-ideology nexus would suggest in respect of his first visit to the Western Wall in 1909. This seems to be a hitherto unpublished opinion— the result of Teveth explaining to me the meaning of an unsubstantiated one-line comment in his second biographical volume, *Ben Gurion: The Burning Ground, 1886–1948.*

Second, when the State of Israel's early independence history is examined, misconceptions are found in the writings of significant commentators. More than one scholar states that a number of the Jewish/Israeli leaders were not really interested in making Jerusalem the capital throughout most of the 1940s. The notion is that it was all a last-minute reaction to the UN's renewed 1949 move for internationalization of the city. From the comments made by key players at the time and thereafter, this is shown to be a problematic explanation.

Third, another line of reasoning asserts that Yitzhak Rabin and other Israeli leaders were acting only out of political expediency when, following the 1967 war, they promoted Jerusalem as "Israel's eternal and undivided capital." Thus their pre-1967 identity and ideological nexuses go unexplored, when in fact they yield a much richer explanation. In each of these cases, glossed-over or ignored issues of identity vis-à-vis Jerusalem arise.

Fourth, impressive parallels are shown to exist between Jewish/Israeli and Palestinian leaders when the role of Jerusalem in their lives and expecta-tions is uncovered. The tendency is to think of the two sides as diametrically opposite foes. Certainly they have many issues that conflict. But one surprising finding here is the similarity of the cases.

In some respects in Yasser Arafat we see echoes of Ben-Gurion: the implacable, single-minded warrior of lifelong influence, equally dedicated to Jerusalem as capital. In the intellectual, maximalist, militaristic, youth-oriented and heart-diseased Jabotinsky, we may recognize Hamas's ascetic, frail, socially dedicated ideologue, Ahmad Yassin. The pragmatic businessman-politician, hawk-turned-dove Shimon Peres and the moderate banker and longtime Arafat supporter Ahmad Quray' share not only these similarities, but also directors' seats on the board of the Peres Center for Peace—and, despite their dovish tendencies, exhibit equivalent intransigence over some of their respective communities' needs in Jerusalem.

The degree to which all these fourteen personalities speak of the centrality of Jerusalem to their cause is striking. Pragmatic men and women, freedom fighters, people of action, express—even given a successful working out of practical modalities in the peace process—that without the resolution of the Jerusalem Question, there can be no peace. It is more than merely a practical matter.

But it is the identity-ideology nexus in combination with the concept of interacting variables that has provided visibility into how identity and ideology affect outcomes, so that stasis is replaced by movement to the benefit of one party or the other, or both. The dynamics of these interactions explain why there is change on the Jerusalem Question at different junctures, and they are instructive as they relate to future opportunities to resolve the continuing impasse. As mentioned throughout, stasis is characterized by the unfavorable interaction of external events and conditions, causing latent identity and ideological imperatives to remain dormant. Evidence of proposition 2 is found in the following representative examples.

Jewish/Israeli:

- Herzl's futile efforts to persuade the sultan to relinquish the Old City to the Jews in 1896
- Weizmann's failure to purchase the Western Wall directly from the Maghribi Arabs in 1918
- Weizmann's unsuccessful attempts to persuade Lord Balfour to "hand over" the Wall to the Jews in 1918
- Ben-Gurion's failed military campaign to capture all of Jerusalem (West and East) in 1948
- The Israeli cabinet's rejection of Ben-Gurion's attempt to initiate a new campaign to capture East Jerusalem in 1948
- Moshe Dayan's unsuccessful bargaining with King Abdullah in 1950 for Israeli sovereignty over the Jewish Quarter and the Western Wall and safe access to Mount Scopus and the Jewish cemetery on the Mount of Olives

Arab/Palestinian:

- The mufti Amin al-Husayni's unsuccessful 1931 campaign to create a Muslim university in Jerusalem in continuity with his promotion of Muslim Jerusalem's holiness and of Muslim religious rights at the Western Wall

- The All-Palestine Government's failure to attain the goal of Jerusalem as capital of the Palestinian state in 1949
- Yasser Arafat's inability to come to a compromise agreement with Ehud Barak on the sovereignty of the Haram/Temple Mount at the Camp David II summit in 2000

When there is movement, on the other hand, it appears to result from a sudden dislocation of current conditions that in turn provide a significant opportunity for expression of latent imperatives, held in check until the breakpoint. In most cases of movement in the long-standing conflict, the presence of force and the lack of effective outside/international intervention were crucial to the gaining of new ground and shifting possession of territory. Sometimes overwhelming threat of territorial loss, elite unity, and serendipitous opportunity also played a role. Taken together, these interacting variables appear to be the triggers that activated latent identity and ideological forces and brought movement to the Jerusalem Question at various times, favoring one side or the other. Thus evidence of proposition 3 is found in the following representative examples.

Jewish/Israeli:

- Ben-Gurion's declaration of Jewish Jerusalem as capital of the State of Israel in 1949
- The 1967 Israeli capture and annexation of East Jerusalem, including the Old City
- Menachem Begin's 1980 reconfirmation of "united" Jerusalem as Israel's "eternal" capital

Arab:

- The capture of Jerusalem by Caliph Omar's forces in 637/38 and the rendering of the city as a Muslim holy enclave

Parallels between personalities on the two sides in the conflict were noted earlier. In a further example of parallelism that emerged in the research, Omar's cleansing of the sacred site in the seventh century, and his setting of the direction of prayer and construction of a mosque, had its equivalent in Israel's capture of the Western Wall and the creation of a broad open plaza for worshipers. There was even a parallel with Islamic prophecy of the end time. In an adaptation of kabbalistic teaching from the nineteenth century by Abraham Isaac Kook (chief rabbi 1921–35), the end of days was being hastened by the coming of the secular Zionists, and Jerusalem was once more central to Jewish messianic hopes.[3] Observed through this prism, the capture of the Wall heralded the Messiah's coming.

However, the focus of efforts to bring about resolution in respect of Jerusalem is on achieving positive outcomes for both Palestinians and Israelis. During the past century, the momentum has seesawed between the two sides. For peace and reconciliation to be effected, there must be movement favorable to both parties. While some of the factors identified in the stasis-movement continuum of the Jerusalem Question anticipate that latent aspects of identity and ideology will continue to exist, other factors will have to change significantly. For example, overwhelming force must give way to mutual security, and territorial possession to new arrangements regarding sovereignty over the respective holy sites.

An encouraging beginning on the long road to resolving the Jerusalem Question arose from the PLO's 1988 decision to engage in the strategy of negotiation, renouncing violence as a means of achieving liberation and recognizing Israel's right to exist. After decades of mutual implacability, it became possible for the two sides to achieve recognition of each other and to actively pursue peace. The peace process that resulted invites analysis in terms of interacting variables that could yet produce a final resolution.

By 1993 the secret Oslo talks were under way, but the Jerusalem Question was kept off the agenda at Israel's insistence. The Palestinians agreed that in order to make progress with the higher priority of establishing the rudiments of a Palestinian state, more difficult issues could be left for final-status talks. Having Israel's agreement to limited independence, with territorial concessions in the form of Gaza and Jericho, allowed the Palestinians to postpone the Jerusalem Question. Just as Ben-Gurion had been willing to swallow temporarily the bitter pill of Jerusalem's proposed internationalization in order to gain international recognition for the State of Israel in 1948, Arafat was also willing to defer the issue of Palestinian sovereignty in Jerusalem. Neither Ben-Gurion nor Arafat denied issues of identity and ideology with respect to Jerusalem; they simply suppressed them, allowing the interactive variable of potential statehood to dominate. But their willingness to engage in an interim constructive series of negotiations required each to shift his parameters of identity and ideology to some degree. Though the issue of Jerusalem was deferred in the Oslo talks, what happened during the process in terms of possible creative solutions meant that the taboo of Jerusalem had been broken. Epistemic communities on both sides began to open the way forward on the most difficult issues. Discussion and compromise became possible, even if deferred for final-status negotiations. Though the Oslo process was eventually declared dead in the wake of the al-Aqsa Intifada, the fact that so much was put on the table by both sides prior to and at Camp David II and Taba meant that the basis for agreement had at least been established. With respect to Jerusalem, Menachem Klein has written that the 1995 Abu Mazen–Beilin plan for the resolution of the Jerusalem Question lies in waiting for the right moment.[4] What was achieved in Oslo, Camp David II and Taba provides further evidence of the movement described by proposition 3, even though the final resolution on Jerusalem remains elusive. In each of these three attempts at furthering the peace process, interacting variables favorable to both sides produced the desire to move toward compromise, thereby releasing latent identifications with the city. The fact that each side recognized what some researchers had already discovered—that Jerusalem signified different things to the respective communities[5]—meant that previously implacably held positions on the city's inviolability fell away to some degree.

Hope for the Future

How ideas are laid down in the human brain and become part of identity and ideology is an important aspect of this study. How identities and ideologies can change is central to the resolution of problems such as the Jerusalem Question. In his seminal work on identity formation, Erikson emphasized the lifelong influence of the example and teaching of parental and/or authority figures during early life and adolescence. His "epigenetic principle" addressed "the unfolding of the genetically social character of the human individual" in interaction with the social environment. Though the individual's identity is most malleable in the early and adolescent years, when five of eight psychosocial crises occur, Erikson stressed that identity modification continues throughout the life cycle. In what may seem a paradox, Erikson wrote that even radical change is possible for the well-established identity.[6] In fact, it is the inner strength of the well-established identity that allows for such change to take place.

Significantly, the feedback loop represented by the epigenetic principle now has a twenty-first-century parallel in research findings in the neuroscience field. The emerging model of brain function echoes Erikson's conceptualization of identity formation, where already-existing individual readiness for each psychosocial crisis interacts with the social world. In this study the term "identity-ideology nexus" was chosen to describe the theoretical framework.

If another concept were to be chosen from the neuroscience field to describe the relationship between identity and ideology at the individual level, it could well be "the self-designing self." Peggy La Cerra and Roger Bingham observe that "adaptive representational networks" in the brain have "combinatorial properties [leading to] the creation of selves and personalities," making us "unique by design."[7] However, since the term "self" has become the synonym for identity in the psychoanalytic field and its use here would not resonate so well with the uses of identity and ideology in the international relations field, the "identity-ideology nexus" is preferred.

The perspective on human nature that is now developing within neuro-science is causing a radical overhaul of another one-hundred-year-old debate—that between nature and nurture. The mapping of the human genome has forced reconsideration of the relationship of heredity to environment in human development. Genes "predetermine the broad structure of the brain," but it seems they also "absorb formative experiences, react to social cues, and even run memory."[8] That is to say, it is no longer nature *versus* nurture, but a sophisticated mutuality. The feedback loop describes nature's relationship with nurture in a more precise way. It is now nature *via* nurture.[9]

As noted earlier, these findings about the neural plasticity of the brain provide greater visibility into its workings, and this in turn has implications for all aspects of human behavior. And as one observer writes, this new model of plasticity "seems crucial if our new understanding of human nature is to inform public policy."[10] It is the possibility of modification in the structures of the adult brain that makes this new finding so important to the case at hand—the resolution of the Jerusalem Question, which is a matter of public policy. Behavior modification studies have shown that rewiring of the brain is possible through self-directed action.[11] How such rewiring might be achieved where political impasses rest on deep-seated issues of identity and ideology is hinted at by Massachusetts Institute of Technology psychologist Steven Pinker. He observes that the new discoveries in neuroscience explain "what makes us what we are" and also invite us to "ponder who we want to be."[12] Identity asks and answers the question "Who am I?" But identity awareness is only the starting point in resolving intercommunal problems. Far more significant is what Pinker touches on when he speaks of "who we want to be." The answer to the question "Who should I be?" is the sine qua non of the resolution of any problem where modification of identity and ideology is essential. Initially this approach to the Jerusalem Question may seem to some idealistic, unrealistic, or imprac-tical. But as Steven Spiegel and David Pervin observe, these are precisely the words that would have been used with regard to the PLO-Israeli volte-face of the 1990s had it been suggested as a real possibility prior to its unveiling.[13] The experience of significant shifts in apparently entrenched identities and ideologies gives hope for the future.

In 2006 the Jerusalem Question is the source of endless commentary and mind-numbing perplexity as the Arab-Israeli conflict continues to challenge world leaders and diplomats and to destroy ordinary men, women, and chil-dren who lead their daily lives in harm's way. Some leaders, such as former Jerusalem deputy mayor Meron Benvenisti, have concluded that the con-flict is an "insoluble but manageable" problem, because it involves "issues of identity, absolute justice, clash of affinity to the same homeland, and conflicting myths."[14]

With respect to the Jerusalem Question, the results of two studies by Jerome Segal et al.[15] offer some hope. These researchers found that while questions about the negotiability of Jerusalem as a whole elicited rejection of any compromise on sovereignty from Israelis and Palestinians alike, questions about which areas of Jerusalem are the most important to the different population groups produced a different picture. Forty-five percent of Israeli Jews "would seriously consider Palestinian sovereignty over Arab settlements and villages previously in the West Bank and now within the borders of Jerusalem." On the other hand, a majority of Palestinians would give serious consideration to a proposal "in which West Jerusalem would be under Israeli sovereignty and East Jerusalem would be under Palestinian sovereignty, with a special arrangement for Israeli control of the Jewish neighborhoods in East Jerusalem."[16] While the Old City was not included in the questions that led to these particular conclusions, the results of this research suggest that because "Yerushalayim/Al-Quds" means different things to different people, compromise on sovereignty in more peripheral areas of the city may be possible.

As to the Old City and its holy sites, however, opinions are far less flexible. The most important areas to both peoples "as part of Jerusalem" are the Temple Mount and the Mount of Olives, and the Old City itself, unless it is disaggregated. The Western Wall is "very important" or "important" to 99 percent of the Israelis, while the al-Aqsa Mosque and the Dome of the Rock are "very important" or "important" to 100 percent of the Palestinians. Here again is the heart of the identity-ideology clash over Jerusalem. Ceding sovereignty in these areas seems impossible at this point. How can the impasse be overcome?

Political Zionism appropriated several elements from the Jewish religion, including obviously the noun "Zion" (both land and city), for its key symbols. According to Baruch Kimmerling, "despite Israel's image as a secular state, most residents are *not* nonreligious, even if they *do not* define themselves as 'religious' "[17] (emphasis added). Aspects of identity common to Judaism and Jewish national history continue to provide unity in the face of Arab opposition. Hence the crescendo of emotion across the Israeli and Jewish spectrum from observant to atheist following the Israeli capture of the Western Wall in 1967.

On the Palestinian side, whether Muslim or Christian (and the majority is, of course, Muslim), religion also plays a role. Though Palestinian religious affiliation is not coincident with national identity, the surveys conducted by Segal et al. indicate the depth of the Palestinian religious feeling for non-Jewish locations in the Old City.[18] The following sites are rated as "very important" by high percentages of Palestinians: Christian Quarter of the Old City (47 percent); Islamic Quarter of the Old City (85 percent);

al-Aqsa Mosque and Dome of the Rock (95 percent); Mount of Olives (66 percent); al-Haram al-Sharif (94 percent). Understandably, 96 percent of the "very religious" rate Jerusalem as "very important to me personally," but the rating remains high (78 percent) for the "not religious."

In the context of identity and ideology, overcoming the impasse over the Jerusalem Question requires deeper understanding on the leadership and public levels of at least two central issues:

- religious origins
- ideology as an identity-securing interpretative system that is nevertheless subject to change

With these thoughts in mind, then, it is unreasonable to suggest that identities and ideologies are destined to clash in perpetuity, and that they can therefore only be "managed" and never resolved.

As English has shown of the Soviet Union, the process of identity modification often begins at the epistemic community level. A first step, then, in resolving the Jerusalem Question would be to draw together a group of experts in identity formation and modification, including neuroscientists, psychologists, and cognitive theorists. They would interact with leaders and dispute-resolution team members from the Palestinian and Israeli sides, together with outside facilitators (likely representing the United States and the EU). The purpose would be to lead Palestinian and Israeli actors in self-understanding about the role that identity and ideology play and have played in the conflict over Jerusalem. It is at the leadership level that such education and introspection must begin.

Three scholars, one Israeli and two Palestinians, are among the few in their communities who have broken the mold in efforts at reconciliation and identity modification. Identity modification is one of the goals of the Israeli organization Peace Now. According to political scientist Menachem Klein, Peace Now seeks to persuade the protagonists on both sides of the conflict to change their identities, so that the Jerusalem Question, among other things, may come to resolution.[19]

On the Palestinian side, the president of Al-Quds University, Sari Nuseibeh, offers a way to open discussion on the Temple Mount/Haram dilemma and religious origins. He explains that for Muhammad there was but one faith, not three monotheistic systems. He viewed Judaism, Christianity, and Islam as manifestations of this primary religion in their own time. Seeking out commonality through mutual respect of origins, Nuseibeh writes:

[T]he more we see ourselves as belonging to different religions—the more monotheism is a tritheism—the harder the chances for reconciliation, and the more Jerusalem will be a potential source of diffusion and destruction. . . . It will be a source of unity, on the other hand, and will shine as the true jewel it is, if it made [*sic*] us aware of the unity of our faith. If the unity of our faith is properly perceived as I have described, then our respective claims on Jerusalem as our political capitals can be regarded as a celebration of this unity, rather than as a point of selfish contention between two ethnocentric tribes.[20]

For his part, the late Edward Said introduced what he described as "the Andalusian model," after his joint cultural project, the "West-Eastern Divan Workshop and Orchestra," founded in 1999 with the Argentine-Israeli pianist and conductor Daniel Barenboim. According to Barenboim, he and Said shared the view "[t]hat there is no military solution in the Middle East, either strategically or morally."[21] Instead they brought together young people through music, creating orchestras where Palestinian, Israeli, Syrian, Lebanese, Egyptian, and other musicians perform in workshops. Their relationship encouraged them to find alternative paths to peace and mutual understanding. The project is located in Seville, which with its history of Jewish, Christian, and Muslim mutual tolerance serves as the inspiration for what Said saw as hope in the Israeli-Palestinian conflict. He readily acknowledged that he had no answer to the ongoing Palestinian-Israeli asymmetry of power[22] and found a new model in the mutuality that cultural interface can bring ("It doesn't pretend to be building bridges. . . . But there it is, a paradigm of coherent and intelligent living together.").[23] Referencing the connection with identity modification, Said noted in a published exchange with Barenboim that in their respective work as performer and interpreter of literature, they both had to "accept the idea that one is putting one's own identity to the side in order to explore the 'other.' "[24] At one of the workshops, an Egyptian attendee sitting next to an Israeli performer said, "Images can be very misleading. The suicide bomber brings to mind a certain image, so does the military operation. But these must not be fixed in one's brain."[25] Another participant was a Palestinian-Israeli pianist discovered by Said in Nazareth. He said, "The way we talk to each other is as important as concrete matters like withdrawal or dividing Jerusalem. The orchestra is an attempt to create a new reality in which this talk would be so normal that the media would have little interest in coming here." In memory of Said, 100 of the musicians performed for the first time in Ramallah in August 2005. This kind of project is a beginning of the recognition that change begins individually in the heart—a rewiring of the brain and its images. It is a small start, but toward the end of his life Said brought forward no other possibility, despite his tireless pursuit of justice for the dispossessed Palestinian people.[26] Said emphasized the need for such healing himself when, after discussing his Andalusian model, he descended into an acrimonious exchange with pro-Israeli members of the audience following a lecture at a California university campus in February 2003. He thus demonstrated an apparent inability to overcome his own deeply held identity and ideology, despite his obvious desire to find a road to peace. It is exactly such ambiguities that, when amplified to a national level, suggest that a workable solution to the impasse is likely to remain elusive unless identity awareness programs are instituted.

If identity and ideology can be modified at the national level, beginning with the leadership on both sides of the conflict, there can be realistic hope for change. But this will be challenging. For instance, in the case of Yasser Arafat, according to U.S. peace-process special adviser Dennis Ross, it was difficult to negotiate. "Here's a man," Ross said, "who's not able to give up the notion of conflict, because struggle is such an essential part of his life's definition." Ross's approach therefore centered on finding "an objective that [was] less than the total resolution of conflict."[27] In other words, Arafat's identity was defined by struggle. When there was no struggle for him, there was identity conflict. And since it appears that Arafat could not function well without struggle, he created struggle to resolve the identity crisis he felt when there was nothing to fight against. The answer to this kind of difficulty in dispute resolution is not gradualism, however—attempting to slowly persuade a man against his will—but rather the leadership of negotiators who grasp how identity can be modified.[28]

This examination of identity and ideology began with observations from some of the latest scholarship on the relationship of identity and foreign policy in the Middle East. That work also provides grist for this study's conclusion. Summarizing, Steven Saideman notes that "[e]lites should consider how their imaginations are constrained by their identities and by those of their country." He adds that they also should seek to understand the role of communal identities in other countries. This, he says, would help leaders in knowing how "to manipulate situations so that identities leading to favorable outcomes increase in salience." But he concludes, "This is not easy," because the causal mechanism linking identity and foreign policy is not clear.[29]

While political manipulation is certainly possible within the identity dynamic, and Ross's comment ("Every negotiation is about manipulation.")[30] notwithstanding, it is surely one of the weakest links in the process of any potential identity change. The kind of meaningful identity modification that is necessary in the case of Jerusalem can begin only with individual identity and then proceed to the collective level. The research in this study highlights the fact that identity formation is a delicate and highly personal process. We defend who we have become. Elite manipulation runs the risk of failing precisely because it is manipulation.

On the other hand, asking and answering the question "Who am I?" with the help of qualified educators and negotiators would be a precursor to understanding the boundaries and limitations of individual identities. Such guidance could lead to more willingness to examine and change the aspects of identity that have perpetuated conflicts such as that between Israelis and Palestinians for far too long.

But as Pinker notes, in reality the question, "Who am I?" is only the beginning of the discussion. If there is to be hope for resolution and reconciliation in any of the world's identity-based conflicts, then "Who am I?" must lead to the much more important question—"Who should I be?" This is about initiating a *process* by which leaders and publics come to understand the role of identity and ideology in their lives. Because the identity-ideology nexus is not easily self-understood, it requires a process of education and introspection to bring its reality and consequences to the surface. The change of heart that would result at the individual identity-securing level, in the personal identity-ideology nexus, is the first essential step to broad political change.

NOTES

Introduction

1. Telhami and Barnett, *Identity and Foreign Policy*, 2.
2. Kissinger, *Foreign Policy*, 26, 165; "Does America Need a Foreign Policy?"
3. Heikal, *Secret Channels*, xi, 95–97.
4. Ashrawi, "Guarded Optimist," 90.
5. Brand, *Palestinians in the Arab World*, 149–85; Lynch, "Jordan's Identity and Interests," 26–57; Barnett, "Israeli Identity," 58–87.
6. Said, *Politics of Dispossession*, 14. Brand, "Palestinians and Jordanians," 46–61.
7. Wallerstein, "Ego Identity Reconsidered," 229, 234. One of the few who acknowledge Erikson's contribution to the study of international affairs is psychiatrist and political psychologist Jerrold Post, who notes that "[t]he psychoanalytic framework of Erik Erikson ([1950] 1963), which relates personality development to the cultural context, is extremely helpful as a model. It emphasizes the intimate dynamic relationship between the developing personality and the environment . . . .Before even considering the particular circumstances surrounding the development of the future leader, however, one must understand thoroughly the culture, especially the political culture, in which the leader's family was embedded" (Post, "Assessing Leaders," 71). See also Post, "Seasons of a Leader's Life" and "Dreams of Glory."
8. See Sasson Sofer, "Invisibility of Ideology," 493–94; Mullins, "Ideology," 500–01.
9. Huntington, *Clash of Civilizations*.
10. Fukuyama, *End of History*.
11. Huntington, "After September 11," 1.
12. See Plamenatz, *Ideology*, 17–23.
13. Mullins, "Ideology," 498–510.
14. Alexander, "Jerusalem as the *Omphalos*," 104–19; Armstrong, *History of Jerusalem*, first color plate.
15. See Ezekiel 38:12 (Septuagint, c. third to first century B.C.E.), where the Greek word *omphalos* describes Jerusalem's location in the world. According to the NIV Study Bible's comment on this verse, "[t]he Hebrew for 'center' also means 'navel,' a graphic image for the belief that Israel was the vital link between God and the world . . . Since the Hebrew for 'land' can also mean 'earth,' theologically Jerusalem is both the center of the land of Israel and the center of the earth" (Grand Rapids, Mich.: Zondervan Bible Publishers, 1985).
16. Friedland and Hecht, "Changing Places," 204.
17. Sharkansky, *Governing Jerusalem*, 20.

Chapter 1:   The Jerusalem Question

1. Cattan, *Jerusalem*, 11.
2. Yehoshua, "Jerusalem," 447.
3. Karmi, "Palestinians Also Lose Jerusalem?" 16.
4. Savir, interview by author.
5. Quray', "Peace Talk," 60.
6. Peres, "Peace Be Within Your Walls," 10.
7. Said, *Politics of Dispossession*, 15, quoting Erikson, *Young Man Luther*, 14.
8. Fitzgerald, *Metaphors of Identity*, 3.
9. *Encyclopaedia Britannica*, 15th ed., Macropaedia, s.v. "ideology."
10. Sasson Sofer, "Invisibility of Ideology," 490.
11. See Mullins, "Ideology"; Sasson Sofer, "Invisibility of Ideology"; Cassels, *Ideology*, 1–8. In the 1990s interest in ideas, ideology, and identity became more pronounced (see Fitzgerald, *Metaphors of Identity*; Katzenstein, *Culture of National Security*; Dittmer and Kim, *China's Quest*; Kull, *Burying Lenin*; English, *Russia*).
12. Morgenthau, *Politics Among Nations*, 5–7, 110–13; "[T]he power drives of nations take hold of ideal principles and transform them into ideologies in order to disguise, rationalize, and justify themselves" (231).
13. Sasson Sofer, "Invisibility of Ideology"; *Zionism*; Cassels, *Ideology*.
14. Sasson Sofer, "Invisibility of Ideology," 490–91.
15. Sasson Sofer, *Zionism*, 4–5, 357.
16. Cassels, *Ideology*, xi, 8, 6–7.
17. See Hirsch, Housen-Couriel, and Lapidoth, *Whither Jerusalem?*
18. Olivas, *Holy City of Jerusalem*. Listed works are in Arabic, Dutch, English, French, German, Hebrew, Latin, Italian, Spanish, and Turkish. Most of the entries are for literature published in the past thirty years.
19. Elon, *Jerusalem*, 34, 249.
20. Gilbert, *Jerusalem in the Twentieth Century*, 37.
21. Benvenisti, *Jerusalem: The Torn City*, quoted in Gilbert, *Jerusalem in the Twentieth Century*, 320.
22. Wasserstein, interview by author.
23. Ibid.
24. Friedland and Hecht, *To Rule Jerusalem*, 489.
25. Lustick, "Reinventing Jerusalem," 57.
26. Brecher, *Decisions*, 24.
27. Ibid., 18 (Brecher's emphasis).
28. Ibid.
29. Ibid, 30, 52.
30. Brecher, *Decisions*, 19, citing "Israel's Proposal" in *Peace of Jerusalem*, 5–17.
31. Lustick, "Reinventing Jerusalem," 57.
32. Brecher, *Decisions*, 14–15.
33. Lustick, "Fetish of Jerusalem."
34. Brecher, *Decisions*, 9.
35. Vertzberger, *World in Their Minds*, 120, 132.
36. Jarausch, *After Unity*, 4.
37. English, *Russia*, 6.
38. Mullins, "Ideology," 503–04.

39. Hemmer and Katzenstein, "No NATO in Asia?" 577.
40. Fearon and Wendt, "Rationalism vs. Constructivism," 57–58.
41. Wallerstein, "Ego Identity Reconsidered," 240–41. See also Schwartz, "Mechanisms of Change."
42. Erikson, *Identity*, 54, 11.
43. Blakeslee, "Brain Power: The Search for Origins" [emphasis added].
44. See Winter and Sivan, *War and Remembrance*, 12; Stiles, "Neural Plasticity"; Schwartz and Begley, *Mind and the Brain*, 88–91. For more detail on the capability of the brain to modify itself physically through experience, see also La Cerra and Bingham, *Origin of Minds*, 5, 17; Flanagan, *Problem of the Soul*, 260–61; Quartz and Sejnowski, *Liars, Lovers and Heroes*, 41; and Ridley, *Nature Via Nurture*, 163–233.
45. See Hemmer and Katzenstein, "No NATO in Asia?" 575–607; Katzenstein, Keohane and Krasner, "Study of World Politics," 645–85; and Fearon and Wendt, "Rationalism vs. Constructivism," 52–72.
46. Gourevitch, "Interacting Variables," 71.
47. Ibid. See also McClelland and Rumelhart, "Interactive Activation Model."
48. Gourevitch, "Interacting Variables," 76.
49. See English, *Russia*, 2–3, 5–6, 241 n. 2.
50. Sasson Sofer, "Invisibility of Ideology," 514.
51. Cassels, *Ideology*, 245.
52. Rashid Khalidi, *Palestinian Identity*, 21, 18, 13.
53. Ibid., 9–62.
54. The writings of Ernest Gellner *(Nations and Nationalism)*, Eric J. Hobsbawm *(Nations and Nationalism Since 1870)*, Eric J. Hobsbawm and Terence Ranger, eds. *(The Invention of Tradition)*, Anthony D. Smith *(The Ethnic Origin of Nations)*, and Benedict Anderson *(Imagined Communities)* inform Khalidi's approach to the construction of national identity in *Palestinian Identity*, x–xii, 211–12 nn. 3–12).
55. Bloom, *Identity*.
56. Mullins, "Ideology."
57. See Coles, *Erikson Reader*, 19.
58. Fitzgerald, *Metaphors of Identity*, 3. See also Jarausch, *After Unity*, 4–5; Gleason, "Identifying Identity," 910–31.
59. Gleason, "Identifying Identity," 910.
60. Erikson, *Identity*, 109, 153, 169.
61. Mullins, "Ideology," 510.
62. Erikson, *Identity*, 168, 173.
63. Bloom, *Identity*, 23, x, 23.
64. Ibid., 47, 110, 103–04.
65. Lasswell, *Psychopathology and Politics*, 7–8.
66. Erikson, *Identity*, 128, 130, 156–57.
67. Erikson, *Insight and Responsibility*, 90.
68. Wallerstein, "Ego Identity Reconsidered," 235–36.
69. Erikson, *Insight and Responsibility*, 96.
70. Daniel Katz, "Nationalism and Strategies," 365–69.
71. Bloom, *Identity*, 20.
72. Erikson, *Identity*, 169, emphasis added.

73. Ibid., 168–69.
74. Bloom, *Identity*, 23.
75. Mullins, "Ideology," 510.
76. Ibid., 509.
77. Bloom, *Identity*, 52.
78. Ibid., 24.
79. Ibid., xi.
80. Post, "Assessing Leaders," 70, 102–04.
81. For another example, see Kimhi, Even and Post, "Yasir Arafat," Methodology.

Chapter 2: Alternative Explanations

1. Kinglake, *Eothen*; Lowthian, *Recent Visit to Jerusalem*; Kitto, *Modern Jerusalem*; Twain, *Innocents Abroad*.
2. Robinson, *Biblical Researches in Palestine*, 1: 418.
3. Sharkansky, *Governing Jerusalem*, 68.
4. Naim Sofer, "Political Status of Jerusalem," 78–90.
5. Sharkansky, *Governing Jerusalem*, 76.
6. As of 2001–02, 8% of Jerusalem employees were engaged in the industrial sector, compared to 10% in Tel-Aviv–Yafo and 17% in Israel. See Choshen and Shahar, *Statistical Yearbook: 2002/2003*.
7. Ibid.
8. Choshen, *Statistical Yearbook: 2005*.
9. Choshen and Shahar, *Statistical Yearbook: 2002/2003*, 17.
10. Israel Ministry of Foreign Affairs mailer, "Sharon Announces NIS 280 m. Jerusalem Development Plan."
11. Sharkansky, *Governing Jerusalem*, 17.
12. Dumper, *Politics of Sacred Space*, 154–55.
13. Peres, *New Middle East*.
14. Ze'ev (Benny) Begin, interview.
15. See Heller, *Israeli Security Policy*, 9.
16. Ze'ev Begin, *A Zionist Stand*, 38.
17. Cited in Widlanski, *Can Israel Survive?* 148.
18. Aronson, "Israeli Settlements," 81.
19. Ibid., 82.
20. Ibid.
21. Chabin, "The Not So Wild, Wild West (Bank)."
22. Ibid.
23. Klein, *Jerusalem*, 25.
24. Nahshon, "City Upon the Hill."
25. Kashriel, interview by author.
26. Nahshon, "Burger King."
27. Kashriel, interview by author.
28. Barak, "Alternate Direction."
29. *Judea Electronic Magazine*, "Barak Changes Wye Maps."
30. Eldar, "Dispute over Ma'aleh Adumim."
31. Moratinos, "The Taba Negotiations."
32. Sontag, "Quest for Mideast Peace."

33. Between September 2000 and July 2002, suicide bombers killed more than 80 people in Jerusalem. See Reuters, "Israeli Defense Chief Unveils Jerusalem Fence Plan."
34. See Makovsky, "Barak's Separate Peace."
35. Reuters, "Israeli Defense Chief."
36. BBC News, "Israel Starts Building Jerusalem Fence."
37. Reuters, "Israeli Defense Chief."
38. BBC News, "Israel Approves Jerusalem Barrier."
39. Gold, "Defensible Borders for Israel."
40. Ibid.
41. Gold, *Jerusalem*, 3.
42. Lapidoth, interview. See also Quigley's comment in Bundy, "Legal Approaches," 48.
43. Hassan Bin Talal, *A Study on Jerusalem* (1979), 27, 29–31, 39–40, cited in Lapidoth, *Whither Jerusalem?* 21.
44. Bundy, "Legal Approaches," 48.
45. Brownlie, *Principles of Public International Law*, 651.
46. Bundy, "Legal Approaches," 46.
47. Quigley, "Jerusalem in International Law," 31.
48. *Reports of the International Court of Justice* (1975), 150, cited in Bundy, "Legal Approaches," 46.
49. Bundy, "Legal Approaches," 46.
50. Quigley, "Jerusalem in International Law," 38.
51. Musallam, *Struggle for Jerusalem*, 7.
52. Savir, interview by author.
53. Bundy, "Legal Approaches," 50.
54. Lapidoth, interview by author.
55. ABC Radio National, "Divided Jerusalem: A Conversation with Bernard Wasserstein."
56. Savir, interview by author.
57. Quray', interview by author.

Chapter 3:   The Meaning and Significance of Jerusalem to the Jewish, Israeli, Arab, and Palestinian Peoples

1. Ps. 137:5–6, New King James Version (Nashville: Thomas Nelson, 1982).
2. Israel Ministry of Foreign Affairs, "Hatikva: The National Anthem."
3. Benvenisti, *City of Stone*, 53.
4. Ps. 48:2, NKJV.
5. Buber, *On Zion*, xvii.
6. Elon, *Jerusalem*, 15.
7. 2 Sam. 24:18–25, NKJV.
8. Elon, *Jerusalem*, 34, 60.
9. Buber, *On Zion*, 33.
10. Schölch, "Jerusalem in the 19th Century," 230.
11. Tibawi, "Jerusalem," 28–30.
12. Elon, *Jerusalem*, 89.

13. Sachar, *History of Israel*, 673.
14. Sprinzak, *Israel's Radical Right*, 40.
15. Benvenisti, *Conflicts and Contradictions*, 10.
16. Gur, *Battle for Jerusalem*, 359, 369, 370.
17. Gorenberg, *End of Days*, 100, 260n, quoting Nadav Shragai, "Rabbi, Stop," *Ha'aretz*, December 31, 1997.
18. Ibid., 100.
19. Benvenisti, *Jerusalem: The Torn City*, 288.
20. Yehoshua, "For a Jewish Border."
21. Ibrahim Mattar, "From Palestinian to Israeli," 59; Said, "Projecting Jerusalem," 6; Rashid Khalidi, "Transforming the Face of the Holy City," Part 2.
22. Meron Benvenisti, *Facing the Closed Wall: Divided and United Jerusalem* (in Hebrew, Jerusalem, 1973), 136, quoted in Elon, *Jerusalem*, 93.
23. Eban, "Freedom and International Morality," 21–22.
24. Hertzberg, "Jerusalem and Zionism," 168.
25. Qur'an 17:1.
26. "[*Hijrah*] has not simply the negative meaning of a flight from Mecca, but the positive one of seeking protection by settling in a place other than one's own. In later Islamic centuries, it would be used to mean the abandonment of a pagan or wicked community for one living in accordance with the moral teaching of Islam" (Hourani, *History of the Arab Peoples*, 17).
27. Duri, "Early Islamic Period," 105.
28. Qur'an 2:144.
29. Duri, "Early Islamic Period," 105.
30. Tibawi, "Jerusalem," 14.
31. The date is the subject of considerable debate, and correspondingly there is a huge literature (see Rashid Khalidi, "Transforming the Face of the Holy City"). Omar's forces besieged the city in 637, and it appears to have succumbed in late 637 or early 638.
32. Jarrar, "Two Islamic Construction Plans," 380.
33. Ibid., 381. Jarrar mentions Muhammad's prophecy of six signs before the Day of Judgment, as recorded by one of the Prophet's companions, 'Awf ibn Malik. The second sign was the conquest of Bayt al-Maqdis, or Jerusalem (Mujir al-Din al-Hanbali, *al-'Uns al-Jalil bi Tarikh al-Quds wa al-Khalil*, 1:244, cited in "Two Islamic Construction Plans," 536 n. 1).
34. Duri, "Early Islamic Period," 105, 126.
35. al-Hadi, "Introduction."
36. Duri, "Early Islamic Period," 109.
37. Armstrong, *History of Jerusalem*, 240.
38. Hasson, "Muslim Literature," 182.
39. Quoted in Tibawi, "Jerusalem," 19.
40. Ibid.
41. W.M. de Slane, *Ibn Khallikan's Biographical Dictionary Translated from the Arabic* (Paris, 1843), 2:636–37, quoted in Little, "Ayyubids and Mamluks," 178.
42. Amitai-Preiss, *Mongols and Mamluks*, 39–45; Keegan, *History of Warfare*, 35.
43. Asali, "Jerusalem Under the Ottomans," 203–04.
44. See Schölch, "Jerusalem in the 19th Century," 238, 229.
45. See Andrew Wheatcroft, *Ottomans*, 167.

46. See Schölch, "Jerusalem in the 19th Century," 239.
47. See Acts 2:5, 10–11, NKJV.
48. See Nathan, "Groundless Claims," 20.
49. Eusebius, *The Life of Constantine*, trans. Samuel Baxter, rev. E.C. Richardson (Grand Rapids, Mich.: Wm. B. Eerdmans, 1955), 2.46.
50. Nathan, "Groundless Claims," 21; Eusebius, *Life of Constantine*, 3.29–33.
51. Eusebius, *Life of Constantine*, 3.30.
52. Dumper, *Politics of Sacred Space*, 108.
53. Tsimhoni, "Christians in Jerusalem," 392.
54. Sabella, "Jerusalem."
55. Holy See and State of Israel, "Fundamental Agreement," Article 4.1.
56. Dumper, *Politics of Sacred Space*, 130.
57. Ibid., 168.

Chapter 4: Jewish and Israeli Personalities

1. Mullins, "Ideology," 506.
2. Ibid., as in Thomas More's *Utopia* and Samuel Butler's *Erewhon* (an anagram of "nowhere").
3. Mullins, "Ideology," 506–07, 509, 510.
4. Wigoder, ed., *New Encyclopedia of Zionism and Israel*, s.v. "Birnbaum, Nathan."
5. Herzl, *Jewish State*, 33, 38–39.
6. Soon known as the World Zionist Organization, though not officially named so until 1960.
7. Shlaim, *Iron Wall*, 3.
8. Ibid.
9. See Sachar, *History of Israel*, 59–63.
10. Kimmerling, *Zionism and Territory*, 9.
11. Shlaim, *Iron Wall*, 5.
12. Patai, *Complete Diaries*, 345–46, 745.
13. Friedland and Hecht, *To Rule Jerusalem*, 49.
14. Patai, *Complete Diaries*, 745–7, 753.
15. Herzl, *Old New Land*, 247.
16. Ibid.
17. Hertzberg, "Jerusalem and Zionism," 154.
18. Reinharz, *Chaim Weizmann*, 9–10.
19. Ibid., 18, 25.
20. Weizmann, *Letters and Papers*, Series A, 7:77.
21. Reinharz, *Chaim Weizmann*, 13.
22. Weizmann, *Trial and Error*, 131. What exactly Weizmann meant by "the capital" is unclear. At the time of writing (1947), Jerusalem was the capital of mandatory Palestine, but the debate over internationalization of the city had begun. Whether Weizmann was expressing his preferences for a future Israeli capital is an interesting question, but the answer is not known.
23. Ibid.
24. Weizmann, *Letters and Papers*, Series A, 8:203–04.
25. Reinharz, *Chaim Weizmann*, 379.
26. Weizmann, *Letters and Papers*, Series A, 6:13.

27. Reinharz, *Chaim Weizmann*, 381.
28. Weizmann, *Letters and Papers*, Series A, 6:175–76.
29. Weizmann, *Trial and Error*, 237.
30. Ibid., 473.
31. Gilbert, *Jerusalem in the Twentieth Century*, 239.
32. Nashashibi, *Jerusalem's Other Voice*, 218.
33. Ze'ev Jabotinsky, *Political and Social Philosophy*, 1.
34. Laqueur, *History of Zionism*, 338.
35. In 1921 the Zionist Executive was the newly named executive body of the Zionist Organization (later the World Zionist Organization).
36. Ovendale notes that members of the British Foreign Office had already begun to distance themselves from the pro-Zionist Balfour Declaration as early as 1919, and that these sentiments were reflected in the 1922 White Paper, "[which] stated that Palestine would not constitute *the* national home, but merely *a* national home for the Jews with no subordination of the Arab population" (Ovendale, *Arab-Israeli Wars*, 57–58, 60. See also Laqueur (*History of Zionism*, 344) for Jabotinsky's worries about the open hostility to Zionism of the 1921 Haycroft report on the Jaffa riots.
37. Eri Jabotinsky, *My Father*, 35–36, quoted in Samuel Katz, *Lone Wolf*, 526–27.
38. Ze'ev Jabotinsky, *Rassvyet*, quoted in Samuel Katz, *Lone Wolf*, 1074.
39. Ze'ev Jabotinsky, quoted in Samuel Katz, *Lone Wolf*, 1078.
40. Samuel Katz, *Lone Wolf*, 1078.
41. Ze'ev Jabotinsky, quoted in Samuel Katz, *Lone Wolf*, 1078.
42. Hertzberg, "Jerusalem and Zionism," 163.
43. Friedland and Hecht, *To Rule Jerusalem*, 158.
44. Ze'ev Jabotinsky, *Political and Social Philosophy*, 101, 98.
45. Shlaim, *Iron Wall*, 14.
46. Ben-Gurion, *Memoirs*, 34, 39.
47. Teveth, *Ben Gurion*, 3–4.
48. Ibid., 96.
49. Quoted in Shlaim, *Iron Wall*, 18.
50. Friedland and Hecht, *To Rule Jerusalem*, 158.
51. Ben-Gurion, *Letters to Paula*, 153–57.
52. Teveth, *Ben-Gurion*, 63.
53. Teveth, e-mails to author, July 2002.
54. Teveth, *Ben-Gurion*, 79.
55. Ben-Gurion, *Memoirs*, 18, 38.
56. Zameret, "Judaism in Israel," 70.
57. Kimmerling, *Zionism and Territory*, 225.
58. Teveth, e-mail to author, July 2002.
59. Ibid.
60. Ben-Gurion, *Memoirs*, 59.
61. Golani, "Jerusalem's Hope."
62. Ibid., 577.
63. Hudson, "Transformation of Jerusalem," 258.
64. Ben-Gurion, *Memoirs*, 136–37.
65. Kurzman, *Ben-Gurion*, 279.
66. Glubb, *Soldier With the Arabs*, 110.

67. Shlaim, *Iron Wall*, 36.
68. Gilbert, *Jerusalem in the Twentieth Century*, 237.
69. Morris, *Righteous Victims*, 242–43.
70. Ibid., 261.
71. Hudson, "Transformation of Jerusalem," 267.
72. Glubb, *Soldier With the Arabs*, 107.
73. Ben-Gurion, *Israel*, 379–82.
74. Ibid., 802.
75. Shlaim, *Iron Wall*, 51.
76. *Divrei Haknesset* (Records of Knesset Proceedings), vol. 4 (2nd Sess.), in Lapidoth and Hirsch, *Jerusalem Question*, 81–82.
77. Ibid., 82–83, in Lapidoth and Hirsch, *Jerusalem Question*, 83.
78. Gilbert, *Jerusalem in the Twentieth Century*, 246.
79. Ibid., 291–92.
80. Benvenisti, *City of Stone*, 136.
81. Kurzman, *Ben-Gurion*, 453.
82. Sachar, *History of Israel*, 713. However, Kurzman disagrees in part, saying that Ben-Gurion's diary entry for June 9, 1967, noted that he didn't believe the Golan Heights were essential to Israel (*Ben-Gurion*, 453). See also Butt, "David Ben-Gurion."
83. Ben-Gurion, *Israel*, 788, 789, 790.
84. Ben-Gurion, *Letters to Paula*, ix.
85. Silver, *Begin*, 3.
86. Dolav, "White Nights, Tempestuous Days," *Ma'ariv*, June 10, 1977, quoted in Silver, *Begin*, 10.
87. Post, "Assessing Leaders," 76.
88. Dolav, "White Nights, Tempestuous Days," quoted in Silver, *Begin*, 10–11.
89. Menachem Begin, "The Pillar of Fire," quoted in Silver, *Begin*, 11.
90. Dolav, "White Nights, Tempestuous Days," quoted in Silver, *Begin*, 4.
91. Smith, *Arab-Israeli Conflict*, 132.
92. Postage stamps as evidence of ideological persuasion are the focus of Kimberly Katz's "Jordanian Jerusalem: Postage Stamps and Identity Construction."
93. Silver, *Begin*, 99.
94. Samuel Katz, *Days of Fire*, 238 quoted in Silver, *Begin*, 100.
95. From the English text of Begin's statement as issued to the press, available in the *Jerusalem Post* archives, quoted in Silver, *Begin*, 112.
96. Knesset debate, March 8, 1949, quoted in Silver, *Begin*, 112.
97. Knesset debate, April 4, 1949, quoted in Silver, *Begin*, 113.
98. Yitzhak Rabin, "Rabin Jerusalem Day Address."
99. Menachem Begin, "Statement to the Knesset."
100. Silver, *Begin*, 182.
101. Bregman and El-Tahri, *Fifty Years War*, 136, quoting Yoel Marcus, *Camp David: The Door to Peace* (in Hebrew, Tel Aviv, 1979): 109–15.
102. Knesset, "Basic Law: Jerusalem, Capital of Israel."
103. Post and Robins, *When Illness Strikes the Leader*, 136.
104. Ibid., 48–50, 136.
105. Silver, *Begin*, 182.
106. Yitzhak Rabin, *Rabin Memoirs*, 30, 31, 32.

107. Ibid., 108, 111.
108. Inbar, *Rabin and Israel's National Security*, 29.
109. Leah Rabin, *Rabin*, 117.
110. Yitzhak Rabin, *Rabin Memoirs*, 111–12.
111. Leah Rabin, *Rabin*, 111.
112. Inbar, *Rabin and Israel's National Security*, 29.
113. Leah Rabin, *Rabin*, 113.
114. Ibid., 117.
115. Yitzhak Rabin, *Memoirs* (Appendix B), 389.
116. Ibid. (Appendix E), 400.
117. Ibid. (Appendix F), 407.
118. Ibid. (Appendix G), 414.
119. Yitzhak Rabin, "Address by Prime Minister Yitzhak Rabin."
120. Yitzhak Rabin, *Memoirs* (Appendix I), 425.
121. Yitzhak Rabin, "Rabin Jerusalem Day Address."
122. Avnery, "The Real Rabin."
123. Yitzhak Rabin, "Rabin Jerusalem Day Address."
124. Gold, "Jerusalem in International Diplomacy," Section 2, "The Political Dimension."
125. Leah Rabin (transcript of question-and-answer session at the April 6, 1997, meeting of the Los Angeles World Affairs Council).
126. Shimon Peres, quoted in Brecher, *Foreign Policy System*, 326.
127. Brecher, *Foreign Policy System*, 358.
128. Ibid., 358–60.
129. Peres, "Address by Foreign Minister."
130. Ibid.
131. Peres, interview with Eric Rouleau, *Le Monde* (Paris), December 28, 1968, translated in *New Middle East* (February 1969): 62 (emphasis added), quoted in Brecher, *Foreign Policy System*, 360–61.
132. Brecher, *Foreign Policy System*, 326.
133. *Jerusalem Post*, June 14, 1966, quoted in Brecher, *Foreign Policy System*, 326.
134. Peres, "Peace Be Within Your Walls," 10–11.
135. Peres, "Interview with Foreign Minister Peres on Israel Radio, April 10, 1993."
136. Peres, *New Middle East*, 172.
137. Peres, "Address by Foreign Minister."
138. Karmi, *Jerusalem Today*, xvi.
139. Peres, "Peace Be Within Your Walls," 10.
140. Ibid., 8.
141. Associated Press, "Peres: No Religion has a Monopoly over Jerusalem."
142. Reuters, "Peres Raises 'World Capital' Solution for Jerusalem."
143. Xinhua, "Annexing East Jerusalem Was Mistake: Peres."
144. Ha'aretz Service, "Peres: No Chance of Clinching Peace Without Dividing J'lem."
145. Peres, "Peace Be Within Your Walls," 11, 10.

Chapter 5: Arab and Palestinian Personalities

1. Benvenisti, *City of Stone*, 3–4.
2. Rashid Khalidi, *Palestinian Identity*, 149, 253 n. 13.

3. 2 Sam. 5:6, NKJV.
4. Gen. 25, NKJV.
5. Hasson, "Muslim Literature"; Rashid Khalidi, *Palestinian Identity*, 151. Porath notes that it was solely inhabitants of Jerusalem who produced this literature (*Emergence*, 3).
6. See Schölch, *Palestine in Transformation*; Rashid Khalidi, *Palestinian Identity*, 29.
7. Rashid Khalidi, *Palestinian Identity*, 19. See also Fishman, "The 1911 Haram Al-Sharif Incident."
8. Porath, *Emergence*, 8–9.
9. Brand, *Palestinians in the Arab World*, 10. See also Rashid Khalidi, *Palestinian Identity*, 149.
10. Mullins, "Ideology," 506–07, 509–10.
11. Philip Mattar, *Mufti of Jerusalem*, 7.
12. Ibid., 9.
13. Al-Husayni, unpublished diaries, quoted in Philip Mattar, *Mufti of Jerusalem*, 11, 12.
14. Porath, *Emergence*, 205–07.
15. Philip Mattar, *Mufti of Jerusalem*, xiii–xv, 31–49.
16. There was evidence of such anticipation in the thinking of certain Zionist supporters. See the report of the International Commission for the Wailing Wall, December 1930, 19–20; Porath, *Emergence*, 261–62, 308.
17. Report of the International Commission for the Wailing Wall, 20.
18. Al-Husayni, quoted in Tibawi, "Jerusalem," 39.
19. Weizmann, Series A, 8:203–04.
20. Philip Mattar, *Mufti of Jerusalem*, 48–49.
21. Hazony, *Jewish State*, 211.
22. Elpeleg, *Grand Mufti*, 70–73; Philip Mattar, 105–07.
23. Philip Mattar, *Mufti of Jerusalem*, 113.
24. Shlaim, *Politics of Partition*, 69–76; Wilson, *Making of Jordan*, 180.
25. Shlaim, *Politics of Partition*, 75.
26. Quoted in Wilson, *Making of Jordan*, 180.
27. Philip Mattar, *Mufti of Jerusalem*, 118.
28. Ibid. In Mattar's account, Abdullah speaks identical words (in respect of the mufti's suggested assassination) to those Shlaim recounts in the earlier meeting with Sasson. It may be that the latter is the only occasion on which he made the suggestion in 1946–47.
29. Quoted in Kurzman, *Genesis 1948*, 21.
30. Ibid., 22.
31. "A Palestine Declaration of Independence was issued on October 1, 1948, which included the following: 'Based on the natural and historical right of the Palestine Arab people for freedom and independence . . . [we declare] total independence of all Palestine . . . and the establishment of an independent, democratic state whose inhabitants will exercise their liberties and rights.' " The declaration was issued by the Palestine National Council convened by the All-Palestine Government. The mufti was elected president of the Council on September 30, 1948 (Philip Mattar, *Mufti of Jerusalem*, 132; see also 133).
32. Beeri, "Palestinian Arab Leadership," 454.
33. Philip Mattar, *Mufti of Jerusalem*, 66–67.
34. Muslih, *Origins of Palestinian Nationalism*, 31.

35. Shukairy, *Statements Made During the 13th Session*, 21–22 (in Portable Document File).
36. The principal sponsor was apparently President Nasir himself (Beeri, "Palestinian Arab Leadership," 455); Elpeleg, *Grand Mufti*, 139.
37. Sicker, *Between Hashemites and Zionists*, 112–14. It has also been suggested that Nasir was anxious to control the Palestinians lest their militancy force Egypt into another war with Israel. Further, based on interviews with PLO leaders Hani Hassan, Khalad Hassan, and Yasser Arafat, Alan Hart writes that the American secretary of state, Dean Rusk, had pressured Nasir to control the Palestinian militants in this way (Hart, *Arafat: Terrorist or Peacemaker?* 160–62).
38. Abu Iyad, *My Home, My Land*, 40; Hart, *Arafat: Terrorist or Peacemaker?* 160–62; Brand, *Palestinians in the Arab World*, 55–56.
39. Philip Mattar, ed., *Encyclopedia of the Palestinians*, s.v. "Shuqayri, Ahmad."
40. Cobban, *Palestinian Liberation Organization*, 29.
41. The meetings actually ran from May 28 to June 2, 1964 (see http://www.ahmad-alshukairy.org/speeches/speeches.html). Laqueur and Rubin date the draft constitution to 1963, prior to the Arab League summit. According to Elpeleg, Nasir had already begun to make plans for the PLO in late 1963 (*Grand Mufti*, 138) and this may be the reason for the draft's date. At the May 1964 meetings in Jerusalem Shuqayri put two documents before the delegates: the Palestinian National Charter/Covenant and the Basic Constitution of the PLO. Both were endorsed (Cobban, *Palestinian Liberation Organization*, 30). However, puzzlingly and presumably in error, Laqueur and Rubin also date the "Arab Summit Conference" to 1963 (*Israel-Arab Reader*, 93).
42. Shuqayri, quoted in Brand, *Palestinians in the Arab World*, 169.
43. First Palestinian Conference, "The Palestinian National Charter," Article 24; Philip Mattar, *Encyclopedia of the Palestinians*, s.v. "Palestine National Charter."
44. Laqueur and Rubin, *Israel-Arab Reader*, 95.
45. Ibid.
46. Sachar, *History of Israel*, 619.
47. Gowers and Walker, *Behind the Myth*, 53–54.
48. Shukairy, *Statements Made During the 13th Session*, 22 (in Portable Document File).
49. Shukairy, *Statements Made During the 16th Session*, 17, 27.
50. Ibid., 35, 42.
51. Shukairy, *Liberation—Not Negotiation*, 19, 20.
52. See Rubinstein, *Mystery of Arafat*, 11–13; Aburish, *Arafat*, 7–9.
53. Wallach and Wallach, *Arafat*, 25.
54. Wallach and Wallach, *New Palestinians*, 52.
55. Rubinstein, *Mystery of Arafat*, 22, 20.
56. Cobban, *Palestinian Liberation Organization*, 272 n.5.
57. Wallach and Wallach, *Arafat*, 71.
58. Wallach and Wallach, *New Palestinians*, 44.
59. Arafat was never a member of the Ikhwan, though he appreciated their support of the Palestinian cause. See Brand, *Palestinians in the Arab World*, 66–67.
60. Hart, *Arafat: Terrorist or Peacemaker?* 78–79.
61. Abu Iyad with Eric Rouleau, *My Home, My Land*, 32–33.
62. Philip Mattar, *Encyclopedia of the Palestinians*, s.v. "Arafat, Yasir."

63. Though some members did attend the initial 1964 PLO meetings in East Jerusalem, Arafat did not (Abu Iyad, *My Home, My Land*, 41).
64. Abu Iyad with Eric Rouleau, *My Home, My Land*, 44.
65. Wallach and Wallach, *Arafat*, 142.
66. Permanent Observer Mission of Palestine to the United Nations, "Background."
67. Aburish, *Arafat*, 142.
68. Shlaim, *Iron Wall*, 460.
69. Ibid.
70. Baker, *Politics of Diplomacy*, 445, 487–513; Ashrawi, *This Side of Peace*, 124–31.
71. Wallach and Wallach, *Arafat*, 49.
72. As told by his son to Wallach and Wallach (*Arafat*, 46).
73. Wallach and Wallach, *Arafat*, 47–48.
74. Philip Mattar *(Mufti of Jerusalem)* makes no reference to Hassan Abu Sa'ud and explains the origins of the riots differently. "Sheik Hasan Effendi Abu Soud" was a representative of the Muslim community at the June-July 1930 hearings of the International Commission for the Wailing Wall in Jerusalem (see the report of the International Commission for the Wailing Wall, 5).
75. Wallach and Wallach, *Arafat*, 28.
76. Ibid., 135–37.
77. Elon, *Jerusalem*, 6.
78. Permanent Observer Mission of Palestine to the United Nations, "Declaration of Independence."
79. Najib and Associated Press, "Arafat: Jerusalem Is 'Life or Death.' "
80. Palestine Liberation Organization, "Political and Religious Leaders Support Palestinian Sovereignty Over Jerusalem."
81. Arafat, "Speech of H.E. Yasser Arafat."
82. Arafat, "The Palestinian Vision of Peace."
83. Doucet, "Arafat: Down But Not Out."
84. Gruber, "Car Bomb Kills Israeli Policeman, Bomber, Ma'ale Adumim."
85. Quoted in Brand, *Palestinians in the Arab World*, 58.
86. Palestine Liberation Organization, "Jerusalem."
87. Erlanger and Altman, "Medical Records Say Arafat Died from a Stroke."
88. Lapidoth, "Jerusalem: Some Legal Aspects," 77.
89. Makovsky, *Making Peace*, 23.
90. Savir, interview by Terry Gross.
91. Yehoshua and Chernitsky, "Ahmad Qurei'—Abu 'Alaa: A Brief Political Profile of the Nominated Palestinian Prime Minister."
92. Ibid., quoting *Al-Quds* (Jerusalem), November 12, 1997.
93. Ahmed Qurei (Ahmad Quray'), "Breaking the Deadlock."
94. Quray', "Peace Talk," 60, 61.
95. Secret discussions lasting almost eighteen months (1994–95) between Israeli Yossi Beilin and Abu Mazen (Mahmoud Abbas) produced the Abu Mazen–Beilin agreement, which included the Abu Dis proposal (see Ross, *Missing Peace*, 208).
96. Quray', "Peace Talk," 60.
97. Statement by the Palestinian Council of Ministers, "Ahmad Qurei Reaffirms Palestinian Position."

98. Wallach and Wallach, *New Palestinians*, 14, 15, 17.
99. Ashrawi, *This Side of Peace*, 27.
100. Ibid., 32, 51.
101. Associated Press, "Hanan Ashrawi Resigns as Arab League Spokeswoman."
102. Ashrawi, *This Side of Peace*, 247.
103. Ibid., 249.
104. Ibid., 267.
105. Ibid., 259.
106. Ibid., 275.
107. Ashrawi, "Lines in the Sand."
108. Ashrawi, "Briefing at Rayburn House Office Building."
109. Ashrawi, *This Side of Peace*, 267.
110. Wallach and Wallach, *New Palestinians*, 43, 48, 49.
111. Ibid., 58.
112. Faysal al-Husayni, interview by Amnon Rubinstein, *Ha'aretz*, March 22, 1968, quoted in Wallach and Wallach, *New Palestinians*, 61–62.
113. al-Husayni, "What's Ahead for the Middle East?"
114. Ashrawi, *This Side of Peace*, 90.
115. Armstrong, *History of Jerusalem*, 419.
116. al-Husayni, "Palestinian Future Vision For Jerusalem."
117. Cable News Network, "Violence Erupts after Sharon Visits Jerusalem Holy Site."
118. PASSIA, "More About Faisal Abdel Qader Al-Husseini."
119. al-Husayni, "The Holy City Must Be Ruled Fairly."
120. Mishal and Sela, *Palestinian Hamas*, 18.
121. See Rangwala, "Short Biographies" s.v. "Hamas."
122. Nüsse, *Muslim Palestine*, xi. According to Mishal and Sela: "literally, enthusiasm" (*Palestinian Hamas*, 35).
123. Hatina, *Islam and Salvation*, 19.
124. Mishal and Sela, *Palestinian Hamas*, 72. See also Hroub, *Hamas*, 204–08; Nüsse, *Muslim Palestine*, 153, 162–63, 172; and Rangwala, "Short Biographies" s.v. "Hamas."
125. Hroub, *Hamas*, 40.
126. Dudkevitch and Mohammed Najib, "Yassin Receives Hero's Welcome."
127. Dudkevitch, "Yassin Offers Temporary Cease-Fire for Full Withdrawal."
128. Yassin, Reuters, May 27, 1998, quoted in Rubin, *Palestinian Politics*, 115.
129. Hroub, *Hamas*, 58.
130. Hamas Charter, Article 1, in Hroub, *Hamas*, 269.
131. Hamas Charter, Article 2, in Hroub, *Hamas*, 269.
132. Hamas Charter, Article 15, in Hroub, *Hamas*, 276–77.
133. Dudkevitch, "Sheikh Yassin."
134. Rodan, "Hamas's Explosive Divide."
135. Rubin, "Yassin's Journeys."
136. Keinon, "Yassin: Is the Sheikh a Real Threat?"
137. Hamas Charter, Article 28, in Hroub, *Hamas*, 285.
138. Hamas Charter, Article 31, in Hroub, *Hamas*, 287.
139. Plotkin, "Hamas would Accept Saudi Peace Plan."

Conclusions

1. Joll, *1914: The Unspoken Assumptions*, quoted in English, *Russia*, 1.
2. Erikson, *Identity*, 178.
3. See Hertzberg, "Jerusalem and Zionism," 162.
4. Klein, *Jerusalem*, 301–09, 335.
5. See Segal et al., *Negotiating Jerusalem*.
6. Erikson, *Insight and Responsibility*, 96.
7. La Cerra and Bingham, *Origin of Minds*, 5.
8. Ridley, *Nature Via Nurture*, front jacket flap.
9. Ibid. Ridley credits David Lykken for the title of his book. See page 286.
10. Ian McEwan, in Ridley, *Nature Via Nurture*, back panel of jacket.
11. Schwartz and Begley, *Mind and the Brain*.
12. Steven Pinker, in Ridley, *Nature Via Nurture*, back panel of jacket.
13. Spiegel and Pervin, *Practical Peacemaking*, 9–10.
14. Benvenisti, "Israeli-Palestinian Conflict," 2.
15. Segal et al., *Negotiating Jerusalem*.
16. Ibid., viii, 189, 195, 221.
17. Kimmerling, "Definitions of the Collective Identity," 263.
18. Segal et al., *Negotiating Jerusalem*, 141–47, 171.
19. Klein, conversation with author, Los Angeles, Calif., February 7, 2003.
20. Nuseibeh, "Islam's Jerusalem," 5–8.
21. Usher, "Hearts and Minds."
22. Said, "Memory, Inequality and Power."
23. Usher, "Hearts and Minds."
24. Barenboim and Said, *Parallels and Paradoxes*, 12.
25. Usher, "Hearts and Minds."
26. Said, "Memory, Inequality, and Power."
27. Ross, "Secrets of the Great Communicators."
28. For an analysis of the strengths and weaknesses of Ross's negotiating techniques in the peace process, based on interviews with him, see Bebchick, "Dennis Ross as an International Mediator."
29. Saideman, "Thinking Theoretically," 200.
30. Ross, *Missing Peace*, 238.

BIBLIOGRAPHY

ABC Radio National. "Divided Jerusalem: A Conversation with Bernard Wasserstein." *The Religion Report*, April 17, 2002. http://www.abc.net.au/rn/talks/8.30/relrpt/stories/s532612.htm (accessed October 28, 2002).

Aburish, Saïd K. *Arafat: From Defender to Dictator.* New York: Bloomsbury, 1998.

Abu Iyad and Eric Rouleau. *My Home, My Land: A Narrative of the Palestinian Struggle.* New York: Times Books, 1978, 1981.

Abu Manneh, B. "The Rise of the Sanjak of Jerusalem in the Late 19th Century." In *The Palestinians and the Middle East Conflict*, edited by Gabriel Ben-Dor, 21–32. Ramat Gan, Israel: Turtledove Publishing, 1979.

Alexander, Philip S. "Jerusalem as the *Omphalos* of the World: On the History of a Geographical Concept." In *Jerusalem: Its Sanctity and Centrality to Judaism, Christianity, and Islam*, edited by Lee I. Levine, 104–19. New York: Continuum, 1999.

Amitai-Preiss, Reuven. *Mongols and Mamluks: The Mamluk-Ilkhanid War, 1260–1281.* Cambridge: Cambridge University Press, 1995.

ArabicNews.com. "Sheikh Yassin Leads Hamas Towards Moderation." January 31, 1998. http://www.arabicnews.com/ansub/Daily/Day/980131/1998013124.html (accessed August 5, 2002).

Arafat, Yasser. "The Palestinian Vision of Peace." Editorial. *New York Times*, February 3, 2002.

———. "Speech of H.E. Yasser Arafat." *The Millennium Assembly of the United Nations: Millennium Summit.* September 6, 2000. http://www.un.org/millennium/webcast/indexe.htm (accessed August 2, 2002).

Armstrong, Karen. *A History of Jerusalem: One City, Three Faiths.* London: Harper Collins, 1997.

Aronson, Geoffrey. "Israeli Settlements In and Around Jerusalem." In *Jerusalem Today: What Future for the Peace Process?* edited by Ghada Karmi, 77–82. Reading, Berks., UK: Garnet Publishing Limited, Ithaca Press, 1996.

Asali, K.J., ed. *Jerusalem in History.* New York: Olive Branch Press, 1990.

———. "Jerusalem Under the Ottomans, 1516–1831 A.D." In *Jerusalem in History*, edited by K.J. Asali, 200–27. New York: Olive Branch Press, 1990.

Ashrawi, Hanan. "Briefing at Rayburn House Office Building." American Committee on Jerusalem. March 13, 2000. http://www.acj.org/briefings/3_13_2000ts.htm (accessed June 7, 2002).

———. "Guarded Optimist on the Peace Process." *Journal of Palestine Studies* 26, no. 3 (1997): 81–91.

Ashrawi, Hanan. "Lines in the Sand." Interview by Charles Krause [online transcript]. *NewsHour*, Public Broadcasting System. March 4, 1997. http://www.pbs.org/newshour/bb/middle_east/march97/ashrawi_3–4.html (accessed September 2, 2005).

———. *This Side of Peace: A Personal Account*. New York: Simon & Schuster, 1995.

Associated Press. "Hanan Ashrawi Resigns as Arab League Spokeswoman." *Jerusalem Post*, March 26, 2002, daily edition.

———. "Peres: No Religion Has a Monopoly over Jerusalem." January 10, 2001. http://www.acj.org/Jan_10.htm#6 (accessed September 7, 2005).

Avnery, Uri. "The Real Rabin." Translation of the unabridged version of an article published in *Ma'ariv*. October 31, 1999. http://www.hagalil.com/israel/rabin/israel/rabin.htm (accessed July 1, 2002).

Barak, Ehud. "Alternate Direction for the Middle East Peace Process." Speech before the Los Angeles World Affairs Council, September 16, 1998. Subsequently published in *World Affairs Journal, Los Angeles* 12, no. 2 (1999).

Barenboim, Daniel and Edward W. Said. *Parallels and Paradoxes: Explorations in Music and Society*. Edited by Ara Guzelimian. New York: Vintage, 2004.

Barnett, Michael N., ed. *Israel in Comparative Perspective: Challenging the Conventional Wisdom*. Albany, N.Y.: State University of New York Press, 1996.

———. "The Israeli Identity and the Peace Process: Re/creating the Un/thinkable." In *Identity and Foreign Policy in the Middle East*, edited by Shibley Telhami and Michael Barnett, 58–87. Ithaca, N.Y.: Cornell University Press, 2002.

Bar-Tal, Daniel, Dan Jacobson, and Aharon Klieman, eds. *Security Concerns: Insights from the Israeli Experience*. Stamford, Conn.: Jai Press Inc., 1998.

BBC News. February 15, 2002–July 11, 2003. http://news.bbc.co.uk.

BBC News, World Edition. "Cleric Condemns Suicide Attacks." July 11, 2003. http://news.bbc.co.uk/1/hi/world/middle_east/3059365.stm (accessed September 2, 2005).

———. "Israel Starts Building Jerusalem Fence." June 30, 2002. http://news.bbc.co.uk/hi/english/world/middle_east/newsid_2076000/2076584.stm (accessed September 2, 2005).

Bebchick, Brian. "The Philosophy and Methodology of Ambassador Dennis Ross as an International Mediator." *International Negotiation* 7, no. 1 (2002): 115–31.

Beeri, Eliezer. "The Emergence of Palestinian Arab Leadership: Husaini, Shuqairi and Arafat." In *The Palestinians and the Middle East Conflict*, edited by Gabriel Ben-Dor, 451–59. Ramat Gan, Israel: Turtledove Publishing, 1979.

Begin, Menachem. "Statement to the Knesset by Prime Minister Begin Upon the Presentation of his Government, June 20, 1977." In *Foreign Relations: Historical Documents*, vol. 4–5, no. 1. State of Israel, Ministry of Foreign Affairs, 1999. http://www.mfa.gov.il/MFA/Foreign%20Relations/Israels%20Foreign%20Relations%20since%201947/1977–1979 (accessed September 2, 2005).

Begin, Ze'ev. *A Zionist Stand*. London: Frank Cass & Co., 1993.

———. Interview by author. Video recording. Jerusalem, March 5, 1990.

Ben-Dor, Gabriel, ed. *Israel in Transition*. The Annals of the American Academy of Political and Social Science, Vol. 555. London: Sage Publications, Inc., March 1998.

———. *The Palestinians and the Middle East Conflict*. Ramat Gan, Israel: Turtledove Publishing, 1979.

Ben-Gurion, David. *Israel: A Personal History*. New York: Funk & Wagnalls Inc., 1971.

———. *Letters to Paula*. Translated by Aubrey Hodes. Pittsburgh: University of Pittsburgh Press, 1971.

———. *Memoirs*. New York: World Publishing Company, 1970.

Benvenisti, Meron. *City of Stone: The Hidden History of Jerusalem*. Berkeley: University of California Press, 1996.

———. *Conflicts and Contradictions*. New York: Villard Books, 1986.

———. "The Israeli-Palestinian Conflict: Ferocious Yet Manageable." *The Fortnightly* (Claremont McKenna College) 18, no. 3 (2002): 2.

——— *Jerusalem: The Torn City*. Minneapolis: University of Minnesota Press, 1976.

———. *Sacred Landscape*. Translated by Maxine Kaufman-Lacusta. Berkeley: University of California Press, 2000.

Beyer, Lisa. "A Hit Gone Wrong." *Time Magazine*, October 13, 1997.

Blakeslee, Sandra. "Brain Power: The Search for Origins." *New York Times*, November 5, 2002.

Bloom, William. *Personal Identity, National Identity and International Relations*. Cambridge: Cambridge University Press, 1990.

Blum, Yehuda Z. *For Zion's Sake*. New York: Herzl Press, 1987.

Brand, Laurie A. *Palestinians in the Arab World: Institution Building and the Search for State*. New York: Columbia University Press, 1988.

———. "Palestinians and Jordanians: A Crisis of Identity." *Journal of Palestine Studies* 24, no. 4 (1995): 46–61.

Brecher, Michael. *Decisions in Israel's Foreign Policy*. New Haven: Yale University Press, 1975.

———. *The Foreign Policy System of Israel: Setting, Images, Process*. New Haven: Yale University Press, 1972.

Breger, Marshall J. and Ora Ahimeir, eds. *Jerusalem: A City and Its Future*. Syracuse: Syracuse University Press, 2002.

Bregman, Ahron and Jihan El-Tahri. *The Fifty Years War: Israel and the Arabs*. London: Penguin Books, 1998.

Brinkhoff, Thomas. "State of Israel." *City Population*. http://www.citypopulation.de/Israel.html (accessed August 28, 2005).

Brownlie, Ian. *Principles of Public International Law*. Oxford: Clarendon Press, 1979.

Buber, Martin. *On Zion: The History of an Idea*. Translated by Stanley Godman. Edinburgh: T & T Clark Ltd., 1952, 1985.

Bundy, Rodman. "Legal Approaches to the Question of Jerusalem." In *Jerusalem Today: What Future for the Peace Process?* edited by Ghada Karmi, 45–50. Reading, Berks., UK: Garnet Publishing Limited, Ithaca Press, 1996.

Butt, Gerald. "David Ben-Gurion." *Israel at Fifty: Profiles*. BBC News. October 19, 1998. http://news.bbc.co.uk/1/hi/special_report/1998/10/98/middle_east/81279.stm (accessed September 2, 2005).

Cable News Network. "Violence Erupts After Sharon Visits Jerusalem Holy Site." *CNN.com*, September 28, 2000. http://www.cnn.com/2000/WORLD/meast/09/28/jerusalem.violence/index.html (accessed August 5, 2002).

Carlsnaes, Walter, Thomas Risse, and Beth A. Simmons, eds. *Handbook of International Relations*. London: Sage Publications, 2002.

Cassels, Alan. *Ideology and International Relations in the Modern World*. London: Routledge, 1996.

Cattan, Henry. *Jerusalem*. London: Saqi Books, 1981, 2000.

Chabin, Michele. "The Not So Wild, Wild West (Bank)." *Jewish Week*, April 20, 2001.

Cheshin, Amir S., Bill Hutman, and Avi Melamed. *Separate and Unequal: The Inside Story of Israeli Rule in East Jerusalem*. Cambridge: Harvard University Press, 1999.

Choshen, Maya. *Jerusalem on the Map: Basic Facts and Trends 1967–1996*. Jerusalem: The Jerusalem Institute for Israel Studies, 1998.

————, ed. *Statistical Yearbook of Jerusalem: 2005*. Jerusalem: The Jerusalem Institute for Israel Studies, 2005. http://www.jiis.org.il (accessed March 17, 2006).

Choshen, Maya and Naama Shahar, eds. *Statistical Yearbook of Jerusalem: 1996*. Jerusalem: The Jerusalem Institute for Israel Studies, 1997.

————. *Statistical Yearbook of Jerusalem: 1998*. Jerusalem: The Jerusalem Institute for Israel Studies, 1999.

————. *Statistical Yearbook of Jerusalem: 2000*. Jerusalem: The Jerusalem Institute for Israel Studies, 2001.

————. *Statistical Yearbook of Jerusalem: 2002–2003*. Jerusalem: The Jerusalem Institute for Israel Studies, 2003. http://www.jerusalemfoundation.org/data/jiis/jerusalem-statistics-2003.html (accessed August 28, 2005).

Cline, Eric H. *Jerusalem Besieged*. Ann Arbor: The University of Michigan Press, 2004.

Cobban, Helena. *The Palestinian Liberation Organisation: People, Power and Politics*. Cambridge: Cambridge University Press, 1984.

Cohen, Erik, Moshe Lissak, and Uri Almagor, eds. *Comparative Social Dynamics*. Boulder, Colo.: Westview Press, 1985.

Coles, Robert, ed. *The Erik Erikson Reader*. New York: W.W. Norton & Company, 2000.

Corbin, Jane. *The Norway Channel: The Secret Talks that Led to the Middle East Peace Accord*. New York: Atlantic Monthly Press, 1994.

Coughlin, Con. *A Golden Basin Full of Scorpions: The Quest for Modern Jerusalem*. London: Little, Brown and Company, 1997.

Dittmer, Lowell, and Samuel S. Kim, eds. *China's Quest for National Identity*. Ithaca, N.Y.: Cornell University Press, 1993.

Doucet, Lyse. "Arafat: Down But Not Out." BBC News. February 15, 2002. http://news.bbc.co.uk/2/hi/world/from_our_own_correspondent/1820716.stm (accessed August 5, 2002).

Dudkevitch, Margot. "Yassin Offers Temporary Cease-Fire for Full Withdrawal." *Jerusalem Post*, October 8, 1997, daily edition.

Dudkevitch, Margot and Mohammed Najib. "Yassin Receives Hero's Welcome." *Jerusalem Post*, October 7, 1997, daily edition.

Dumper, Michael. *The Politics of Jerusalem Since 1967*. New York: Columbia University Press, 1997.

————. *The Politics of Sacred Space: The Old City of Jerusalem in the Middle East Conflict*. Boulder, Colo.: Lynne Rienner Publishers, Inc., 2002.

Duri, Abdul Aziz. "Jerusalem in the Early Islamic Period: 7th–11th Centuries A.D." In *Jerusalem in History*, edited by K.J. Asali, 105–29. New York: Olive Branch Press, 1990.

Eban, Abba. " 'Never Have Freedom and International Morality been so Righteously Protected': Text of the Address by Israel's Foreign Minister, Mr. Abba Eban, in the General Assembly of the United Nations on 19 June, 1967." New York: Israel Information Services, 1967.

Eldar, Akiva. "Dispute over Ma'aleh Adumim." Ha'aretz, English edition, February 19, 2002.

Elon, Amos. The Israelis: Founders and Sons. New York: Holt, Rinehart and Winston, 1971.

————. Jerusalem: City of Mirrors. Boston: Little, Brown and Company, 1989.

Elpeleg, Zvi. The Grand Mufti: Haj Amin al-Hussaini, Founder of the Palestinian National Movement. Translated by David Harvey. London: Frank Cass & Co., 1993.

English, Robert D. Russia and the Idea of the West: Gorbachev, Intellectuals, and the End of the Cold War. New York: Columbia University Press, 2000.

Erikson, Erik H. Identity and the Life Cycle. New York: W.W. Norton & Company, 1959, 1994.

————. Insight and Responsibility: Lectures on the Ethical Implications of Psychoanalytic Insight. New York: W.W. Norton & Company, 1964.

————. Young Man Luther. New York: W.W. Norton & Company, 1958, 1962.

Erlanger, Steven and Lawrence K. Altman. "Medical Records Say Arafat Died from a Stroke." New York Times, September 8, 2005.

Fearon, James D. and Alexander Wendt. "Rationalism vs. Constructivism: A Skeptical View." In Handbook of International Relations, edited by Walter Carlsnaes, Thomas Risse, and Beth A. Simmons, 52–72. London: Sage, 2002.

First Palestinian Conference. "The Palestinian National Charter," 1964. Available online at Permanent Observer Mission of Palestine to the United Nations: Palestine Liberation Organization. 1999. http://www.palestine-un.org/plo/pna_two.html (accessed July 30, 2002).

Fishman, Louis. "The 1911 Haram al-Sharif Incident: Palestinian Notables Versus the Ottoman Administration." Journal of Palestine Studies 34, no.3 (2005): 6–22.

Fitzgerald, Thomas. Metaphors of Identity: A Culture-Communication Dialogue. Albany, N.Y.: State University of New York Press, 1993.

Flanagan, Owen. The Problem of the Soul: Two Visions of Mind and How to Reconcile Them. New York: Basic Books, 2002.

Franklin, Shai. "The Palestinian Refugee Issue: Possible Outcomes, Achievable Goals." In The Environment, Water, Refugees, and Economic Cooperation and Development. Vol. 2 of Practical Peacemaking in the Middle East, edited by Steven L. Spiegel and David J. Pervin, 215–32. New York: Garland Publishing, 1995.

Friedland, Roger and Richard Hecht. "Changing Places: Jerusalem's Holy Places in Comparative Perspective." In Israel: The Dynamics of Change and Continuity, edited by David Levi-Faur, Gabriel Sheffer, and David Vogel, 200–25. London: Frank Cass & Co., 1999.

Friedland, Roger and Richard Hecht. To Rule Jerusalem. Cambridge: Cambridge University Press, 1996.

Friedman, Lawrence J. Identity's Architect: A Biography of Erik H. Erikson. Cambridge: Harvard University Press, 1999.

Fukuyama, Francis. The End of History and the Last Man. New York: Avon Books, 1993.

Gilbert, Martin. *Jerusalem in the Twentieth Century.* New York: John Wiley & Sons, Inc., 1996.

Gleason, Philip. "Identifying Identity: A Semantic History." *Journal of American History* 69, no. 4 (1983): 910–31.

Glubb, John Bagot. *A Soldier with the Arabs.* London: Hodder and Stoughton, 1957.

Golani, Motti. "Jerusalem's Hope Lies Only in Partition: Israeli Policy on the Jerusalem Question, 1948–67." *International Journal of Middle East Studies* 31 (1999): 577–604.

———. "Zionism Without Zion: The Jerusalem Question, 1947–1949." *The Journal of Israeli History* 16, no. 1 (1995): 39–52.

Gold, Dore. "Defensible Borders for Israel." *Jerusalem Letter/Viewpoints*, no. 500 (2003). http://www.jcpa.org/jl/vp500.htm (accessed August 28, 2005).

———. *Jerusalem.* Final Status Issues: Israel-Palestinians, Study No. 7. Tel Aviv: Jaffee Center for Strategic Studies, 1995.

———. "Jerusalem in International Diplomacy." New York: UnitedJerusalem.com, Inc. 2000. http://www.unitedjerusalem.com/US_ISRAEL_RELATION/Jerusalem_in_International_Dip/jerusalem_in_international_dip.asp#whiteline anchorHome (accessed April 24, 2002).

Goldhill, Simon. *The Temple of Jerusalem.* Harvard: Harvard University Press, 2005.

Gorenberg, Gershom. *The End of Days: Fundamentalism and the Struggle for the Temple Mount.* New York: The Free Press, 2000.

Gourevitch, Peter. "Interacting Variables: September 11 and the Role of Ideas and Domestic Politics." *International Organization* (Spring 2002): 71–80.

Gowers, Andrew and Tony Walker. *Behind the Myth: Yasser Arafat and the Palestinian Revolution.* New York: Olive Branch Press, 1992.

Gruber, Yehuda. "Car Bomb Kills Israeli Policeman, Bomber, Ma'ale Adumim." *Reuters*, February 18, 2002.

Guardian Newspapers (United Kingdom). November 1, 2001.

Gur, Mordechai. *The Battle for Jerusalem.* Translated by Philip Gillon. New York: Ibooks, Inc., 2002.

Ha'aretz (Jerusalem), English edition. February 19, 2002–July 24, 2005.

Ha'aretz Service. "Peres: No Chance of Clinching Peace Without Dividing J'lem." *Ha'aretz*, July 24, 2005. http://www.haaretz.com/hasen/objects/pages/PrintArticleEn.jhtml?itemNo=603903 (accessed September 1, 2005).

al-Hadi, Mahdi Abd. "Introduction," in Nuseibeh, Sabella, and Reiter, *Jerusalem: Religious Aspects.* Jerusalem: Palestinian Academic Society for the Study of International Affairs, 1995.

Hammer, Reuven. *The Jerusalem Anthology: A Literary Guide.* Philadelphia: Jewish Publication Society, 1995.

Hart, Alan. *Arafat: Terrorist or Peacemaker?* London: Sidgwick & Jackson, 1984.

Hasson, Isaac. "Muslim Literature in Praise of Jerusalem." In *The Jerusalem Cathedra: Studies in the History, Archaeology, Geography and Ethnography of the Land of Israel.* Vol. 1. Edited by Lee I. Levine, 168–84. Jerusalem: Yad Izhak Ben-Zvi Institute, 1981.

Hatina, Meir. *Islam and Salvation in Palestine: The Islamic Jihad Movement.* Tel Aviv: The Moshe Dayan Center for Middle Eastern and African Studies, Tel Aviv University, 2001.

Hazony, Yoram. *The Jewish State: The Struggle for Israel's Soul.* New York: Basic Books, 2000.

Heikal, Mohamed. *Secret Channels: The Inside Story of Arab-Israeli Peace Negotiations.* London: Harper Collins Publishers, 1996.

Heller, Mark A. *Continuity and Change in Israeli Security Policy.* Oxford: Oxford University Press, 2000.

Hemmer, Christopher and Peter J. Katzenstein. "Why Is There No NATO in Asia?: Collective Identity, Regionalism, and the Origins of Multilateralism." *International Organization* 56, no. 3 (2002): 577–607.

Hertzberg, Arthur. "Jerusalem and Zionism." In *City of the Great King: Jerusalem from David to the Present,* edited by Nitza Rosovsky, 149–77. Cambridge: Harvard University Press, 1996.

———, ed. *The Zionist Idea: A Historical Analysis and Reader.* 1959. Reprint, with a foreword by Emanuel Neumann. New York: Atheneum, 1976.

Herzl, Theodor. *The Jewish State (Der Judenstaat).* Translated by Harry Zohn. New York: Herzl Press, 1970.

———. *Old New Land.* Updated ed. Translated by Lotta Levensohn. Princeton: Markus Wiener Publishers, 1960, 1997.

Hirsch, Moshe, Deborah Housen-Couriel, and Ruth Lapidoth. *Whither Jerusalem? Proposals and Positions Concerning the Future of Jerusalem.* Translated by Ralph Mandel. Dordrecht, The Netherlands: Martinus Nijhoff Publishers, 1995.

Holy See and State of Israel. "Fundamental Agreement Between the Holy See and the State of Israel, December 30, 1993." In *Foreign Affairs: Historical Documents,* vol. 13–14, no. 151. State of Israel, Ministry of Foreign Affairs, 1999. http://www.israel.org/mfa/go.asp?MFAH00rs0 (accessed September 23, 2003).

Horovitz, David, ed. (In conjunction with the *Jerusalem Report* staff.) *Shalom, Friend: The Life and Legacy of Yitzhak Rabin.* New York: Newmarket Press, 1996.

———. (In conjunction with the *Jerusalem Report* staff.) *Yitzhak Rabin: Soldier of Peace.* London: Peter Halban, 1996.

Hourani, Albert. *A History of the Arab Peoples.* Cambridge: Harvard University Press, Belknap Press, 1991.

Hroub, Khaled. *Hamas: Political Thought and Practice.* Washington, D.C.: Institute for Palestine Studies, 2000.

Hudson, Michael C. "The Transformation of Jerusalem." In *Jerusalem in History,* edited by K.J. Asali, 249–78. New York: Olive Branch Press, 1990.

Huntington, Samuel P. *The Clash of Civilizations and the Remaking of World Order.* New York: Simon & Schuster, 1998.

———. "Religion, Culture, and International Conflict after September 11: A Conversation with Samuel P. Huntington." *Center Conversations* (An Occasional Publication of the Ethics and Public Policy Center), no. 14 (2002): 1–4.

al-Husayni, Faysal. "The Holy City Must Be Ruled Fairly." Op-Ed. *Los Angeles Times,* July 3, 2000. http://pqasb.pqarchiver.com/latimes/search.html (accessed May 14, 2002).

———. "Palestinian Future Vision for Jerusalem." In *About the Orient House: Articles and Speeches of Faisal Husseini.* The Orient House, December 15, 1999. http://www.orienthouse.org/about/Articles/ALECSO.html (accessed April 30, 2003).

———. "What's Ahead for the Middle East?" (Part 1). Interview by author. *The World Tomorrow.* Ambassador Television Production, June 17, 1990.

Inbar, Efraim. *Rabin and Israel's National Security.* Baltimore: The Johns Hopkins University Press, 1999.

International Commission for the Wailing Wall. "Report . . . to Determine the Rights and Claims of Moslems and Jews in Connection with the Western or Wailing Wall at Jerusalem." London: H.M. Stationery Office, December 1930. http://domino.un.org/unispal.nsf/0/59a92104ed00dc468525625b00527fea?O penDocument (accessed September 25, 2003).

International Policy Institute for Counter-Terrorism. "Terrorist Organization Profiles." *International Terrorism.* 2001. http://www.ict.org.il (accessed August 1, 2002).

Isaacs, Ronald H. and Kerry M. Olitsky. *Critical Documents of Israeli History: A Sourcebook.* Northvale, N.J.: Jason Aronson Inc., 1995.

Israel Ministry of Foreign Affairs. "Hatikva: The National Anthem." In *Facts About Israel: The State,* 2003 edition. State of Israel, Ministry of Foreign Affairs, 1999. http://www.israel-mfa.gov.il/mfa/go.asp?MFAH00k90 (accessed September 11, 2003).

Israel Ministry of Foreign Affairs mailer. "Sharon Announces NIS 280 m. Jerusalem Development Plan." June 1, 2005.

Jabotinsky, Eri. *My Father, Ze'ev Jabotinsky* (in Hebrew). Jerusalem: Hotsaat Stimatski, 1980.

Jabotinsky, M. Vladimir (Ze'ev). *Evidence Submitted to the Palestine Royal Commission.* London: New Zionist Press, 1937.

———. *The Political and Social Philosophy of Ze'ev Jabotinsky: Selected Writings.* Edited by Mordechai Sarig. Translated by Shimshon Feder. London: Vallentine Mitchell, 1999.

Jarausch, Konrad H., ed. *After Unity: Reconfiguring German Identities.* Providence, R.I.: Berghahn Books, 1997.

Jarrar, Sabri. "Two Islamic Construction Plans for al-Haram al-Sharif." In *City of the Great King: Jerusalem from David to the Present,* edited by Nitza Rosovsky, 380–416. Cambridge: Harvard University Press, 1996.

Jerusalem Post. April 14, 1997–July 19, 2002.

Jewish Post of New York. April 2001–February 2002. http://www.jewishpost.com.

Jewish Week. April 20, 2001.

Judea Electronic Magazine. "Barak Changes Wye Maps." Vol. 7, no. 4, July–August 1999. http://womeningreen.org/judea/index1.htm#arch (accessed April 23, 2002).

Karmi, Ghada, ed. *Jerusalem Today: What Future for the Peace Process?* Reading, Berks., UK: Garnet Publishing Limited, Ithaca Press, 1996.

———. "Must the Palestinians also Lose Jerusalem?" *Middle East International* 501, no. 26 (1995): 16.

Karsh, Efraim, ed. *From Rabin to Netanyahu: Israel's Troubled Agenda.* London: Frank Cass & Co., 1997.

———, ed. *Israel's Transition from Community to State.* Vol. 1 of *Israel: The First Hundred Years.* London: Frank Cass & Co., 2000.

Kashriel, Benny. Interview by author. Video recording. Ma'aleh Adumim, June 22, 1999.

Katz, Daniel. "Nationalism and Strategies of International Conflict Resolution." In *International Behavior: A Social-Psychological Analysis,* edited by Herbert C. Kelman, 356–90. New York: Holt, Rinehart and Winston, 1965.

Katz, Kimberly. "Jordanian Jerusalem: Postage Stamps and Identity Construction." *Jerusalem Quarterly File*, no. 5. (1999). http://www.jqf-jerusalem.org/1999/jqf5/katz.html (accessed February 4, 2003).

Katz, Samuel (Shmuel). *Battleground: Fact and Fantasy in Palestine.* New York: Bantam Books, 1973.

———. *Days of Fire.* London: W.H. Allen, 1968. Quoted in Silver, *Begin.*

———. *Lone Wolf: A Biography of Vladimir (Ze'ev) Jabotinsky.* 2 vols. New York: Barricade Books, 1996.

Katzenstein, Peter J., ed. *The Culture of National Security: Norms and Identity in World Politics.* New York: Columbia University Press, 1996.

Katzenstein, Peter J., Robert O. Keohane, and Stephen J. Krasner. "International Organization and the Study of World Politics." *International Organization* 52, no. 4 (1998): 645–85.

Katzman, Kenneth. "Shaykh Ahmad Yassin." In *CRS Report for Congress: Terrorism: Middle Eastern Groups and State Sponsors, 1999.* Congressional Research Service, August 9, 1999. www.fas.org/irp/crs/Crsterr3.htm (accessed July 9, 2002).

Keegan, John. *A History of Warfare.* London: Pimlico, 1994.

Keinon, Herb. "Yassin: Is the Sheikh a Real Threat?" *Jerusalem Post*, June 12, 1998, daily edition.

Kelman, Herbert C., ed. *International Behavior: A Social-Psychological Analysis.* New York: Holt, Rinehart and Winston, 1965.

Khalidi, Rashid. "The Centrality of Jerusalem to An End of Conflict Agreement." *Journal of Palestine Studies* 30, no.3 (2001): 82–87.

———. *Palestinian Identity: The Construction of Modern National Consciousness.* New York: Columbia University Press, 1997.

———. "Transforming the Face of the Holy City: Political Messages in the Built Topography of Jerusalem," Part 2. *Jerusalem Quarterly File.* no. 4 (1999). http://www.jqf-jerusalem.org/1999/jqf4/khalidi.html (accessed September 2, 2005).

Khalidi, Walid, ed. *From Haven to Conquest: Readings in Zionism and the Palestine Problem Until 1948.* Beirut: Institute for Palestine Studies, 1971.

Kimhi, Shaul, Shmuel Even, and Jerrold Post. "Yasir Arafat: Psychological Profile and Strategic Analysis." In *International Policy Institute for Counter Terrorism: Research Reports.* June 25, 2003. http://www.ict.org.il/articles/yasir_arafat.htm (accessed September 26, 2003).

Kimmerling, Baruch. "Between the Primordial and the Civil Definitions of the Collective Identity: *Eretz Israel* or the State of Israel?" In *Comparative Social Dynamics*, edited by Erik Cohen, Moshe Lissak, and Uri Almagor, 262–83. Boulder, Colo.: Westview Press, 1985.

Kimmerling, Baruch, ed. *The Israeli State and Society: Boundaries and Frontiers.* Albany, N.Y.: State University of New York Press, 1989.

———. *Zionism and Territory: The Socio-Territorial Dimensions of Zionist Politics.* Berkeley: Institute of International Studies, University of California, 1983.

Kimmerling, Baruch and Joel S. Migdal. *Palestinians: The Making of a People.* New York: Macmillan, The Free Press, 1993.

Kinglake, Alexander W. *Eothen.* London: John Ollivier, 1844.

Kissinger, Henry. *Does America Need a Foreign Policy? Toward a Diplomacy for the 21st Century.* New York: Simon & Schuster, 2001.

Kissinger, Henry. "Does America Need a Foreign Policy?" Speech before the Los Angeles World Affairs Council, July 18, 2001.

Kitto, John. *History of Ancient and Modern Jerusalem.* London: Religious Tract Society, ca. 1847.

Klein, Menachem. *Jerusalem: The Contested City.* Translated by Haim Watzman. New York: New York University Press, 2001.

———. Interview by author. Video recording. Jerusalem, January 9, 2000.

———. Interview by author. Video recording. Oxford, January 8, 2002.

Knesset. "Basic Law: Jerusalem, Capital of Israel." In *The Law: Basic Laws.* State of Israel, Ministry of Foreign Affairs, 1999. http://www.israel-mfa.gov.il/mfa/jerusalem%20capital%20of%20israel/ (accessed September 2, 2002).

Kramer, Martin, "The Temples of Jerusalem in Islam." *Peacewatch.* no. 277. (September 18, 2000). The Washington Institute for Near East Policy. http://www.washingtoninstitute.org/templateC05.php?CID=1968 (accessed September 2, 2005).

Kull, Steven. *Burying Lenin: The Revolution in Soviet Ideology and Foreign Policy.* Boulder, Colo.: Westview Press, 1992.

Kurzman, Dan. *Ben-Gurion: Prophet of Fire.* New York: Simon & Schuster, 1983.

———. *Genesis 1948.* New York: New American Library, Inc., in association with the World Publishing Company, 1970.

Lapidoth, Ruth. *Jerusalem: Past, Present and Future.* Paris: Revue Internationale de Droit Comparé, 1996.

———. *Jerusalem and the Peace Process.* Jerusalem: The Jerusalem Institute for Israel Studies, 1994. Reprinted from *Israel Law Review* 28 (1994).

———. "Jerusalem: Some Legal Aspects." In *Jerusalem: A City and Its Future,* edited by Marshall J. Breger and Ora Ahimeir, 61–90. Syracuse, N.Y.: Syracuse University Press, 2002.

———. Interview by author. Video recording. Jerusalem, June 20, 1999.

Lapidoth, Ruth and Ora Ahimeir, eds. *Freedom of Religion in Jerusalem.* Jerusalem: The Jerusalem Institute for Israel Studies, 1999.

Lapidoth, Ruth and Moshe Hirsch, eds. *The Jerusalem Question and Its Resolution: Selected Documents.* Dordrecht, The Netherlands: Martinus Nijhoff Publishers, in cooperation with The Jerusalem Institute for Israel Studies, 1994.

Laqueur, Walter. *A History of Zionism.* New York: Holt, Rinehart and Winston, 1972.

Laqueur, Walter and Barry Rubin, eds. *The Israel-Arab Reader: A Documentary History of the Middle East Conflict.* 6th ed. New York: Penguin Books, 2001.

Lasswell, Harold D. *Psychopathology and Politics.* Chicago: University of Chicago Press, 1930, 1977.

La Cerra, Peggy and Roger Bingham. *The Origin of Minds: Evolution, Uniqueness, and the New Science of the Self.* New York: Harmony Books, 2002.

Levi-Faur, David, Gabriel Sheffer, and David Vogel. *Israel: The Dynamics of Change and Continuity.* London: Frank Cass & Co., 1999.

Levine, Lee I., ed. *The Jerusalem Cathedra: Studies in the History, Archaeology, Geography and Ethnography of the Land of Israel.* Vol. 1. Jerusalem: Yad Izhak Ben-Zvi Institute, 1981.

———. *The Jerusalem Cathedra: Studies in the History, Archaeology, Geography and Ethnography of the Land of Israel.* Vol. 2. Jerusalem: Yad Izhak Ben-Zvi Institute, 1982.

———. *The Jerusalem Cathedra: Studies in the History, Archaeology, Geography and Ethnography of the Land of Israel.* Vol. 3. Jerusalem: Yad Izhak Ben-Zvi Institute, 1983.

———. *Jerusalem: Its Sanctity and Centrality to Judaism, Christianity, and Islam.* New York: Continuum, 1999.

Little, Donald P. "Jerusalem under the Ayyubids and Mamluks: 1187–1516 A.D." In *Jerusalem in History*, edited by K.J. Asali, 177–99. New York: Olive Branch Press, 1990.

Lowthian, John. *A Narrative of a Recent Visit to Jerusalem and Several Parts of Palestine in 1843–44.* London, 1845.

Lustick, Ian S. "The Fetish of Jerusalem: A Hegemonic Analysis." In *Israel in Comparative Perspective: Challenging the Conventional Wisdom*, edited by Michael N. Barnett, 143–72. Albany: State University of New York Press, 1996.

———. "Reinventing Jerusalem." *Foreign Policy* 93 (Winter 1993–94): 41–59.

Luz, Ehud. "Through the Jewish Historical Prism: Overcoming a Tradition of Insecurity." In *Security Concerns: Insights from the Israeli Experience*, edited by Daniel Bar-Tal, Dan Jacobson, and Aharon Klieman, 55–72. Stamford, Conn.: Jai Press Inc., 1998.

Lynch, Marc. "Jordan's Identity and Interests." In *Identity and Foreign Policy in the Middle East*, edited by Shibley Telhami and Michael Barnett, 26–57. Ithaca, N.Y.: Cornell University Press, 2002.

Ma'ariv (Jerusalem). June 10, 1977.

Makovsky, David. "Barak's Separate Peace." *Washington Post*, July 16, 2000, Outlook section.

———. *Making Peace with the PLO: The Rabin Government's Road to the Oslo Accord.* Boulder, Colo.: Westview Press, 1996.

Mattar, Ibrahim. "From Palestinian to Israeli: Jerusalem 1948–1982." *Journal of Palestine Studies* 12, no. 4 (1983): 57–63.

Mattar, Philip, ed. *Encyclopedia of the Palestinians.* New York: Facts On File, Inc., 2000.

———. *The Mufti of Jerusalem: Al-Hajj Amin Al-Husayni and the Palestinian National Movement.* Rev. ed. New York: Columbia University Press, 1988.

McCarthy, Justin. *The Ottoman Turks: An Introductory History to 1923.* London: Addison Wesley Longman Limited, 1997.

———. *The Population of Palestine: Population History and Statistics of the Late Ottoman Period and the Mandate.* New York: Columbia University Press, 1990.

McClelland, James L. and David E. Rumelhart. "An Interactive Activation Model of Context Effects in Letter Perception: Parts 1 and 2." *Psychological Review* 88, no. 5 (1981): 375–407; 89, no. 1 (1982): 60–94.

Mishal, Shaul and Avraham Sela. *The Palestinian Hamas: Vision, Violence, and Coexistence.* New York: Columbia University Press, 2000.

Moratinos, Miguel. "The Taba Negotiations (January 2001)." *Journal of Palestine Studies* 31, no. 3 (2002): 79–89.

Morgenthau, Hans J. *Politics Among Nations: The Struggle for Power and Peace.* 6th ed. Revised by Kenneth W. Thompson. New York: McGraw-Hill, 1985.

Morris, Benny. *Righteous Victims: A History of the Zionist-Arab Conflict, 1881–1999.* New York: Alfred A. Knopf, 1999.

Mullins, Willard A. "On the Concept of Ideology in Political Science." *The American Political Science Review* 66, no. 2 (1972): 498–510.

Musallam, Sami F. *The Struggle for Jerusalem: A Programme of Action for Peace.* Jerusalem: Palestinian Academic Society for the Study of International Affairs, 1996.

———. Interview by author. Video recording. Jericho, January 6, 2000.

Muslih, Muhammad Y. *The Origins of Palestinian Nationalism.* New York: Columbia University Press, 1988.

———. *Toward Coexistence: An Analysis of the Resolutions of the Palestine National Council.* Washington: The Institute for Palestine Studies, 1990.

Nahshon, Gad. "Burger King: Alive and Well in Maale-Adomim." *Jewish Post of New York,* April 2001.

———. "City Upon the Hill." *Jewish Post of New York,* February 2002.

Najib, Mohammed and Associated Press. "Arafat: Jerusalem Is 'Life or Death.' " *Jerusalem Post,* July 2, 1998, daily edition.

Nashashibi, Nasser Eddin. *Jerusalem's Other Voice: Ragheb Nashashibi and Moderation in Palestinian Politics, 1920–1948.* Exeter, UK: Ithaca Press, 1990.

Nathan, Peter. "Groundless Claims." *Vision—Journal for a New World* 3, no. 2 (2001): 19–23.

New York Times, May 15, 1948–May 8, 2003.

Nuseibeh, Sari. "Islam's Jerusalem." In *Jerusalem: Religious Aspects,* by Sari Nuseibeh, Bernard Sabella, and Yitzhak Reiter. Jerusalem: Palestinian Academic Society for the Study of International Affairs, 1995.

Nuseibeh, Sari, Bernard Sabella, and Yitzhak Reiter. *Jerusalem: Religious Aspects.* Jerusalem: Palestinian Academic Society for the Study of International Affairs, 1995.

Nüsse, Andrea. *Muslim Palestine: The Ideology of Hamas.* Amsterdam: Overseas Publishers Association, N.V., Harwood Academic Publishers, 1998.

Olivas, Veronika, ed. *The Holy City of Jerusalem: A Bibliography With Indexes.* Huntington, N.Y.: Nova Science Publishers, Inc., 2001.

Oren, Michael B. *Six Days of War: June 1967 and the Making of the Modern Middle East.* Oxford: Oxford University Press, 2002.

Ovendale, Ritchie. *The Origins of the Arab-Israeli Wars.* 2nd ed. London: Longman, 1984, 1992.

Palestine Liberation Organization. "Jerusalem." *Permanent Status Issues.* PLO, Negotiation Affairs Department, 2001. www.nad-plo.org/permanent/jerusalem.html (accessed August 5, 2003).

———. "Political and Religious Leaders Support Palestinian Sovereignty Over Jerusalem." *Eye on the Negotiations.* PLO, Negotiation Affairs Department, August 29, 2000. http://www.nad-plo.org/eye/pol-jerus.html (accessed August 2, 2003).

Palestinian Council of Ministers. "Palestinian Prime Minister Ahmad Qurei Reaffirms Palestinian Position Regarding the Disengagement and Calls for Israeli Clarifications." Press release (MIFTAH, August 13, 2005). http://www.miftah.org/Display.cfm?DocId=8180&CategoryId=2 (accessed September 8, 2005).

PASSIA. "More About Faisal Abdel Qader Al-Husseini." *In Memoriam: Faisal Husseini.* Palestinian Academic Society for the Study of International Affairs. (2001.) www.passia.org/faisl/index.html (accessed May 2, 2003).

———. "Shuqeiri, Sheikh As'ad." *Palestine Facts and Info: Personalities.* Palestinian Academic Society for the Study of International Affairs, n.d. http://www.passia.org/index_pfacts.htm (accessed September 11, 2003).

Patai, Raphael, ed. *The Complete Diaries of Theodor Herzl.* 5 vols. Translated by Harry Zohn. London: Herzl Press and Thomas Yoseloff, 1960.

Peleg, Ilan. *Begin's Foreign Policy, 1977–1983: Israel's Move to the Right.* New York: Greenwood Press, 1987.

Peres, Shimon. "Address by Foreign Minister Shimon Peres at a Foreign Ministry Seminar Marking the First Anniversary of the Signing of the Declaration of Principles," (Jerusalem, September 11, 1994). State of Israel, Ministry of Foreign Affairs, 1999. http://www.mfa.gov.il/mfa/ (accessed June 24, 2003).

———. "Interview with Foreign Minister Peres on Israel Radio, April 10, 1993." In *Foreign Relations: Historical Documents, 1992–1994,* vol. 13–14, no. 67. State of Israel, Ministry of Foreign Affairs, 1999. http://www.mfa.gov.il/mfa/ (accessed September 2, 2005).

———. *The New Middle East.* New York: Henry Holt and Company, Inc., 1993.

———. "Peace Be Within Your Walls." Interview by author. *Vision—Journal for a New World* 2, no. 1 (2000): 7–11.

Permanent Observer Mission of Palestine to the United Nations. "Background." In *Palestine Liberation Organization,* 1999. http://www.palestine-un.org/plo/frindex.html (accessed July 30, 2003).

———. "Declaration of Independence" In *Palestine Liberation Organization: Documents,* 1999. http://www.palestine-un.org/plo/frindex.html (accessed July 30, 2003).

Pinker, Steven. *The Blank Slate: The Modern Denial of Human Nature.* New York: Viking Penguin, 2002.

Plamenatz, John. *Ideology.* London: Praeger Publishers, Inc., 1970.

Plett, Barbara. "Israel Fence Revives Old Controversies." BBC News, June 19, 2002. http://news.bbc.co.uk/2/hi/middle_east/2054113.stm (accessed November 12, 2003).

Plotkin, Robert. "Hamas Would Accept Saudi Peace Plan, Spokesman Says: Group Would Stop Attacks on Israelis If Occupation Ends." *San Francisco Chronicle,* April 28, 2002.

Porath, Yehoshua. *The Emergence of the Palestinian-Arab National Movement, 1918–1929.* London: Frank Cass & Co., 1974.

———. *The Palestinian Arab National Movement: From Riots to Rebellion.* Vol. 2, *1929–1939.* London: Frank Cass & Co., 1977.

Post, Jerrold M. "Assessing Leaders at a Distance: The Political Personality Profile." In *The Psychological Assessment of Political Leaders,* edited by Jerrold M. Post, 69–104. Ann Arbor, Mich.: University of Michigan Press, 2003.

———. "Dreams of Glory and the Life Cycle: Reflections on the Life Course of Narcissistic Leaders." *Journal of Political and Military Sociology* 12 (Spring 1984): 49–60.

Post, Jerrold M, ed. *The Psychological Assessment of Political Leaders.* Ann Arbor, Mich.: University of Michigan Press, 2003.

———. "The Seasons of a Leader's Life: Influences of the Life Cycle on Political Behavior." *Political Psychology* 2, no. 3/4 (1980): 35–49.

Post, Jerrold M. and Robert S. Robins. *When Illness Strikes the Leader: The Dilemma of the Captive King.* New Haven: Yale University Press, 1993.

Prince of Asturias Foundation. "Daniel Barenboim and Edward Said, Prince of Asturias Award for Concord 2002." In *Prince of Asturias Awards: 2002.*

September 4, 2002. http://www.fundacionprincipedeasturias.org/ing/salaprensa/noticias/noticia343.html (accessed September 11, 2003).

Prior, Michael. *Zionism and the State of Israel: A Moral Inquiry.* New York: Routledge, 1999.

Quartz, Steven R. and Terrence J. Sejnowski. *Liars, Lovers, and Heroes: What the New Brain Science Reveals About How We Become Who We Are.* New York: William Morrow, 2002.

Quigley, John. *The Case for Palestine: An International Law Perspective.* Durham: Duke University Press, 1990, 2005.

————. "Jerusalem in International Law." In *Jerusalem Today: What Future for the Peace Process?* edited by Ghada Karmi, 25–43. Reading, Berks., UK: Garnet Publishing Limited, Ithaca Press, 1996.

Quray', Ahmad (Abu Ala'). *Hanging Peace: Readings in the Political Economy of Palestine* (in Arabic). Amman: Dar al-Faris, 1999.

————. "Peace Talk." Interview by author. *Vision—Journal for a New World* 2, no. 2 (2000): 60–61.

Qurei, Ahmed (Ahmad Quray') "Breaking the Deadlock," *Peace Watch*, no. 166: Special Forum Report (The Washington Institute for Near East Policy, May 20, 1998). http://www.washingtoninstitute.org/templateC05.php?CID=1857 (accessed September 8, 2005).

Rabin, Leah. *Rabin: Our Life, His Legacy.* New York: G.P. Putnam's Sons, 1997.

Rabin, Yitzhak. "Address by Prime Minister Yitzhak Rabin (Middle East/North Africa Economic Summit, Casablanca, October 30–November 1, 1994). State of Israel, Ministry of Foreign Affairs, 1999. http://www.israel-mfa.gov.il/mfa/ (accessed June 24, 2003).

————. "Rabin Jerusalem Day Address to Knesset" (May 29, 1995). State of Israel, Ministry of Foreign Affairs, 1999. http://www.israel-mfa.gov.il/mfa/ (accessed June 24, 2003).

————. *The Rabin Memoirs.* Expanded ed. Berkeley: University of California Press, 1996.

Ragionieri, Rodolfo. "International Constraints and National Debates in the Israeli-Palestinian Peace Process." *Quaderni Forum* 11, no. 1 (1997).

Rangwala, Glen. "Short Biographies of Some of the Major Palestinian Political Leaders Since 1967." 2003. http://middleeastreference.org.uk/palbiograph.html (accessed September 26, 2003).

————. "Short Institutional Biographies of Some of the Major Palestinian Political Groupings Since 1967." 2003. http://www.middleeastreference.org.uk/palestiniangroups.html (accessed September 26, 2003).

Reinharz, Jehuda. *Chaim Weizmann: The Making of a Zionist Leader.* New York: Oxford University Press, 1985.

Reinharz, Jehuda and Anita Shapira, eds. *Essential Papers on Zionism.* London: Cassell, 1996.

Renshon, Stanley. "Life History and Character Development." In *New Directions in Psychohistory*, edited by Mel Albin, 60–68. Lexington, Mass.: D.C. Heath and Company, Lexington Books, 1980.

Reuters. "Israeli Defense Chief Unveils Jerusalem Fence Plan." *New York Times*, June 30, 2002.

———. "Peres Raises 'World Capital' Solution for Jerusalem," July 22, 2003. http://www.acj.org/Daily%20News/2003/July/July%2022.htm#2 (accessed September 1, 2005).

Ridley, Matt. *Nature Via Nurture: Genes, Experience, and What Makes Us Human.* New York: Harper Collins, 2003.

Robins, Robert S. and Jerrold M. Post. *Political Paranoia: The Psychopolitics of Hatred.* New Haven: Yale University Press, 1997.

Robinson, Edward. *Biblical Researches in Palestine and the Adjacent Regions: A Journal of Travels in the Years 1838 and 1852.* Vol. 1. 3rd ed., with additional notes and a new introduction by William G. Dever. Jerusalem: The Universitas Booksellers, 1970.

Rodan, Steve. "Hamas's Explosive Divide." *Jerusalem Post,* April 10, 1998, daily edition.

Rosovsky, Nitza, ed., *City of the Great King: Jerusalem from David to the Present.* Cambridge: Harvard University Press, 1996.

Ross, Dennis. *The Missing Peace: The Inside Story of the Fight for Middle East Peace.* New York: Farrar, Straus and Giroux, 2004.

———. "Secrets of the Great Communicators." Interview by Lise Funderburg. *O Magazine,* March 2003.

Rubin, Barry. *The Transformation of Palestinian Politics: From Revolution to State-Building.* Cambridge: Harvard University Press, 1999.

Rubinstein, Danny. *The Mystery of Arafat.* Translated by Dan Leon. South Royalton, Vt.: Steerforth Press, 1995.

Sabella, Bernard. "Jerusalem: A Christian Perspective." In *Jerusalem: Religious Aspects,* by Sari Nuseibeh, Bernard Sabella, and Yitzhak Reiter. Jerusalem: Palestinian Academic Society for the Study of International Affairs, 1995, 2000.

Sachar, Howard M. *A History of Israel: From the Rise of Zionism to Our Time.* 2nd ed. New York: Alfred A. Knopf, 1996.

Safieh, Afif. *Christian Voices from the Holy Land: O Jerusalem!* London: Palestinian General Delegation to the U.K. and the Office of Representation of the P.L.O. to the Holy See, 2000.

———. Interview by author. Video recording. London, January 3, 2002.

Said, Edward W. "Memory, Inequality and Power: Palestine and the Universality of Human Rights," public lecture, UCLA, February 20, 2003.

———. *The Politics of Dispossession: The Struggle for Palestinian Self-Determination, 1969–1994.* New York: Vintage Books, 1994, 1995.

———. "Projecting Jerusalem." *Journal of Palestine Studies* 25, no. 1 (1995): 5–14.

———. *The Question of Palestine.* New York: Vintage Books, 1992.

Said, Edward W. and Christopher Hitchins. *Blaming the Victims.* London: Verso, 1988.

Saideman, Stephen. "Thinking Theoretically About Identity and Foreign Policy." In *Identity and Foreign Policy in the Middle East,* edited by Shibley Telhami and Michael Barnett, 169–200. Ithaca, N.Y.: Cornell University Press, 2002.

San Francisco Chronicle, April 28, 2002.

Savir, Uri. *Fresh Air.* Interview by Terry Gross. National Public Radio, May 14, 1998.

———. *The Process: 1,100 Days That Changed the Middle East.* New York: Random House, 1998.

———. "Remarks by Mr. Uri Savir, Head of Israel's Delegation to the Permanent Status Negotiations Between Israel and the Palestinian Authority." Opening

Session, May 5, 1996. http://www.israel-mfa.gov.il/mfa/ (accessed September 25, 2003).

―――. Interview by author. Video recording. Jerusalem, June 21, 1999. Condensed interview: "Peace Talk." *Vision—Journal for a New World* 2, no. 2 (2000): 62–63.

Schölch, Alexander. "Jerusalem in the 19th Century (1831–1917 A.D.)" In *Jerusalem in History*, edited by K.J. Asali, 228–48. New York: Olive Branch Press, 1990.

―――. *Palestine in Transformation 1856–1882: Studies in Social, Economic and Political Development.* Washington, D.C.: Institute of Palestine Studies, 1993.

Schwartz, Jeffrey M. and Sharon Begley. *The Mind and the Brain: Neuroplasticity and the Power of Mental Force.* New York: Regan Books, 2002.

Schwartz, Seth J. "In Search of Mechanisms of Change in Identity Development: Integrating the Constructivist and Discovery Perspectives on Identity." *Identity* 2, no. 4 (2002): 317–39.

Segal, Jerome M., Shlomit Levy, Nader Izzat Sa'id, and Elihu Katz. *Negotiating Jerusalem.* New York: State University of New York Press, 2000.

Sharkansky, Ira. *Governing Jerusalem: Again on the World's Agenda.* Detroit: Wayne State University Press, 1996.

Shaw, Stanford J. and Ezel Kural Shaw. *Reform, Revolution and Republic: The Rise of Modern Turkey, 1808–1975.* Vol. 2 of *History of the Ottoman Empire and Modern Turkey.* Cambridge: Cambridge University Press, 1977.

Shindler, Colin. *Ploughshares into Swords? Israelis and Jews in the Shadow of the Intifada.* London: I.B. Tauris & Co Ltd, 1991.

Shlaim, Avi. *The Iron Wall: Israel and the Arab World.* London: Penguin Books, 2000.

―――. *The Politics of Partition: King Abdullah, the Zionists and Palestine, 1921–1951.* New York: Columbia University Press, 1990.

Shtayyeh, Mohammad, ed. *Scenarios on the Future of Jerusalem.* Jerusalem: Palestinian Center for Regional Studies, 1998.

Shukairy, Ahmad. *Liberation—Not Negotiation.* Beirut: Research Centre, Palestine Liberation Organization, 1966.

―――. *Statements Made During the 12th Session of the United Nations General Assembly and the Third Emergency Special Session of the United Nations By His Excellency Ahmad Shukairy.* New York: Saudi Arabian Mission to the united Nations, 1958.

―――. "Statements Made During the 13th Session of the United Nations General Assembly 1958." In *Speeches.* Eyad Shukairy, n.d. http://www.ahmad-alshukairy.org/speeches/speeches.html (accessed August 1, 2003).

―――. *Statements Made During the 16th Session of the United Nations General Assembly by His Excellency Ahmad Shukairy.* New York: Saudi Arabian Mission to the United Nations, 1962.

Shukairy, Eyad. "Biography of Ahmad Al-Shukairi." N.d. www.ahmad-alshukairy.org (accessed May 2, 2003).

Sicker, Martin. *Between Hashemites and Zionists: The Struggle for Palestine, 1908–1988.* New York: Holmes & Meier, 1989.

Silver, Eric. *Begin: The Haunted Prophet.* New York: Random House, 1984.

Smith, Charles D. *Palestine and the Arab-Israeli Conflict.* 3rd ed. New York: St. Martin's Press, 1996.

Sofer, Naim. "The Political Status of Jerusalem in the Hashemite Kingdom of Jordan." *Middle Eastern Studies* 12 (1976): 73–94.

Sofer, Sasson. "International Relations and the Invisibility of Ideology." *Millennium: Journal of International Studies* 16, no. 3 (1988): 489–523.

———, ed. *Peacemaking in a Divided Society: Israel after Rabin.* London: Frank Cass & Co., 2001.

———. *Zionism and the Foundations of Israeli Diplomacy.* Translated by Dorothea Shefet-Vanson. Cambridge: Cambridge University Press, 1998.

Sontag, Deborah. "Quest for Mideast Peace: How and Why It Failed." *New York Times,* July 26, 2001.

Spiegel, Steven L. and David J. Pervin, eds. *The Environment, Water, Refugees, and Economic Cooperation and Development.* Vol. 2 of *Practical Peacemaking in the Middle East.* New York: Garland Publishing, 1995.

Sprinzak, Ehud. *The Ascendance of Israel's Radical Right.* Oxford: Oxford University Press, 1991.

Stein, Kenneth W. *Heroic Diplomacy: Sadat, Kissinger, Carter, Begin and the Quest for Arab-Israeli Peace.* New York: Routledge, 1999.

Stiles, Joan. "Neural Plasticity and Cognitive Development." *Developmental Neuropsychology* 18, no. 2 (2000): 237–72.

Telhami, Shibley. "Camp David II: Assumptions and Consequences." *Current History* (January 2001).

Telhami, Shibley and Michael Barnett, eds. *Identity and Foreign Policy in the Middle East.* Ithaca, N.Y.: Cornell University Press, 2002.

Teveth, Shabtai. *Ben-Gurion: The Burning Ground, 1886–1948.* Boston: Houghton Mifflin, 1987.

Tibawi, A.L. "Jerusalem: Its Place in Islam and Arab History." In *The Arab-Israeli Confrontation of June 1967: An Arab Perspective,* edited by Ibrahim Abu-Lughod, 10–48. Evanston, Ill.: Northwestern University Press, 1970.

Trevelyan, G.M. *History of England.* New Illustrated Ed. London: Longman, 1973.

Tsimhoni, Daphne. *Christian Communities in Jerusalem and the West Bank Since 1948: An Historical, Social, and Political Study.* Westport, Conn.: Praeger, 1993.

———. "Christians in Jerusalem: A Minority at Risk." *Journal of Human Rights* 4 (2005): 391–417.

Twain, Mark. *The Innocents Abroad, or, The New Pilgrims' Progress.* Hartford, Conn.: American Publishing Co., 1869.

Usher, Rod. "Hearts and Minds." *Time Magazine,* September 2, 2002. http://www.time.com/time/europe/magazine/article/0,13005,901020902–340702,00.html (accessed April 22, 2003).

Vertzberger, Yaacov Y.I. *The World in Their Minds: Information Processing, Cognition, and Perception in Foreign Policy Decisionmaking.* Stanford: Stanford University Press, 1990.

Wallach, Janet and John Wallach. *Arafat: In the Eyes of the Beholder.* Rev. ed. New York: Carol Publishing Group, Birch Lane Press, 1990, 1997.

———. *The New Palestinians: The Emerging Generation of Leaders.* Rocklin, Calif.: Prima, 1992.

Wallerstein, Robert S. "Erikson's Concept of Ego Identity Reconsidered." *Journal of the American Psychoanalytic Association* 46, no. 1 (1998): 229–47.

Wallerstein, Robert S. and Leo Goldberger, eds. *Ideas and Identities: The Life and Work of Erik Erikson*. Madison, International Universities Press, Inc., 1998.

Washington Post, July 16, 2000–July 24, 2001.

Wasserstein, Bernard. "Divided Jerusalem: A Conversation with Bernard Wasserstein." In *The Religion Report*. ABC Radio National, April 17, 2002. http://www.abc.net.au/rn/talks/8.30/relrpt/stories/s532612.htm (accessed April 25, 2003).

———. *Divided Jerusalem: The Struggle for the Holy City*. London: Profile Books, 2001.

———. Interview by author. Video recording. Glasgow, January 7, 2002.

Weizmann, Chaim. *The Letters and Papers of Chaim Weizmann*. Series A: Letters. Vol. 6, March 1913–July 1914. Edited by Gedalia Yogev, Shifra Kolatt, and Evyatar Friesel. Jerusalem: Israel Universities Press, 1974.

———. *The Letters and Papers of Chaim Weizmann*. Series A: Letters. Vol. 7, August 1914–November 1917. Edited by Leonard Stein. London: Oxford University Press, 1975.

———. *The Letters and Papers of Chaim Weizmann*. Series A: Letters. Vol. 8, November 1917–October 1918. Edited by Dvorah Barzilay and Barnet Litvinoff. New Brunswick, N.J.: Rutgers University, Transaction Books, 1977.

———. *The Letters and Papers of Chaim Weizmann*. Series B: Papers. Vol. 1, August 1898–July 1931. Edited by Barnet Litvinoff. New Brunswick, N.J.: Rutgers University, Transaction Books, 1983.

———. *The Letters and Papers of Chaim Weizmann*. Series B: Papers. Vol. 2, December 1931–April 1952. Edited by Barnet Litvinoff. New Brunswick, N.J.: Rutgers University, Transaction Books, 1984.

———. *Trial and Error: The Autobiography of Chaim Weizmann*. New York: Harper & Brothers, 1949.

Wheatcroft, Andrew. *The Ottomans*. London: Viking, 1993.

Wheatcroft, Geoffrey. *The Controversy of Zion: Jewish Nationalism, the Jewish State, and the Unresolved Jewish Dilemma*. Reading, Mass.: Addison-Wesley Publishing Company, 1996.

Widlanski, Michael A., ed. *Can Israel Survive a Palestinian State?* Jerusalem: Institute for Advanced Strategic and Political Studies, 1990.

Wigoder, Geoffrey, ed. *New Encyclopedia of Zionism and Israel*. Cranbury, N.J.: Associated University Presses, 1994.

Wilson, Mary C. *King Abdullah, Britain and the Making of Jordan*. Cambridge: Cambridge University Press, 1987.

Winter, Jay and Emmanuel Sivan, eds. *War and Remembrance in the Twentieth Century*. Cambridge: Cambridge University Press, 1999.

Xinhua. "Annexing East Jerusalem Was Mistake: Peres." *People's Daily Online*, June 6, 2005. http://english.people.com.cn/200506/06/print20050606_188608.html (accessed September 1, 2005).

Yehoshua, Avraham B. "Jerusalem." In *The Jerusalem Anthology: A Literary Guide*, compiled by Reuven Hammer, 443–53. Philadelphia: Jewish Publication Society, 1995.

———. "For a Jewish Border." *Jerusalem Post*, July 19, 2002.

Yehoshua Y. and B. Chernitsky, "Ahmad Qurei'—Abu 'Alaa: A Brief Political Profile of the Nominated Palestinian Prime Minister." Inquiry and Analysis

Series, no. 147 (Middle East Media Research Institute, September 18, 2003). http://memri.org/bin/articles.cgi?Page=archives&Area=ia&ID=IA14703 (accessed September 8, 2005), quoting *Al-Hayat Al-Jadida* (P.A.), January 22, 1997.

Zameret, Zvi. "Judaism in Israel: Ben-Gurion's Private Beliefs and Public Policy." Translated by Moshe Tlamim. *Israel Studies* (University of Indiana) 4, no. 2 (1999): 64–89.

INDEX

Note: Numbers in italic indicate maps or tables. References to "Jerusalem Question" are abbreviated as "JQ."

47, 64–65, 113, 115, 117, 123,
148, 151, 158–60, 166
Oslo II Agreement (1995), 170
Taba talks (2001), 2, 44, 156, 183, 184
Ottoman Empire, 3–5, 8, 21, 36, *37*,
46, 53, 60–62, 64, 71, 73, 74, 79,
86, 128, 130, 138, 143
Ovendale, Ritchie, 198n36

Pale of Settlement, 74, 122
Palestine
Egyptian rule of, 36
flag of, 136
Hamas territorial goal of, 172, 174
history of, 7, 51–65
identity-ideology nexus and, 3
Jerusalem and international law and,
47
Jewish immigration to, 69–71, 75,
86–87, 107, 116
see also Palestine, partition of; *and*
specific areas, cities, events,
governing authorities, and
organizations
Palestine, partition of, 46
Ben-Gurion and, 87–89
British proposal on (1937), 80–82, *81*
al-Husayni, Amin, and, 134, 136
Shuqayri and, 139
UN proposal on (1947), 79, 89–91,
90, 99, 108, 135, 139, 160
Weizmann and, 87
Palestine Liberation Army (PLA),
140, 163
Palestine Liberation Organization
(PLO), 47, 105, 113, 117, 119,
128, 129, 139–40, 146–53,
155–58, 161, 163–64, 167–69,
173, 183, 185, 202n41, 203n63
Executive Committee, 140, 147,
153, 164
Public Organization Department,
163
Palestine National Council (PNC),
136, 137, 147–50, 169, 201n31

Palestine National Fund, 140
Palestinian Academic Society for the
Study of International Affairs, 166
Palestinian Arabs, 5–6
Begin and, 106
Christian, *37*, 62–65, 129, 142,
157–62, 176
declaration of independence (1988),
148, 164
disparity in military and economic
power, 5, 35
early Zionists and, 71, 80, 86–87,
95
expropriation of land of, 41, 43, 55
leaders, 6, 127–76, 180–81
legal issues and, 35
limits on Jewish access to holy sites
and, 53–54
Muslim, meaning of Jerusalem to, in
religion and history, 56–62
population of Jerusalem, *37*
Peres and, 117, 118, 120, 121
Rabin and, 114
war of 1948 and, 79, 91
see also Palestinian National
Authority; Palestinian state;
and specific events, individuals,
and organizations
Palestinian Congress, First (Amman,
1948), 136
Palestinian Council of Ministers, 156
Palestinian Economic Council for
Development and Reconstruction
(PECDAR), 153
Palestinian General Assembly, 139
Palestinian Independent Commission
for Citizens' Rights, 158
Palestinian Initiative for the Promotion
of Global Dialogue and
Democracy (MIFTAH),
158, 161
Palestinian-Israeli underground
political organization, 158, 161
Palestinian Legislative Council (PLC),
8, 150, 154, 156, 158